DESIGNING
RESISTANCE
TRAINING
PROGRAMS

DESIGNING RESISTANCE TRAINING PROGRAMS

Steven J. Fleck
United States Olympic Committee

William J. Kraemer
University of Connecticut

Human Kinetics Books
Champaign, Illinois

6/94

Fleck, Steven J., 1951-
  Designing resistance training programs.

  Bibliography: p.
  Includes index.
  1. Isometric exercise.   I. Kraemer, William J.,
  1953-   . II. Title.
  GV505.F58   1987   613.7'1   87-2850
  ISBN 0-87322-113-3

Developmental Editor: Sue Wilmoth, PhD; Production Director: Ernie
Noa; Projects Manager: Lezli Harris; Copy Editor: Claire Mount; Assistant
Editor: Julie Anderson; Typesetter: Theresa Bear; Text Design: Keith
Blomberg; Text Layout: Denise Mueller; Cover Photo: Bill Morrow;
Printed By: Versa Press, Inc. and R & R Bindery Service, Inc.

Interior photo credits: Many thanks to the University of Oregon and Boston
College Sports Information photographers. Sam Bowie p. 47, David Weintraub
p. 74, David Zahn pp. 78, 80, and 177. Ricky Stewast p. 103, Sam Glass p. 106,
Greg Scwab p. 177, Lenore Morrison and Diane Schulz p. 218. Thanks also to
the YMCA of the USA for the photos on pp. 13, 83, 121 (right photo), and 149
(bottom photo).

ISBN: 0-87322-113-3

Printed in the United States of America   10 9 8 7 6

Human Kinetics Publishers
Box 5076, Champaign, IL 61825-5076
1-800-747-4457

Canada: Human Kinetics Publishers, P.O. Box 2503, Windsor, ON N8Y 4S2
1-800-465-7301 (in Canada only)

Europe: Human Kinetics Publishers (Europe) Ltd., P.O. Box IW14,
Leeds LS16 6TR, England
0532-781708

Australia: Human Kinetics Publishers, P.O. Box 80, Kingswood 5062,
South Australia
618-374-0433

New Zealand: Human Kinetics Publishers, P.O. Box 105-231,
Auckland 1
(09) 309-2259

Dedications

To my parents Marv and Elda

Steven Fleck

To Joan and my children Daniel, Anna, and Maria

William Kraemer

Acknowledgments

The completion of this work has been aided by many friends and colleagues who gave us encouragement and helpful criticism when needed. To all of these individuals we say thank you. We would like to give special thanks to Dr. Carl Maresh and Mr. Ken Kontor for their helpful comments on the manuscript during the review process. Thanks to Dr. Tom Baechle, Ms. Dini McCurry, Mr. Keith Kephart, Mr. Mike Carter, and Mr. Leo Totten for their assistance and expertise in the preparation of portions of the manuscript concerning the practical aspects and special topics of resistance training. To Mr. Wes Emmert, Mr. Mike Clark, and the National Strength and Conditioning Association national office staff a special thanks for assisting us with photographs included in the text.

A very speical thanks to Dr. Gary Dudley for encouragement and just being a friend during some difficult times of my career.

Thanks to Dr. James A. Vogel, Director of the Exercise Physiology Division for his support of this project and for allowing the flexibility needed to complete this work.

Thank you to Dr. Rainer Martens, Dr. Sue Wilmoth, and the rest of the Human Kinetics staff for their expertise and patience in bringing this work to publication.

To Mrs. Dora Ward, thanks for her patience and careful typing of parts of the manuscript.

Thanks to Dr. Robert Bartels and Dr. Bruce Noble for fostering our scientific interest in physiology and at the same time making us aware of the applied aspects of exercise physiology.

Contents

Preface

The past ten years have witnessed a popularity explosion in the use and acceptance of resistance training by people of all ages. Athletes, fitness enthusiasts, students, and patients have all realized benefits from the use of various resistance training programs. Because resistance training appeals to such a wide variety of people, the goals of weight lifting programs have become quite diverse. In order to meet these diverse needs, resistance training programs are designed specifically for the individual. This book addresses the scientific and theoretical basis of program design in resistance training. It is our hope that an increased factual understanding of both the scientific and empirical evidence related to resistance training will enhance the ability to prescribe exercise and design programs to meet individual and team needs.

Chapters 1 and 2 introduce the basic principles and concepts in resistance training. In chapter 1, basic terms and concepts are discussed and defined. Chapter 2 is an overview of the different types of resistance training along with the major research that has been conducted in this area. These two chapters provide the basic facts needed to further develop your understanding of program design in subsequent chapters.

Chapter 3 discusses the basic structure of variables in program design of both daily training sessions and long-range training plans or periodization. This gives you the blueprint from which to design a program. In the development of a resistance training program, there are many questions to answer concerning the needs and goals of an individual or team. The more questions that are answered, the more likely the individual or team will reach specific training goals. Subsequent chapters introduce you to other major topics in resistance training.

Chapter 4 describes some of the standard programs which have gained acceptance in the world of resistance training and analyzes them in the context of the variable structure outlined in chapter 3. This type of analysis demonstrates that any program can be quantified and examined in a systematic manner related to the choices made on the different program variables. Chapter 5 describes the basic concepts of exercise prescription in other forms of training such as aerobic conditioning, interval training, and stretching. In addition, we discuss how you might integrate these different types of training with resistance training as well as what is known about the compatibility of these different types of training programs.

Chapters 6 and 7 give a basic understanding of physiology and physiological changes involved with training. We do more than just explain muscle physiology. The physiological structures and mechanisms are discussed in the context of where they might be involved with resistance training. This information (along with chapter 2) gives you a solid foundation regarding the scientific understanding of resistance training. From this you should be able to be more creative in your program design and to answer some of your own questions and those of others including: "How come I have to do this?" "Why are you having me do it this way?" "What can I expect from this type of program?" "Why is this workout so exhausting?" or "What does this do to the muscle?". Your scientific understanding of the structure and function of resistance training along with adaptations involved will give you more insights into program design and exercise prescription.

Chapter 8 acquaints you with the effects of detraining so that proper maintenance programs can be designed to maintain training gains. This, along with the periodization concepts presented in chapter 3, is important for developing programs which can be used on a yearly basis for fitness and/or athletics.

Chapters 9 and 10 address the different concepts concerning the use of resistance training in specific populations. Chapter 9 discusses considerations when developing resistance training programs for women. Chapter 10 examines the different aspects that need to be considered when designing a program for children. Each of these chapters attempts to make you aware of special considerations which are important when designing a program for these specific groups.

Much of the empirical evidence for resistance training has been accumulated by training programs for competitive resistance sports. Chapter 11 gives you a basic understanding about the sports of body building, power lifting, and Olympic lifting. By examining the training programs for each of these sports you will see that each sport's programs are specific to the needs and goals of the sport. This knowledge will allow you to incorporate training ideas from these specific sports when the goals of your program and these sports are similar.

Designing a successful resistance training program is a major challenge. In writing this book, we identified three goals. First, we wanted to provide a source that would help in the decision-making process that is involved in program design. Second, we wanted to document the specific knowledge base associated with resistance training. Finally, we wanted to develop a structured system which will help individuals develop resistance programs based on the needs and goals. It is our hope that the time spent in the weight room is as productive as possible and that your needs and goals are met with the program you design. Good luck and good training!

Chapter 1

Basic Principles of Resistance Training and Exercise Prescriptions

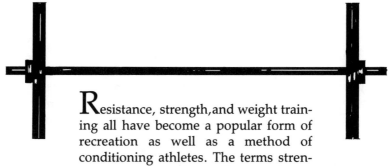

Resistance, strength, and weight training all have become a popular form of recreation as well as a method of conditioning athletes. The terms strength, weight, and resistance training are all terms which have been used to describe a type of exercise which requires the body's musculature to move (or attempt to move) against some type of opposing force presented by various types of equipment. We use the term *resistance training* in order to encompass a wide range of training modalities rather than *weight training*, which really refers to one type of resistance modality. The term *strength* really refers to a performance characteristic of muscle function and will be defined in this book as the maximal force a muscle or muscle group can generate at a specified velocity (Knuttgen & Kraemer, 1987). The most commonly used forms of resistance exercise are free weights and various weight machines. The increased number of private, high school, and college resistance training facilities attest to the popularity of this form of physical conditioning. Individuals who participate in a resistance training program expect the program to produce certain benefits; among the most common are increased strength, muscular hypertrophy (increased muscle size), and sports performance, as well as changes in body composition. A well-designed and consistently performed resistance training program may produce all of these benefits.

Both the recreational weight lifter and the athlete expect gains in strength or muscular hypertrophy from a resistance training program. All types of resistance training (e.g., isokinetic, variable resistance, isometric) along with many different training systems (e.g., combinations of sets, repetitions, and loads) produce significant increases in strength or muscular hypertrophy.

Most athletes and many recreational lifters expect the gains in strength or muscular hypertrophy produced by a resistance training program to lead to increases in sport performance. Resistance training can cause increases in motor performance (e.g., ability to sprint, throw an object, or jump); these increases in basic motor skills can lead to better performance in various games and sports.

Body compositional changes are also goals of many recreational lifters and athletes performing a resistance training program. Normally the changes in body composition desired by all individuals are a decrease in the amount of body fat and an increase in muscle mass. However, some individuals desire a gain in total body weight and some a decrease in total body weight. All of these changes are achieved by a properly planned and performed resistance training program.

Resistance training can produce changes in body composition, strength, muscular hypertrophy, and motor performance desired by many individuals. To produce optimal changes in these areas it is necessary to adhere to some basic principles. These principles apply regardless of the type of resistance training or the type of system utilized.

Maximal Muscular Contractions

Voluntary maximal muscular contractions appear to be the most effective way to increase muscular strength (Fleck & Schutt, 1985). This does not mean that the individual must lift the maximal amount of resistance possible for one repetition termed a one repetition maximum (1 RM). Rather the muscle must move as much resistance as its present condition will allow. The force generated by a fatigued muscle during a voluntary maximal muscular contraction is not as great as that of a nonfatigued muscle. The last repetition in a set to failure is a voluntary maximal muscular contraction even though the force produced would not be the maximal force possible if the muscle was not partially fatigued. An X RM refers to the amount of resistance that allows the performance of X repetitions in good form, with X-plus-one repetitions in good form being impossible. Many resistance training systems use sets to failure and/or RMs to assure the performance of voluntary maximal contractions and, subsequently, the associated training effects. The need to perform voluntary maximal contractions is often referred to as overloading the muscle. In other words, the muscle must contract against a resistance it normally does not encounter. This process stimulates physiological changes which cause an increase in strength.

Some resistance training machines have been specifically developed to force the muscle to perform voluntary maximal contractions either through a greater range of motion (see chapter 2, Variable Resistance) or during more repetitions than the last repetition in a set to failure (see chapter 2, Isokinetics). Developments in equipment attest to a belief in the necessity for voluntary maximal contractions. All competitive weight lifters use voluntary maximal contractions at some point in their training programs, indicating that competitive lifters realize the need for voluntary maximal contractions to bring about optimal gains in strength or muscular hypertrophy.

Intensity

Closely related to voluntary maximal contractions is the intensity of training. Intensity is the power output (rate of performing work) of an exercise. Intensity can under certain circumstances be increased by using a heavier resistance and in other circumstances by moving a given load faster. The closer a given load is moved to the maximal possible velocity the greater the intensity and the training effect on the muscle. This is true for both single-joint and multi-joint exercises (Komi, 1979). Increasing the intensity of an exercise by increasing the velocity of movement is important when a major goal is to increase the power output of the muscle and not just its ability to lift maximal loads.

Volume of Training

Volume of training is estimated by summing the total number of repetitions performed during a specific time period. Frequency (number of training sessions per week, month, or year) and duration (length of each training session) have a direct bearing on the volume of training. Larger volumes of training appear to be important when the goal of a resistance program includes decreases in percentage of body fat and increases in lean body mass or muscular hypertrophy (Stone, O'Bryant, & Garhammer, 1981; Stone, O'Bryant, Garhammer, McMillan, & Rozenek, 1982). That body builders use large volumes of training to develop substantial muscular hypertrophy suggests that a relationship exists between volume of training and muscular hypertrophy. Volume of training is discussed in greater detail in chapter 3.

Variation of Training

Variation in the volume and intensity of training (periodization) is extremely important for optimal gains in strength (Stone et al., 1981; Matveyev, 1981). The use of periodization is discussed in chapter 3.

Slight variations in the position of the foot, hand, or other body parts that do not affect the safety of the lifter is also valuable in producing continued gains in strength (Garhammer, 1981). The use of several exercises as a means to vary the conditioning stimulus of a particular muscle group are also a valuable means to assure continual increases in strength (see chapter 6, Order of Fiber Type Recruitment).

The use of several different types of muscular contractions (e.g., concentric, eccentric) is also a valuable means by which to vary training. The use of a combination of concentric and eccentric contractions as opposed to only concentric contractions in the training program produces superior gains in strength (Hakkinen & Komi, 1981). Several types of variations in training thus appear to be useful to achieve optimal gains in strength.

Progressive Resistance Exercise

Progressive resistance exercise refers to the need to continually increase the stress placed on the muscle as it becomes capable of producing greater force. For example, at the start of a training program the five RM for arm curls might be 50 lb, a sufficient stimulus to produce an increase in strength. Later on in the training program five repetitions at 50 lb would not be a sufficient stimulus to produce further gains. The muscles involved can easily perform five repetitions with 50 lb and consequently 50 lb is no longer a five RM. If the training load is not increased at this point, no further gains in strength will be realized.

There are several prescribed methods for progressively overloading the muscle. The resistance (amount of weight utilized) to perform a certain number of repetitions can be increased. The use of RMs automatically provides progressive overload because as the muscle's strength increases the amount of resistance necessary to perform a true

RM also increases. A five RM of 50 lb may increase to 60 lb after several weeks of training. Another method is to progressively overload the muscle by increasing the volume of training performed (i.e., the number of sets and repetitions of a particular exercise). Due to the possibility of *overtraining* care must be exercised when progressively overloading the muscle. This is especially true when the progressive resistance is in the form of an increased volume of training (Stone et al., 1982).

Rest Periods

Recovery both between sets of exercises and between training sessions are important factors. The rest periods allowed between sets of exercises are in large part determined by the goals of the training program. If the goal of the program is to increase the ability to exhibit maximal strength, relatively long rest periods (several minutes) and heavy resistances should be used. When the goal is to increase the ability to perform high-intensity exercise, rest periods between sets should be less than one minute. If enhancement of long-term endurance (aerobic power) is the goal then short rest periods and relatively light resistances are prescribed.

Traditionally, one day of recovery is allowed between training sessions for a particular muscle group. This is still a good rule of thumb, though some evidence indicates that other patterns of training sessions and recovery periods are equally beneficial (see chapter 3 for more information). Residual muscular soreness, when present to the extent that it interferes with performance of the following training session, is a good indication that the rest between workouts was insufficient (see chapter 3 for more information concerning rest periods between sets and training sessions).

Speed Specificity

Most coaches and athletes maintain that resistance training should be performed at the velocity encountered during the actual sporting event. They believe that resistance training produces its greatest strength gains at the velocity at which the training is performed. Though there is scientific evidence that supports this view (see chapter 2, Isokinetics) an intermediate training velocity is best if the aim of the program is to increase strength at all velocities of movement. For an individual interested in general strength, an intermediate training velocity is recommended.

Contraction Specificity

If an individual trains isometrically, and progress is evaluated with a static contraction, a large increase in strength may seem apparent. However, if this same individual's progress is determined by dynamic testing little or no increase in strength may be demonstrated. This is called *testing specificity* (see chapter 2, Comparisons of Types of Training). This testing specificity indicates that gains in strength are specific to the type of training (e.g., isometric, variable resistance, isokinetic) performed. Therefore, a training program for a specific sport should consist predominantly of the types of muscular contractions encountered in that sport (see chapter 3). As an example, because isometric contractions are frequently performed while wrestling, it is beneficial to incorporate some isometric training into the resistance program for wrestling.

Muscle Group Specificity

Muscle group specificity simply means that each muscle group requiring strength gains must be specifically trained. If an increase in strength is desired in the abductors of the upper arm, exercises such as dumbbell lateral raises must be incorporated into the training program. There must be exercises in a training program specifically chosen for each muscle group in which an increase in strength is desired.

Energy Source Specificity

There are two anaerobic sources and one aerobic source of energy for muscular contractions (see chapters 6 and 7). If an increase in the ability of a muscle to perform anaerobic exercise is desired, the bouts of exercise should be of short duration and high intensity. If increases in the muscle's ability to perform aerobic exercise is desired the training performed will be of a longer duration and lower intensity. Resistance training is usually associated with training of the anaerobic energy sources. The number of sets and repetitions and the length of rest periods between sets and exercises chosen should be consistent with the energy source in which training adaptations are desired. This is discussed in more detail in chapter 3.

Safety Aspects of Lifting

Successful resistance training programs have one prominent feature in common—safety. Without safe lifting techniques, spotting, and proper breathing, the quality of the training program is reduced.

Spotting

Proper spotting is necessary to ensure the safety of the participants in a resistance training program. Spotters serve two important functions: to assist the trainee with the exercise and to summon help if an accident does occur.

A detailed description of spotting techniques for all exercises is beyond the scope of this text. However, several factors should be considered when spotting. The spotter must be strong enough to assist the trainee if needed. During the performance of certain exercises (e.g., back squats) more than one spotter may be necessary to ensure the safety of the lifter. Spotters should know the proper technique of the lift they are spotting and must be attentive to the lifter and his or her performance of the exercise. Following these simple guidelines will aid in the avoidance of injury in a resistance training program.

Breathing

A valsalva maneuver (holding your breath with a closed glottis) during performance of resistance training is not recommended. Extremely high blood pressures up to 480/350 mm Hg during the performance of a double leg press have been reported (MacDougall, Tusen, Sale, Moroz, & Sutton, 1985). Figure 1.1 depicts the intraarterial blood pressure response during maximal isometric contractions of the leg extensors of one leg. The blood pressure response during an isometric contraction in which breathing was allowed is substantially lower than the response observed from an isometric contraction performed simultaneously with a valsalva maneuver as well as a valsalva maneuver in the absence of an isometric contraction. This demonstrates that the elevation of blood pressure during resistance training is much lower if breathing is performed during the contraction as opposed to the performance of a valsalva maneuver during the contraction. Elevated blood pressure makes the work of pumping blood by the heart more difficult and requires substantially more energy than pumping the same volume of blood at a lower pressure. Normally, it is recommended to exhale during the lifting of the resistance and inhale during the lowering of the resistance portions of each repetition.

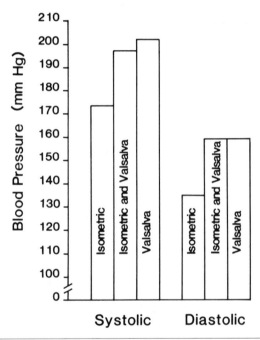

Figure 1.1 Systolic and diastolic blood pressures are depicted during an isometric contraction only, simultaneous isometric contraction and valsalva maneuver, and valsalva maneuver only. Unpublished data of Fleck and Dean, 1985, N = 6.

Proper Form

The proper form of various resistance training exercises is partially determined by the desire to train specific muscle groups with specific exercises. Altering the proper form of an exercise allows the utilization of other muscle groups to perform the exercise movement. This decreases the training stimulus on the muscles normally associated with a particular exercise. Breaking of proper form is used in several advanced systems of resistance training (burn system, forced repetition system). These systems are not recommended for beginning resistance trainers (see chapter 4, Systems of Resistance Training).

Proper form is also necessary as an injury prevention measure. This is especially true in exercises such as squats, deadlifts, and power cleans. Breaking of proper form in these types of exercises normally places undue stress on the lower back region. Improper form in these types of exercises should be avoided and is normally associated with individuals who try to perform the exercise with resistances presently greater than their capabilities.

Full Range of Motion

Normally exercises are performed through the full range of motion allowed by the body position and the joints involved. Although no definitive studies are available, it is assumed that to develop strength throughout the full range of motion of a joint, training must be performed through the full range of motion. Studies involving the joint angle specificity of isometric training indicate that if training is only performed at a specific joint angle, strength gains will be realized in a narrow range around that specific joint angle and not throughout the joint's range of motion (see chapter 2, Isometric Training).

These basic principles apply to all training programs and types of training. They should be considered and applied to the types of training discussed in chapter 2.

Chapter 2

Types of Strength Training

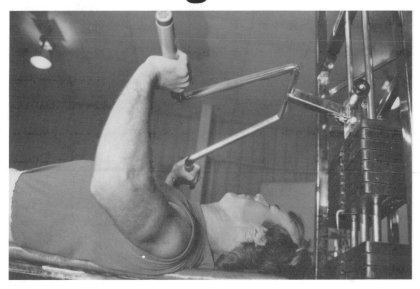

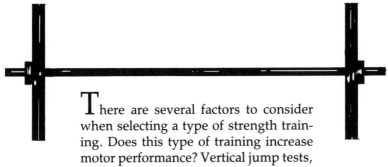

There are several factors to consider when selecting a type of strength training. Does this type of training increase motor performance? Vertical jump tests, a 40-yard dash, and throwing a ball for distance are common motor performance tests. Most athletes perform strength training as a portion of their overall training program. Their main interest is not how much weight they can lift, but whether increased strength brought about by training results in better performances in their particular sport.

Is strength increased throughout the range of motion and at all velocities of movement? Most sports require strength through the entire range of joint motion, or at least a major portion of it. If strength is not increased throughout the entire range of motion, performance may not be enhanced as much as possible by a particular type of training. The majority of athletic events require strength at a variety of movement speeds, particularly at fast velocities. If strength is not increased over a range of movement speeds once again improvements in performance may not be optimal.

Other questions to consider include: How much equipment is needed and what is the cost of the equipment? Does this type of training cause changes in percentage of body fat and, if so, to what extent? How much of an increase in strength can be expected over a specified training period with this type of training? How does this type of training compare with other types of training in the preceding factors?

There has been a considerable amount of research concerning resistance training. The emergence of conclusions from this research, however, is hampered by several intervening factors. The vast majority of studies have been short term in duration (8 to 12 weeks), which makes direct application of the results of these studies to long-term training (years) controversial. Some of the elements that can affect gains in strength are the number of muscular contractions performed, the load or intensity utilized in training, and the pretraining status of the individual. These elements vary considerably from study to study and make interpretation of the results difficult. Enough research has been conducted, however, to reach some tentative conclusions concerning the types of strength training. This chapter addresses the major research in the field of strength training and the various conclusions that it demonstrates.

Isometrics

Isometric or static resistance training refers to a muscular contraction where no change in the length of the muscle takes place. The muscle does not generate enough force against the mass to cause movement. This type of resistance training is normally performed against an immovable object such as a wall, a barbell, or a weight machine loaded beyond the maximal concentric strength of an individual. Isometrics can also be performed by having a weak muscle group contract against a strong muscle group. For example, trying to bend the left elbow and resisting the movement by pushing down on the left hand with the right hand. The left elbow flexors are weaker than the right elbow extensors, so the left biceps would be performing an isometric contraction. The cost of using isometrics can range from minimal (use of a wall as an immovable object) to quite expensive (use of a weight machine).

Isometrics came to the attention of the American public in the early 1950s, when Steinhaus (1954) introduced the work of two Germans, Hettinger and Muller (1953). Hettinger and Muller concluded that gains in strength of 5% per week were produced by one daily two-thirds of maximal isometric contraction six seconds in duration. Gains in strength of this magnitude with such little training time and effort seemed unbelievable. Subsequent studies demonstrated that isometric training leads to static strength gains but that the gains are substantially less than 5% per week (Fleck & Schutt, 1985).

Increases in strength from isometric training are related to the number of contractions performed, the duration of the contractions, whether the contraction is maximal or submaximal, and the frequency of training. Most studies involving isometric training manipulate several of these simultaneously. It is difficult, therefore, to evaluate the importance of any one factor. Enough research has been conducted, however, to allow for certain recommendations concerning isometric training.

Voluntary Maximal Contractions

Some increases in strength can be achieved with submaximal isometric muscular contractions (Davies & Young, 1983; Hettinger & Muller, 1953). However, the majority of research supports the idea that maximal are superior to submaximal isometric contractions in bringing about increases in strength (Rasch & Morehouse, 1957; Ward & Fisk, 1964).

Number of Contractions and Training Duration

Hettinger and Muller (1953) proposed that only a six-second contraction per day was necessary to produce maximal gains in strength. Other studies have experimented with various combinations of number and duration of contractions: Bonde-Peterson (1960) used one five-second contraction, and Davies and Young (1983) tried seven sixty-second contractions per training day. The majority of research has utilized contractions of three to ten seconds in duration and a relatively small number of contractions per day (see Table 2.1). The duration of the contraction and the number of training contractions per day individually show a weak correlation to increases in strength when compared with the product of the contraction duration times the number of contractions (MacDonagh & Davies, 1984). This means that optimal gains in strength are the result of either a small number of long duration contractions or a higher number of short duration contractions. Table 2.1 also indicates that one contraction per day is ineffective in causing increases in strength.

Frequency of Training

The optimal training frequency (i.e., the number of training sessions per week) has also received attention. Hettinger (1961) calculated that both alternate-day and once-a-week isometric training programs are 80% and 40%, respectively, as effective as daily training sessions. He also concluded that training once every two weeks does not cause increases in strength though it does serve to maintain strength. The exact percentages are controversial but the superiority of daily training with isometrics is well established (Atha, 1981). To bring about increases in maximal strength the optimal isometric program should consist of maximal isometric contractions performed on a daily basis. In addition the product of the number of training contractions times the duration of the contractions should be large (i.e., greater than 30).

Table 2.1 Effect of Isometric Training on Maximal Voluntary Isometric Contractions

Reference	Duration of contraction(s)	Contractions per day	Duration × contractions per day	Number of training days	M.V.I.C. increase (%)	M.V.I.C. increase % day	Muscles
Ikai & Fukunaga, 1970	10	3	30	100	92	0.9	Elbow flexors
Komi et al., 1978	3-5	5	15-25	48	20	0.4	Quadriceps
Bonde-Peterson, 1960	5	10	50	36	15	0.4	Elbow flexors
Bonde-Peterson, 1960	5	1	5	36	0	0	Elbow flexors
Davies & Young, 1983	3	42	126	35	30	0.86	Triceps surae
McDonagh et al., 1983	3	30	90	28	20	0.71	Elbow flexors
Grimby et al., 1973	3	30	90	30	32	1.1	Triceps

MVIC = maximal voluntary isometric contraction

Note. From "Adaptive Responses of Mammalian Skeletal Muscle to Exercise With High Loads," by M.J.N. McDonagh and C.T.M. Davies, 1984, *European Journal of Applied Physiology,* **52**, p. 140. Copyright 1984 by Springer-Verlag. Adapted by permission.

Muscular Hypertrophy

Significant increases in limb circumferences (Kanehisa & Miyashita, 1983; Meyers, 1967; Rarick & Larson, 1958) and total body weight (Kanehisa & Miyashita, 1983) can occur due to isometric training. These changes (especially the increases in limb circumferences) are usually associated with muscular hypertrophy. Significant increases in static strength due to isometric training with no increase in limb circumference have been reported (Ward & Fisk, 1964). Increases in strength with no similar increases in muscular hypertrophy are normally attributed to some adaptation of neural factors (see chapter 6, Order of Fiber Type Recruitment and Proprioceptors). It is evident that isometric training can bring about increases in hypertrophy and neural adaptations, both of which can increase strength.

Joint Angle Specificity

Static strength increases due to isometric training are joint angle specific (Gardner, 1963; Meyers, 1967; Williams & Stutzman, 1959). If isometric training is performed at a joint angle of 90 degrees, strength will be increased at this joint angle but not necessarily at other joint angles. This joint angle specificity appears to have a carryover of plus and minus 20 degrees of the training joint angle (Knapik, Mawdsley, & Ramos, 1983). In addition, twenty six-second isometric contractions cause a greater carryover or transfer to joint angles besides the training angle than six six-second contractions (Meyers, 1967). This demonstrates that a greater number of contractions leads to a greater carryover of strength to joint angles other than the training angle. Isometric training of the elbow flexors at four different angles does increase static strength at all four angles and significantly increases dynamic power of the elbow flexors (Kaneshisa & Miyashita, 1983). The above studies demonstrate that if isometric training is used to increase strength throughout a joint's range of motion, training must take place at several joint angles and a large number of training contractions should be used.

It is at times possible to take advantage of isometric training's joint angle specificity. Each dynamic exercise has a sticking point. Sticking point refers to the joint position in a movement where the mechanical advantage is at its lowest point and therefore is the most difficult portion of the movement to perform. Performance of isometric training at the sticking point will increase strength at this joint angle and therefore aid in performance of the dynamic exercise.

Motor Performance

Isometric training does not increase motor performance ability (Clarke, 1973; Fleck & Schutt, 1985). This may be due in part to two factors. Isometric training can reduce the maximal speed of a limb's movement (Swegan, 1957). In addition a limb's maximal speed, with little resistance to its movement, is not increased due to isometric training (DeKoning, Binkhorst, Vissers, & Vos, 1982). Motor performance tests involve movement at maximal speeds with little resistance. A decrease in a limb's maximal speed or a lack of improvement in maximal speed with small resistance will lead to *no* increase in motor performance ability. The aforementioned studies involved isometric training at only one joint angle. Dynamic power over a wide range of resistance can be increased due to isometric training at four different joint angles within the range of motion (Kanehisa & Miyashita, 1983). The possibility exists therefore that increases in motor performance may occur if isometric training is performed at several joint angles.

Miscellaneous Considerations

Because elaborate equipment is not necessary, isometrics can be performed virtually anywhere. The lack of movement of an external object can lead to motivational problems with some trainees. This can also make it difficult for the coach to assess whether the trainee is performing at the desired maximal intensity.

Dynamic Constant Resistance

Isotonic is traditionally defined as a muscular contraction in which the muscle exerts a constant tension. The execution of free-weight exercises and exercises on various weight training machines, though usually considered isotonic, are not by nature isotonic. The tension exerted by a muscle in the performance of such exercises is not constant but varies with the mechanical advantage of the joint involved in the movement. A more workable definition of isotonic is a resistance training exercise where the external resistance or weight does not vary. Because there is confusion concerning the term isotonic, most people have adopted the term dynamic constant resistance training. The cost of this type of training ranges from quite inexpensive to relatively expensive equipment. This wide range is due to the wide variety of equipment that can be used to perform dynamic constant resistance training.

Number of Sets and Repetitions

The optimum number of sets and repetitions using dynamic constant external resistance training necessary to achieve optimal gains in strength has received a great deal of attention. This line of inquiry assumes that (a) an optimum number of sets and repetitions actually exists (b) once found it will work for all individuals and exercises, and (c) it will promote increases in strength for an indefinite period of time. In reviewing the research concerning this topic it should be kept in mind that the majority of studies examining this subject used novice, college-aged individuals as trainees and covered a relatively short time period (eight to twelve weeks.) The effects of pretraining status and the duration of the study may have on the results of a research project are shown in Figure 2.1.

Berger's studies in the 1960s focused on the bench press and back squat exercises, trained with repetition maximums, and used one RM as the testing criterion. A repetition maximum is the maximal amount of resistance that can be lifted for a specific number of repetitions. At a seven RM the resistance is such that only seven repetitions can be

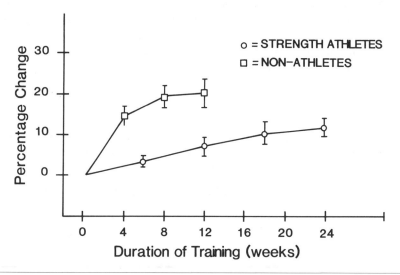

Figure 2-1 The percentage change in maximal squat ability from the pretraining value is dependent upon pretraining status of the trainees and duration of the training. *Note.* From ''Factors Influencing Trainability of Muscular Strength During Short-Term and Prolonged Training'' by K. Hakkinen, 1985, *National Strength and Conditioning Association Journal, 7,* p. 33. Copyright 1985 by the National Strength and Conditioning Association. Adapted by permission.

completed and an eighth repetition is not possible. Berger's research indicated that the optimum number of sets and repetitions for the bench press and the back squat was three and six, respectively (Berger, 1962a, 1962b). In a later study Berger seems to contradict his earlier findings (Berger 1963). Groups were trained utilizing six sets at two RM, three sets at six RM and three sets at ten RM. All groups gained significantly according to the one RM testing criterion but no significant difference was demonstrated between the training groups. This demonstrates that there may be various combinations of sets and repetitions that cause optimal gains in strength.

Other researchers have substantiated the conclusion that there is no one optimal combination of sets and repetitions. No difference in increases of one RM was found when training consisted of three sets of six RM and two sets of nine RM (Henderson, 1970) five sets at three RM, four sets at five RM or three sets at seven RM (Withers, 1970) or three sets of two to three, five to six, or nine to ten RM (O'Shea, 1966). Common to all of these studies is the fact that the sets were all performed at an RM and therefore performed to failure. This means at the end of the set the muscles were performing a voluntary maximal contraction.

Tables 2.2 and 2.4 depict changes in the bench and leg press due to dynamic constant resistance training. These tables and the aforementioned studies indicate that the optimum number of repetitions for strength improvement is somewhere between two and ten RM and the optimum number of sets is between two and five.

Maximal Contractions

The need for voluntary maximal muscular contractions to produce optimal gains in strength is demonstrated by Berger and Hardage's study

Table 2.2   Effect of Frequency of Training on One RM Bench Press

Reference	Subjects (by sex)	Days per week of training and percent improvement					
Gilliam, 1981	Male	Days	1	2	3	4	5
		% Improvement	19	24	32	29	41
Hunter, 1985	Male	Days	3	4			
		% Improvement	12	17			
Hunter, 1985	Female	Days	3	4			
		% Improvement	20	33			

Table 2.3   Changes in Bench Press Strength Due to Training

Reference	Sex of subjects	Type of training	Length of training (weeks)	Days of training/ week	Sets and repetitions	Equipment trained on % increase	Comparative test Type of equipment	% increase
Brown & Wilmore, 1974	F	IT	24	3	8 wk = 1 × 10,8,7,6,5,4 16 wk = 1 × 10,6,5,4,3	38	—	—
Mayhew & Gross, 1974	F	IT	9	3	2 × 20	26	—	—
Wilmore, 1974	F	IT	10	2	2 × 7-16	29	—	—
Wilmore et al., 1978	F	IT	10	3	40%-55% 1 RM for 30 s	20	—	—
Berger, 1962a	M	IT	12	3	3 × 6	30	—	—
Fahey & Brown, 1973	M	IT	9	3	5 × 5	12	—	—
Wilmore, 1974	M	IT	10	2	2 × 7-16	16	—	—
Allen et al., 1976	M	IT	12	3	2 × 8, 1 × exhaustion	44	—	—
Ariel, 1977	M	IT	20	5	4 × 8-3	14	—	—
Wilmore et al., 1978	M	IT	10	3	40%-55% 1 RM for 30 s	8	—	—
Gettman et al., 1978	M	IT	20	3	50% 1 RM, 6 wk = 2 × 10-20 14 wk = 2 × 15	32	IK (12/s)	27
Coleman, 1977	M	IT	10	3	2 × 8-10 RM	12	—	—
Coleman, 1977	M	VR	10	3	1 × 10-12 RM	—	IT++	12
Ariel, 1977	M	VR	20	5	4 × 8-3	—	IT	29
Gettman & Ayres, 1978	M	IK (60°/s)	10	3	3 × 10-15	—	IT	11
Gettman & Ayres, 1978	M	IK (120°/s)	10	3	3 × 10-15	—	IT	9
Gettman et al., 1979	M	IK	8	3	4 wk = 1 × 10 at 60° s 4 wk = 1 × 15 at 90° s	22	IT	11

IT = isotonic

VR = variable resistance

IK = isokinetic

+ = values for 10 RM

+ + = values for average training weights

RM = repetition maximum

(1967). They selected two groups to undergo a training program of one set of ten repetitions. For Group 1 the initial repetition was at the one RM level, and each following repetition was adjusted so that a maximum effort was required; Group 2 trained with one full set at ten RM. Both groups trained three times per week for eight weeks. Though both groups made significant gains in strength, Group 1 improved significantly more than Group 2. This demonstrates the need for voluntary maximal contractions to achieve optimal strength improvement.

Frequency of Training

The frequency of dynamic constant resistance training is the subject of several studies. Studies which compared three versus two training sessions per week suggest that either three is superior to two (Henderson, 1970) or two is superior to three (Berger, 1965) in causing increases in strength. A comparison of frequencies of five, three, and two training sessions demonstrates that five and three bring about significantly greater increases in strength than two (Barham, 1960). This study demonstrated no difference, however, between five and three training sessions per week.

Table 2.2 presents two studies concerning frequency of training. One of these studies (Gilliam, 1981) compared frequencies from one to five times per week. The study showed five to be superior to the lower frequencies in causing increases in a one RM bench press. The other significant difference reported in this particular study is that three is superior to two training sessions per week. A study comparing four and three training sessions per week using male and female subjects reports that both sexes gain significantly more in their one RM bench press with more frequent training sessions (Hunter, 1985). Interestingly, the four-sessions-per-week subjects trained two consecutive days twice a week, (i.e., Monday, Tuesday, and Thursday, Friday), while the three-sessions-per-week groups trained in the traditional alternate-day method (i.e., Monday, Wednesday, Friday).

These studies of training frequency have certain shortcomings: They all examined beginning resistance exercisers (novice subjects); they examined short time periods (up to 12 weeks); and most of them did not equate the total amount of sets and repetitions performed by the different training groups. A tentative conclusion that arises from these studies is that the greater frequency groups realized greater increases in strength. The majority of research indicates that three training sessions per muscle group per week is the minimum frequency which causes maximum gains in strength.

Motor Performance

Dynamic constant resistance training has been proven to increase motor performance. Countless studies show increases in motor performance tests of the vertical jump (Campbell, 1962; Capen, 1950; Chu, 1950; Stone, O'Bryant, & Garhammer, 1981), the standing long jump (Capen, 1950; Chu, 1950; Schultz, 1968), shuttle run (Campbell, 1962; Kusintz & Kenney, 1958), the short sprint (Capen, 1950; Schultz, 1967), and the shot put (Chu, 1950; Schultz, 1967). Statistically insignificant changes in short sprint time (Chu, 1950) and decreases in standing long jump ability (Schultz, 1971) have also been demonstrated. Overhead baseball throwing ability for speed and accuracy, according to two studies, is not significantly affected by dynamic constant resistance training with weighted-ball or pulley-type exercises (Brose & Hanson, 1967; Straub, 1968). Though conflicting results emerge from this research, as a whole it demonstrates that dynamic constant resistance training can significantly improve motor performance ability.

Direct practice, alone or combined with resistance or sprint training, increases standing long jump ability to a significantly greater degree than resistance training alone (Schultz, 1967). This study noted no significant difference in the various combinations of direct practice training. These results indicate that if a major goal of a resistance training program is to optimally improve motor performance, direct practice of the skill and resistance training should be combined in the training program.

Strength Changes

Increases in strength for both sexes due to dynamic constant resistance training are well documented. Tables 2.2, 2.3, and 2.4 present changes in a one RM bench press and leg press due to short-term dynamic constant resistance training. Women experience substantial increases in one RM leg strength; one project measured a 48% increase in only nine weeks of training (Mayhew & Gross, 1974). Increases in one RM leg strength for men range from 71% in twelve weeks (Allen, Byrd, & Smith, 1976) to 7% in ten weeks (Wilmore et al., 1978). Using a one RM bench press as the testing criterion, women have reportedly increased by 38% in 24 weeks of training (Brown & Wilmore, 1974). Similarly, men experienced increases ranging from 44% in twelve weeks (Allen et al., 1976) to 8% in ten weeks (Wilmore et al., 1978). The range of possible increases in strength is most likely due to differences in the subjects' pretraining status.

Table 2.4 Changes in Leg Press Strength Due to Training

Reference	Sex of subjects	Type of training	Length of training (weeks)	Days of training/ week	Sets and repetitions	Equipment trained on % increase	Comparative test type of equipment	% increase
Mayhew & Gross, 1974	F	IT	9	3	2 × 10	48*	—	—
Brown & Wilmore, 1974	F	IT	24	3	8 wk = 1 × 10,8,7,6,5,4 16 wk = 1 × 10,6,5,4,3	29	—	—
Wilmore et al., 1978	F	IT	10	3	40%-55% 1 RM for 30 s	27	—	—
Allen et al., 1976	M	IT	12	3	2 × 8 1 × exhaustion	71++	—	—
Wilmore et al., 1978	M	IT	10	3	40%-55% 1 RM for 30 s	7	—	—
Gettman et al., 1978	M	IT	20	3	50% 1 RM, 6 wk = 2 × 10-20 14 wk = 2 × 15	—	IK	43.0
Coleman, 1977	M	IT	10	3	2 × 8-10 RM	17	—	—
Coleman, 1977	M	VR	10	3	1 × 10-12 RM	—	IT	18.0
Pipes, 1978	M	VR	10	3	3 × 8	27	IT	7.5
Gettman et al., 1980	M	VR	20	3	3 × 8	18*	IK	17.0
Gettman et al., 1979	M	IK	8	3	4 wk = 1 × 10 at 60° s 4 wk = 1 × 15 at 90° s	38	IT	18.0
Gettman et al., 1980	M	IK	20	3	2 × 12 at 60° s	42	VR	10.0

IT = isotonic

VR = variable resistance

IK = isokinetic

+ = values for 10 RM

+ + = values for average training weights

* = values for number of weight plates

RM = repetition maximum

Body Compositional Changes

The normal pattern of changes in body composition due to short-term dynamic constant resistance training includes small increases in lean body mass and small decreases in percent body fat. Because these two changes occur simultaneously the result is little or no change in total body weight (see Table 7.1).

Eccentric Training

Eccentric (also called negative resistance) training refers to a muscular contraction in which the muscle lengthens. This type of contraction is found in daily life. Walking down a flight of stairs, for example, requires the thigh muscles to perform eccentric contractions. Performance of normal dynamic constant resistance training requires eccentric contractions whenever the resistance is lowered. The lifting of a resistance causes the muscle to shorten as it contracts and is called a concentric contraction. As with dynamic constant resistance training equipment the financial cost of eccentric training can vary considerably. If free weights are used the cost is quite modest. If a weight machine is used the cost can range from modest to quite expensive.

Strength Changes

Advocates of eccentric training believe that, due to the application of a greater amount of resistance during eccentric training, it leads to greater increases in strength when compared with concentric and normal dynamic resistance training. Muscle tension is higher during eccentric contractions than it is during either isometric or concentric contractions (Olson, Schmidt, & Johnson, 1972). Short-term eccentric training (8 to 12 weeks) causes significant increases in strength of maximal eccentric, concentric, dynamic constant resistance, and isometric contractions (Atha, 1981; Clarke, 1973; Fleck & Schutt, 1985). On a percentage-increase basis, six eccentric contractions performed four times per week for seven weeks causes greater increases in maximal eccentric, concentric, and isometric force than the same program using only concentric contractions (Komi & Buskirk, 1972). However, the vast majority of studies report no significant difference in gains in isometric, concentric, and eccentric strength due to training isometrically, concentrically, with constant dynamic resistance, and eccentrically (Atha, 1981; Clarke, 1973; Fleck & Schutt, 1985).

Optimal Eccentric Resistance

The optimal resistance to be used for eccentric training has received some study. Jones (1973) believes the optimal resistance to be a load the subject could lower slowly and halt at will. Using this definition others claim that a resistance of 120% of the dynamic constant resistance one RM is appropriate (Johnson, Adamczy, Tennoe, & Stromme, 1976).

Motor Performance and Body Composition

Few studies have examined the effects that negative resistance training has on motor performance and lean body mass, but some research has suggested a positive relationship. Vertical jumping ability did increase with negative resistance training of the legs (Bonde-Peterson & Knuttgen, 1971). Upper arm circumference showed significant increases with eccentric training, but the increase did not differ significantly from increases due to concentric training (Komi & Buskirk, 1972). Increases in limb circumference are usually associated with muscular hypertrophy.

Postexercise Soreness

A disadvantage of eccentric training is the development of greater postexercise soreness than that which accompanies isometric, isotonic, or concentric-only training (Fleck & Schutt, 1985; Talag, 1973). This soreness peaks 48 hours after exercise and lessens after each subsequent training session for a period of one to two weeks. After this time soreness is no worse than that which follows isometric training (Komi & Buskirk, 1972).

Motivational Considerations

Several other factors should be considered with regard to eccentric training. It is necessary to have a partner or some kind of equipment to assist in lifting the heavier resistance encountered in eccentric training. These heavier resistances are a potential safety hazard, especially with the use of free weights. Some individuals derive great satisfaction from training with very heavy resistance. Eccentric training for these individuals will be a positive motivational factor.

Miscellaneous Considerations

If one aim of the training program is to increase one RM bench press and squat the incorporation of eccentric training is appropriate. One of the factors that divides great from good power lifters in the bench press and squat is technique: Those who can lift greater quantities of weight are found to lower the resistance more slowly (Madsen & McLaughlin, 1984; McLaughlin, Dillman, & Lardner, 1977). It is suggested that the performance of eccentric training may facilitate both the process of lowering the resistance slowly and the keeping of proper form while this process takes place.

Variable Resistance

Variable resistance equipment operates through a lever arm, cam or pulley arrangement. Its purpose is to alter the resistance throughout the range of motion of an exercise in an attempt to match the increases and decreases in strength (strength curve) throughout the range of motion of the exercise. Ideally, by increasing and decreasing the resistance to match the strength curve of the exercise, the muscle is forced to contract maximally throughout the range of motion resulting in maximal gains in strength. Due to variations in limb length, point of attachement of the muscle's tendon to the bones, and body size, it is hard to conceive of one mechanical arrangement that would match the strength curve of all individuals for each particular exercise. Recent biomechanical research indicates that for at least one type of variable resistance equipment considerable modification of the five examined exercise machines is needed to approximate the strength curves of the exercise movement (Harman, 1983). The financial cost of variable resistance training ranges from modest to very expensive because of the variety of variable resistance machines that are now available.

Strength Changes

Significant strength gains from short-term variable resistance training (4 to 16 weeks) have been demonstrated. Researchers have experimented with various combinations of sets and repetitions: 1 × 10-12 RM (sets multiplied by repetitions) (Peterson, 1975); four sets with increasing resistance and decreasing repetitions from eight to three in a half pyramidal program (Ariel, 1977); 2 × 12 at 50% of one RM (Gettman, Culter, & Strathman, 1980); 2 × 10-12 RM (Coleman, 1977); 1 × 8-12 RM (Hurley et al., 1984); and 1 × 12-15 RM (Stone, Johnson, & Carter, 1979). One of these studies reports a substantial increase for male trainees of 50% in upper body exercises and 33% in lower body exercises after 16 weeks of training (Hurley et al., 1984). Increases in strength in the bench and leg presses due to variable resistance training are depicted in Tables 2.3 and 2.4, respectively. It is apparent that this type of training can cause substantial increases in strength.

Motor Performance

Concerning motor performance tests, both improvement and no change have been reported with variable resistance training (Peterson, 1975; Silvester, Stiggins, McGown, & Bryce, 1985). In the Peterson study a group of football players participated in a combined program of in-season football training and variable resistance strength training. The control group participated only in the in-season football training. The resistance training program consisted of a series of 20 exercises designed to increase the strength of all the major muscle groups. A training session consisted of 2 × 8-12 RM for all 20 exercises. The resistance training group showed a mean decrease of 0.05 seconds in the 40-yard dash and a mean increase of 3.2 cm (1.3 inches) in a vertical-jump test. Within the control group the mean in the 40-yard dash was decreased by 0.03 seconds and the mean vertical jump increased 0.7 cm (0.3 inches). Whether the changes were statistically significant or whether a significant difference existed between the two groups is not addressed. This leads us to conclude that this study offers little concrete evidence concerning the relationship between motor performance and variable resistance training.

The second of these studies (Silvester et al., 1984) studied two groups: Group 1 trained on a cam-type variable resistance machine, and Group 2 trained on an increasing level arm-type variable resistance machine. Group 1 trained three days per week for six weeks followed by two days per week for five weeks (this protocol was recommended by a representative of the manufacturers of the machine). Participants did leg extensions immediately followed by leg presses, performing each exercise for 1 set of 12 repetitions to failure. Group 2 trained 3 days per week for the entire 11 weeks on the leg press using 1 set of 7-10 repetitions followed by one set to failure. No difference in static leg strength was demonstrated between the two groups. Group 1 and Group 2 increased their mean vertical jump, 0.69 cm (0.3 inches) and 2.91 cm (1.1 inches), respectively. The increase in vertical jump of Group 2 was significantly greater than Group 1. The data suggests that motor performance can increase due to variable resistance training, but this depends on the training protocol and/or equipment used.

Body Composition

Increases in lean body mass and decreases in fat percentage occur with variable resistance training. These changes in body composition are depicted in Table 7.1 and are of the same magnitude as the changes which occur due to dynamic constant resistance training.

Safety Considerations

It is possible to overstretch a muscle or joint on some variable resistance machines without proper instruction and supervision. However, overall safety is not a major concern with this type of training, and a spotter is not normally necessary.

Isokinetics

Isokinetics refers to a muscular contraction performed at constant angular limb velocity. Unlike other types of resistance training, there is no set resistance to meet; rather, the velocity of movement is controlled. The resistance offered by the isokinetic machine cannot be accelerated; any force applied against the equipment results in an equal reaction force. The reaction force mirrors the force applied to the equipment throughout the range of movement of an exercise, making it theoretically possible for the muscle(s) to exert a continual, maximal force. Advocates of isokinetic training believe that the ability to exert maximal force throughout the range of motion leads to optimal strength increases. Other advantages are that it allows for speeds of contraction closer to the speeds encountered during athletic performance while producing minimal muscle and joint soreness. This allows difficult training sessions to be more tolerable.

Strength Changes

Strength gains occur with short-term isokinetic training. Various combinations of sets, repetitions, and speeds of movement reportedly cause significant increases in strength: 1 set of 30 repetitions at 22.5

degrees/second (1 × 30 at 22.5) (Moffroid, Whipple, Hofkosh, Lowman, & Thistle, 1969); 2 × 12 at 60 (Gettman et al., 1980); 2 × 10 at 60 for four weeks, followed by 2 × 15 at 90 for four additional weeks (Gettman, Ayres, Pollock, Durstine, & Grantham, 1979); 3 × 15 at 90 (Gettman & Ayres, 1978); 3 × 15 at 60 (Gettman & Ayres, 1978); 5 × 5 at 60 (Ciriello, Holden, & Evans, 1983); 15 × 10 at 60 (Ciriello, Holden, & Evans, 1983); and 1 × 10 at 60, 1 × 30 at 179, and 1 × 50 at 299 (Kanehisa & Miyashita, 1983). Gains in strength have also been achieved by performing as many repetitions as possible in set periods of time of 6 and 30 seconds at 180 degrees per second (Lesmes, Costill, Coyle, & Fink, 1978). Increases in strength have also been achieved by performing a set of voluntary maximal contractions until a given percentage of peak force could no longer be generated. One set continued until peak force of at least 60%, 75%, or 90% could no longer be generated at each velocity of 30, 60, and 90 degrees per second (Fleck, 1979) and until 50% of peak force could no longer be maintained during slow speed training (1 set at each velocity of 30, 60, and 90 degrees/second) or fast speed training (1 set at each velocity of 180, 240, and 300 degrees/second) (Smith & Melton, 1981). Tables 2.3 and 2.4 include changes in strength in the bench press and leg press (squat) due to isokinetic training. It is apparent that many combinations of sets and repetitions of isokinetic training can cause increases in strength.

Number of Sets and Repetitions

Despite the vast quantity of research concerning the effects of isokinetic training, little has been said about the optimal number of sets and reptitions. One study (Lesmes et al., 1978) shows no difference in gains of peak torque between 10 sets of 6-second duration, performing as many repetitions as possible (approx 3), and 2 sets of 30-second duration, performing as many repetitions as possible (approx 10). Both groups trained at 180 degrees per second four times a week for seven weeks. Another study compared all combinations of 5, 10, and 15 repetitions along with slow, intermediate, and fast velocities of movement. After training three days per week for nine weeks no significant differences existed in strength among any of the groups (Davies, 1977). Five sets of 5 repetitions (Group A) and 15 sets of 10 repetitions (Group B), both at 60 degrees per second have also been compared (Ciriello, Holden, & Evans, 1983). In this study training was performed three times per week for 16 weeks. They tested peak torque at eight velocities ranging from 0 to 300 degrees per second. Both groups improved significantly at all test velocities; only one significant difference existed between the two: At 30 degrees per second, Group B showed greater gains than Group A. All three of these studies agree on at least one point: The number of repetitions performed appears to have little to do with increases in peak torque. (Note: the minimal number of repetitions performed per set in these studies was three.)

Training Velocity

Previously cited studies firmly support the idea that isokinetic training effects an increase in strength. Two questions inherent to isokinetic training have yet escaped unequivocal answers. What is the optimal training speed: fast or slow? Do strength increases obtained at a particular training speed carry over to speeds above and below it?

Though several studies have investigated the first of these questions no conclusive answer has emerged. After comparing 36 and 108 degrees per second Moffroid and Whipple (1970) determined that fast speed training is superior to slow speed training. Alternatively, two studies favor slow speed over fast speed training for gains in peak torque. One of these (Oteghen, 1975) used the bench press to compare a slow speed training group (10 seconds to complete one repetition) and a fast speed training group (2 seconds to complete one repetition). The second project compared 60 and 120 degrees per second (Gettman & Ayres, 1978). Finally, some research suggests that there is no evidence to favor either slow or fast speeds when considering gains in peak torque (Katch, Pechar, Pardew, & Smith, 1975). This specific project compared a slow speed training group (10 seconds to complete one repetition) and a fast speed training group (2 seconds to complete one repetition). Besides the conflicting reports of these studies other factors impede any conclusions favoring slow or fast speed training. All of the research covered a short duration of no more than 10 weeks making conclusions concerning long-term training difficult. Because the majority of these studies experimented with such slow speeds in general, any comparison between slow and fast speeds is artifical. During many physical activities angular limb velocities of greater than 300 degrees per second are easily achieved. A conclusion favoring either a slow or a fast speed of training, in terms of velocities below 300 degrees per second, has little practical application for most athletes.

Two studies do however provide some insight into the fast- versus-slow-velocity question. Kanehisa and Miyashita (1983) trained three groups at specified velocities of 60, 179, and 300 degrees per second, six times per week for eight weeks. The slowest of these, Group 1, performed 10 voluntary maximal contractions per session. Groups 2 and 3 performed 30 and 50, respectively. All were tested for peak torque at 60, 119, 179, 239, and 300 degrees per second both before and after the training program. Groups 1 and 2 increased significantly in average power of a repetition at all test speeds. Group 3 increased significantly in average power of a repetition only at the fastest test speeds (i.e., 239 and 300 degrees per second). In addition, Groups 2 and 3 showed a significantly greater increase in average power of a repetition than Group 1 at the test speeds of 239 and 300 degrees per second. The fact that this study varied the number of repetitions prohibits any set conclusions. From the immediate results, however, it appears than an intermediate speed (approx 179 degrees per second) is the most advantageous for gains in average power over a range of movement.

The last study considered in this context also utilized three groups (Coyle et al., 1981). Group A, a slow speed group, trained at 60 degrees per second with five sets of six maximal contractions; Group B, a fast speed group, trained at 300 degrees per second with five sets of 12 maximal contractions. Group C used a combination of slow and fast speeds: two or three sets of six repetitions at 60 degrees per second and two or three sets of 12 repetitions at 300 degrees per second. The results of the tests for peak torque are presented in Table 2.5. It is evident that each group showed its greatest gains at its specific training velocity. At 0 degrees per second (isometric) all three groups experienced similar gains, demonstrating that the velocity of training is dictated by the velocity of desired peak torque increases. In other words, if an individual wants peak torque increases at slow speeds, slow speed training is prescribed. Likewise, if the goal is peak torque increases at fast speeds, fast speed training is the key.

Velocity and Strength Carryover

The second question concerning isokinetic training is whether increases in peak torque carry over to velocities beyond the training velocity. Recall the Moffroid and Whipple study that compared 36 and 108 degrees per second (1970). They found that increases in peak torque only carried over to speeds of movement below the training velocity (see Figure 2.2). The study depicted in Table 2.5 also lends support to this finding, but it should be noted that the slow group (60 degrees per second) demonstrated some increases at speeds greater than its training velocity. These studies all determined peak torque irrespective of the joint angle at which peak torque occurred. One might question whether the torque was actually increased at a specific joint angle and therefore a specific muscle length, an indication that the mechanisms controlling muscle tension at that length have been altered.

Table 2.5 Percent Increases in Peak Torque Due to Isokinetic Training at Specific Velocities

Degrees of peak torque	Peak torque increases (in percentages)		
	Group A	Group B	Group C
PT/0	Fast	Slow	Mixed
	23.6	20.3	18.9
PT/60	Slow	Mixed	Fast
	31.8	23.6	15.1
PT/180	Fast	Slow	Mixed
	16.8	9.2	7.9
PT/300	Fast	Mixed	Slow
	18.5	16.1	0.9

PT/0-PT/300 = peak torque at 0 to 300 degrees per second

Bracketed groups exhibit no statistically significant difference in peak torque.

Note. From "Specificity of Power Improvements Through Slow and Fast Isokinetic Training" by E.F. Coyle, D.C. Feiring, T.C. Rotkins, R.W. Cote, III, F.B. Roby, W. Lee, and J.H. Wilmore, 1981, *Journal of Applied Physiology: Respiratory, Environmental and Exercise Physiology,* **51,** p. 1440. Copyright 1981 by the American Physiological Society. Adapted by permission.

Peak torque of the knee extensors at velocities from 30 to 300 degrees per second is slightly higher than torque at a knee angle 30 degrees from full extension (Yates & Kamon, 1983). When subjects are grouped according to whether they have greater or less than 50% fast-twitch fibers, the two groups show no significant difference in the torque velocity curves for peak torque. For torque at a specific angle, however, the torque velocity curves are significantly different between the two groups (Yates & Kamon, 1983). These data suggest that torque at a specific angle is influenced to a greater extent than peak torque by muscle fiber-type composition.

A study which determined torque at a specific angle trained two groups at 96 and 239 degrees per second respectively (Caiozzo, Perrine, & Edgerton, 1981). Table 2.6 depicts the improvement (in percentages) which occurred at the testing velocities. The first group (96 deg/second) showed significant increases in torque above and below the training speed. The second group (239 deg/s) showed significant

Table 2.6 Isokinetic Versus Variable Resistance Training: Strength Changes

Test and group		Test (% improvement)	
Knee Extension	Isometric	60°/s	240°/s
VR	14.6	3.1	2.3
SIK	.5	21.3	24.7
FIK	6.7	3.4	60.9
Knee Flexion			
VR	10.9	14.5	13.6
SIK	15.5	17.4	10.2
FIK	9.0	8.6	51.3

VR = variable resistance

SIK = slow speed isokinetic

FIK = fast speed isokinetic

Note. Data compiled from "Isokinetic Versus Isotonic Variable Resistance Training" by M.J. Smith and P. Melton, 1981, *American Journal of Sports Medicine, 9*, p. 276. Copyright 1981 by the American Orthopaedic Society of Sports Medicine. Adapted by permission.

increases at the two testing speeds immediately below the training speed and insignificant increases at all other testing speeds. When the test criterion is torque at a specific angle, training at a slow velocity causes significant increases in torque at faster velocities.

The results of research concerning velocity and carryover using peak torque and torque at a specific angle are not necessarily contradictory (see Figures 2.2 and 2.3). Both demonstrate that fast velocity training (108 and 239 degrees per second) causes significant increases in torque below the training velocity. Differences in the amount (significant or insignificant) of carryover below the training velocity may be attributed to the velocities that were defined as fast (108 or 239 degrees per second). Both studies also demonstrate that slow velocity training (36 and 96 degrees per second) causes significant carryover in torque below the training velocity. Both the insignificant carryover by the slowest of these (36 degrees per second) and the significant carryover by the group that trained at 96 degrees per second to velocities above their respective training velocity may be attributed to the difference in training speed, even though each group had a slow speed designation. (Note that 96 degrees per second is 2.5 times faster than 36 degrees per second.) We consider 96 degrees per second to be an intermediate rather than a slow velocity of training. A previously cited study (Kanehisa & Miyashita, 1983) demonstrated that an intermediate train-

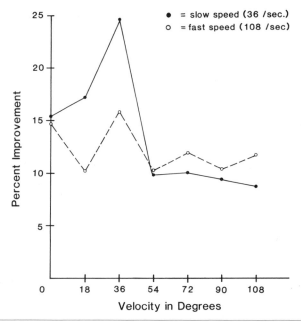

Figure 2.2 Percent change in peak torque due to slow and fast speed training. *Note.* Data from ''Specificity of Speed of Exercise'' by M.T. Moffroid and R.H. Whipple, 1970, *Physical Therapy,* **50**, p. 1695.

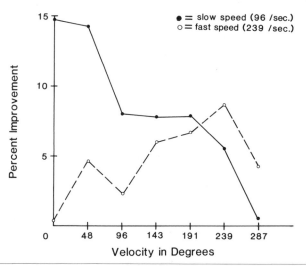

Figure 2.3 Percent change in peak torque at a specific joint angle due to slow and fast speed training. *Note.* Data from ''Training-Induced Alterations of the In Vivo Force Velocity Relationship of Human Muscle'' by V.J. Caiozzo, J.J. Perrine, and V.R. Edgerton, 1981, *Journal of Applied Physiology: Respiratory, Environmental, and Exercise Physiology,* **51**, p. 752.

ing velocity caused the greatest carryover of average power to a wider range of velocities both above and below the training velocity. Research strongly suggests that an intermediate training velocity is recommended for strength carryover. This seems to be the case for both changes in peak torque and changes in angle-specific torque.

Body Composition

Changes in body composition due to isokinetic training are included in Table 7.1. These changes include increases in lean body mass and decreases in percent fat and are of the same magnitude as those induced by other types of training.

Motor Performance

Improved motor performance, specifically, significant increases in the vertical jump (Blatther & Noble, 1979; Perrine & Edgerton, 1975; Smith & Melton, 1981), the standing broad jump (Smith & Melton, 1981), and the 40-yard dash (Smith and Melton, 1981) occur with isokinetic training. Reportedly, motor performance is increased by fast speed training more than it is by slow speed training (Smith & Melton, 1981). Training in this study consisted of one set to 50% fatigue in peak torque at 180, 240, and 300 degrees per second for the fast speed group and one set to 50% fatigue in peak torque at 30, 60, and 90 degrees per second for the slow speed group. Each group trained three times weekly for six weeks. The fast speed and slow speed groups improved, respectively, 5.4% and 3.9% in a vertical jump test, 9.1% and 0.4% in the standing long jump, and −10.1% and +4.1% in the 40-yard dash. The results suggest that fast speed isokinetic training may be more effective than slow speed training in increasing motor performance.

Miscellaneous Considerations

There are other factors to examine when considering isokinetic training. Training isokinetically has been reported to cause minimal muscular soreness (Atha, 1981). Because neither a free weight nor a weight stack has to be lifted in isokinetic training, the possibility of injury is minimal and no safety spotter is required. It is, however, difficult to judge an individual's effort unless the machine has an accurate feedback system of either the force generated or the actual work performed. Furthermore, motivation is a problem with some trainees because of the lack of visible movement of a weight or weight stack.

Comparisons of Types of Training

Studies comparing the various types of resistance training are rare. There are several problems in identifying the most beneficial type of training for strength gains. A major issue is specificity of training. When training and testing are performed using the same type of resistive equipment, a large increase in strength is demonstrated. If training and testing are performed on two different types of equipment, however, the increase in strength is substantially less, and sometimes nonexistent. Problems in comparison also arise in equating total volume of training (i.e., sets and repetitions), total work (i.e., total repetitions times resistance), and total training time. These discrepancies make it difficult to prove the superiority of one type over another of resistance training. Several of these problems are illustrated in one particular study (Leighton, Holmes, Benson, Wooten, & Schmerer, 1967). Subjects were trained twice a week for eight weeks using several isometric and dynamic constant resistance training regimes. Two of these, in particular, were an isometric program consisting of one six-second voluntary maximal contraction, and the *DeLorme dynamic constant resistance program*. The DeLorme program uses 3 sets of 10 repetitions progressing in resistance from 50% to 75% and finally to 100% of 10 RM resistance. Each of the training groups exercised three muscle groups. The isometric and DeLorme programs produced changes of 9.76% and 8.32%, respectively, in strength. According to these results isometric training proved to be superior to dynamic constant resistance training, at least in this instance. Another dynamic constant resistance program, however, resulted in a 38% increase in strength. The overall results are, then, ambiguous: Isometric training is both inferior and superior to dynamic constant resistance training. This study demonstrates that the result of a study comparing two types of training is in part dependent on the effectiveness of the training programs used for each type of training.

Isometric Versus Dynamic Constant Resistance

Comparisons of strength gains between isometric training and dynamic constant resistance training follow a pattern of test specificity. When isometric testing procedures are used isometric training is superior (Berger, 1963b; Moffroid et al., 1969), and when dynamic constant resistance testing (one RM) is used dynamic constant resistance training is superior (Berger, 1963c). Isokinetic testing for increases in strength are inconclusive. When isokinetically tested at 22.5 degrees per second, both isometric and dynamic constant resistance training groups improved 3% in peak torque (Moffroid et al., 1969). A second study demonstrated a 13% increase in peak torque for an isometrically trained group and a 28% increase for an isotonically trained group (the velocity of isokinetic testing was not given) (Thistle, Hislop, Moffroid, & Lowman, 1967). A review of the current literature finds that the better-quality dynamic constant resistance programs are more effective than the standard isometric programs for increasing strength (Atha, 1981). Regarding the most effective resistance training program, comparisons have as yet to be made. Finally, it is clear that motor performance is improved by dynamic constant resistance training to a greater extent than it is improved by isometric training (Campbell, 1962; Chu, 1950; Fleck & Schutt, 1985).

Isometric Versus Variable Resistance

The authors are aware of no studies that directly compare isometric and variable resistance training. Because various studies report no improvement in motor performance with isometric training (Clarke, 1973; Fleck & Schutt, 1985) along with some improvement in motor performance with variable resistance training (Peterson, 1975), the most that can be said is that variable resistance training may be superior to isometric training in this parameter. If an individual seeks improved motor performance, evidence suggests that variable resistance training provides more positive results than isometric training.

Isometric Versus Isokinetic Resistance

Comparisons of isometric and isokinetic resistance training follow a pattern of test specificity. Isometric is superior to isokinetic training in isometric tests (Moffroid et at., 1969). Isometric force of the knee extensors at a knee angle of 90 degrees increased 17% with isometric training and 14% with isokinetic training. At a knee angle of 45 degrees, the increases were 14% and 24%, respectively. Likewise, knee flexor strength increased, respectively, 26% and 11% at a knee angle of 90 degrees and 24% and 19% at a knee angle of 45 degrees. The isometrically trained group demonstrated superior isometric force improvements over the isokinetically trained group in three of these four tests.

Isokinetic is superior to isometric training in the development of isokinetic torque (Moffroid et al., 1969; Thistle et al., 1969). For example, knee extensor strength for isokinetically and isometrically trained groups increased 47% and 13%, respectively (Thistle et al., 1967). An additional project reported that isokinetically and isometrically trained groups increased 11% and 3%, respectively, for knee extension at 22.5 degrees per second. For knee flexion the increases were 15% and 3%, respectively, at 22.5 degrees per second (Moffroid et al., 1969). The phenomenon of test specificity is evident in the strength increases for both isometric and isokinetic training.

As with previous comparisons, the issue of improved motor performance has not been addressed in comparisons between isometric and isokinetic training. Research has indicated that isometric programs lead to no improvement in motor performance (Clarke, 1973; Fleck & Schutt, 1985) whereas some improvement has been measured with isokinetic training (Blatther & Noble, 1979; Perrine & Edgerton, 1975; Smith & Melton, 1981). The evidence suggests that isokinetic training is superior in this parameter.

Isometric Versus Eccentric Resistance

Measured isometrically there is no difference in the strength gains derived from isometric and eccentric training (Bonde-Peterson, 1960; Laycoe & Marteniuk, 1971). Bonde-Peterson trained both males and females with elbow flexions and knee extensions for 36 training sessions in 60 days. The participants trained either with isometric resistance or with eccentric resistance. All trainees performed 10 maximal 5-second contractions per day. The isometrically trained individuals experienced the following rates of improvement in isometric strength: elbow flexion, 13.8% for males and 1% for females; knee extension, 10% for males and 8.3% for females. The eccentrically trained individuals exhibited the following rates of improvement in isometric strength: elbow flexion, 8.5% for males and 5% for females; knee extension, 14.6% for males and 11.2% for females. There is no significant difference between these two types of training with regard to isometric strength.

Laycoe and Marteniuk (1971) reached the same conclusion after training two groups three times per week for six weeks with 3-second maximal contractions of the knee extensors. The isometric and eccentric groups improved 17.4% and 17%, respectively, in an isometric knee extension. Other studies also report no difference in strength gains between these two training methods (Atha, 1981).

Dynamic Constant Resistance Versus Variable Resistance

Comparisons of strength increases due to these two types of training are equivocal. After 20 weeks of training, variable resistance training demonstrated a clear superiority over dynamic constant resistance training in a one RM free-weight bench press (Ariel, 1977). Dynamic constant resistance and variable resistance training produced gains of 14% and 29.5%, respectively. Further information concerning this study is presented in Table 2.3.

Leg press strength illustrates the phenomenon of test specificity for these two types of training (Pipes, 1978). After 10 weeks of training a variable resistance group increased 27% when tested with variable resistance methods and 7.5% when tested with dynamic constant resistance methods. Conversely, a group trained with dynamic constant resistance improved 7.5% when tested by variable resistance methods and 28.9% when tested by dynamic constant resistance methods. More information concerning this study is presented in Table 2.4. Three other exercises tested and trained for in the aforementioned study demonstrated a similar test specificity pattern.

In a five-week program of three training sessions per week, dynamic constant resistance training was found to be superior to variable resistance training in producing strength gains determined by dynamic constant resistance testing (Stone et al., 1979). No difference between the two types of training was shown when tested for variable resistance strength improvements. Another study compared six exercises in a 10-week program of three training sessions per week. Tests of both variable resistance and dynamic constant resistance methods concluded that both types of training resulted in equal strength gains. The dynamic constant resistance group used the DeLorme method and the variable resistance group used one set of 10 to 12 repetitions at 10 to 12 RM (Rogers, 1980).

Another study compared groups trained on cam-type variable resistance equipment, increasing lever arm variable resistance equipment, and free weights (Silvester et al., 1984). The cam-type group performed 12 repetitions at a 12 RM. The increasing lever arm group performed 1 set of 7 to 10 repetitions and 1 set to failure at 10 RM. The free-weight group did 3 sets of 6 repetitions at a 6 RM. All groups performed the same two exercises (leg extensions and leg press). (The training regimes used by the variable resistance groups were those recommended by the equipment manufacturers.) All three groups trained for 11 weeks. The results showed no significant difference among the groups in static leg strength. This same study used four other groups to compare static elbow flexor strength. Group 1 trained with free weights for 11 weeks using 1 set to failure of 10 to 12 repetitions, and Group 2 used free weights for 3 sets of 6 repetitions at a 6 RM. Groups 3 and 4 trained for elbow flexion using cam-type variable resistance equipment along with the free-weight training regimens of Groups 1 and 2. No significant difference in static elbow strength was demonstrated among the four groups at any of four different testing angles.

Table 7.1 indicates that body compositional changes from these two types of training are of the same magnitude. A 10-week comparative study noted no significant difference between dynamic constant resistance and variable resistance training with regard to changes of percent fat, body mass, and total body weight (Pipes, 1978).

Concentric Versus Eccentric Resistance

Comparative studies indicate there is no significant difference between gains in strength between concentric and eccentric training (Atha, 1981). After a seven-week program of four times per week with six contractions of the elbow flexors per training session, no significant difference in maximal isometric, eccentric, or concentric tension was demonstrated between concentric and eccentric training (Komi & Buskirk, 1972). No significant difference exists between the two in maximal constant dynamic resistance arm curls, arm presses, knee flexions, and knee extensions after six weeks, training three times per week (Johnson et al., 1976). Concentric training consisted of 2 sets of 10 repetitions at 80% of 1 RM. Eccentric training consisted of 2 sets of 6 repetitions at 120% of 1 RM. Eccentric training does, however, produce more muscular soreness than that which results from concentric training, especially during the first few weeks of the program (Atha, 1981).

Hakkinen and Komi (1981) compared three groups: Group 1 trained with concentric resistance, performing a squat exercise; Group 2 used primarily concentric with some additional eccentric contractions; and Group 3 trained primarily with eccentric plus some concentric contractions. The results of the study are presented in Figure 2.4. The groups that trained with both eccentric and concentric contractions made greater gains than the group that trained only with concentric contractions. This suggests that several types of contractions may be necessary to bring about maximal gains in strength.

Dynamic Constant Resistance Versus Isokinetic Resistance

Studies comparing these two types of training indicate no clear superiority of either type over the other. After eight weeks of training, the knee extensors of an isokinetically trained group increased 47.2% in isokinetic torque whereas a dynamic constant resistance group increased by 28.6% (Thistle et al., 1967). Daily training of the knee ex-

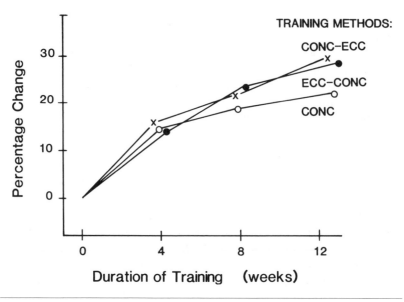

Figure 2.4 Percentage change in maximal squatting ability due to concentric-only, concentric and some eccentric and eccentric and some concentric training. *Note.* From "Effect of Different Combined Concentric and Eccentric Muscle Work Regimens on Maximal Strength Development" by K. Hakkinen and P. Komi, 1981, *Journal of Human Movement Studies*, **7**, p. 36. Copyright 1981 by Teviot Scientific Publications. Adapted by permission.

tensors and flexors for four weeks shows that isokinetic training (22.5 degree/second) is superior to constant dynamic resistance training in isokinetic and isometric strength increases (Moffroid et al., 1969). The isokinetic and constant dynamic resistance groups exhibited increases in isometric knee extension force of 24% and 13%, respectively, and 19% and 1%, respectively, in isometric knee flexion force. Isokinetic peak torque at 22.5 degrees per second of the isokinetic and dynamic constant resistance groups increased 11% and 3%, respectively, in knee extension and 16% and 1%, respectively, in knee flexion. Dynamic constant resistance training has been demonstrated to increase isokinetic torque at a medium and fast velocity to a significantly greater extent than isokinetic training at a medium and fast (but not at a slow) velocity (Davies, 1977). No significant difference in isokinetic torque at any velocity was shown between the dynamic constant resistance and slow isokinetic groups.

A biomechanical examination of free-weight and isokinetic bench pressing has been performed (Lander, Bates, Sawhill, & Hamill, 1985). Subjects performed a free-weight bench press at 90% and 75% of their one RM. The same subjects also performed maximal isokinetic bench presses at a speed corresponding to the individual subject's movement speed during 90% and 75% free-weight bench press. Velocity of movement varied from 26 to 48 degrees per second, and 45 to 92 degrees per second for the isokinetic bench presses, corresponding to the 90% and 75% of one RM free-weight bench presses. No significant difference in maximal force existed between the isokinetic bench press and the 90% and 75% of one RM free-weight bench press. The study indicated that free weights may affect muscles in a manner similar to isokinetic devices, at least in the context of force production during the major portion of a movement.

Body compositional changes from dynamic constant resistance and isokinetic training are of the same magnitude. See Table 7.1 for information concerning comparative changes in percent fat, body mass, and total body weight.

Isokinetic Versus Variable Resistance

Comparisons of isokinetic and variable resistance training demonstrate a test specificity phenomenon. One study compared groups of slow and fast speed isokinetic training with variable resistance training. Slow speed isokinetic training consisted of one set to 50% of peak torque at the velocities of 30, 60, and 90 degrees per second. Fast speed isokinetic training followed the same format as slow speed training velocities of 180, 240, and 300 degrees per second. Variable resistance training initially consisted of 3 sets of 10 repetitions at 80% of a 10 RM; once all sets could be completed, more resistance was added. All groups performed leg extensions and flexions only. Tables 2.6 and 2.7 present the results of this study. In measures of strength the isokinetic groups demonstrated a relatively consistent pattern of test speed specificity. The variable resistance group demonstrated consistent increases in knee flexion, irrelevant of the test criterion, but knee extension showed large increases in isometric force only. Another study involving changes in leg press strength illustrates more clearly a test specificity phenomenon between these two types of training (Gettman, Culter, & Stratmam, 1980). See Table 2.4 for information concerning this study. These results attest to the difficulty in choosing the group which possesses superiority with regard to strength increases.

Table 2.7 depicts a comparison of the benefits of isokinetic and variable resistance training for motor performance. Fast speed isokinetic training demonstrated increases in three of four motor performance tests which surpassed improvement brought about by the slow speed isokinetic or variable resistance training. According to these results fast

Table 2.7   Isokinetic Versus Variable Resistance: Motor Performance Changes

Test	Group (% change)		
	VR	SIK	FIK
Leg press	10.5	9.8	6.7
Vertical jump	1.6	3.9	5.4
Standing long jump	.3	.4	9.1
40-yard dash	− 1.4	+ 1.1	− 10.1

VR = variable resistance

SIK = slow speed isokinetic

FIK = fast speed isokinetic

Note. Data compiled from "Isokinetic Versus Isotonic Variable Resistance Training" by M.J. Smith and P. Melton, 1981, *American Journal of Sports Medicine, 9*, p. 277. Copyright 1981 by the American Orthopaedic Society of Sports Medicine. Adapted by permission.

speed isokinetic training may be superior to slow speed isokinetic and variable resistance training in the context of motor performance improvement.

The information presented in this chapter concerning the types of resistance training, motor performance, body compositional changes, gains in strength, and the concept of test specificity should be considered at the onset of any resistance training program. The next chapter specifies the process involved in developing a program of resistance training. Several decisions have to be made regarding a needs-analysis, goals, and finally, the appropriate resistance training program to meet both an individual's needs and an individual's goals can be designed.

Chapter 3

Individualizing Exercise Prescriptions in Resistance Training

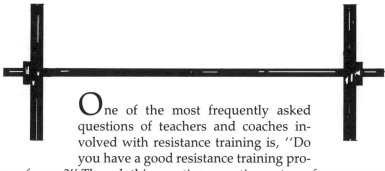

One of the most frequently asked questions of teachers and coaches involved with resistance training is, ''Do you have a good resistance training program for me?'' Though this question sometimes stems from a general lack of understanding, more often it indicates confusion concerning the basic outcomes derived from resistance training programs. It is not an uncommon belief that there is a secret program which will unlock unbelievable strength gains. This is true to a certain extent: Consistent training with proper variation and adherence to the prescribed basic principles of resistance training will allow for optimal gains in strength according to each individual's genetic potential.

The gains made in any variable related to muscular performance will be linked to genetic potential (e.g., fiber types) and the present location of an individual on the theoretical training curve (see Figure 3.1).

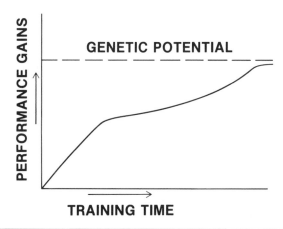

Figure 3.1 A theoretical training curve is presented. Notice that at the start of a training program large gains in fitness are made. After this period of rapid initial fitness gains further improvement occurs at a slower rate.

As an individual starts to train (at the bottom of the curve), the initial gains are great because of the large potential to be realized. As training proceeds, gains slow down as one approaches his or her potential (at the top of the curve).

Each exercise program must be designed according to individual specifications. It is especially important that the individual's fitness level be evaluated and understood by the teacher or coach. One of the most serious mistakes made in designing a workout is placing too much stress on the individual before he or she can tolerate it. Though it is easy to design a training program for an individual, a good coach or teacher must be sensitive to that person's fitness levels and ability to tolerate the training stress. Even when designing training programs for an athletic team, the coach must take into account individual responses to the generalized program, making adjustments to achieve optimal results and reduce the chance of injury or overtraining. Progress in a resistance training program should follow the staircase principle (Figure 3.2). An individual begins a training session with a

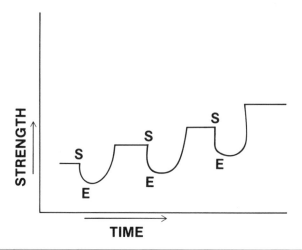

Figure 3.2   A resistance training program should allow for a staircase effect. The S and E designate the start and end of a workout, respectively.

particular amount of strength. During the training session strength decreases due to fatigue; at the conclusion of the session strength is at its lowest point. After recovering from the first session the individual should begin the next training session at a slightly higher strength level. This staircase process is repeated for each training session. Designing training programs which allow this staircase effect is the biggest challenge for teachers and coaches in the field of resistance training.

The exercise prescription of resistance training has for a long time been more of an art than a science. However, as with the prescription of any exercise, a solid understanding of the underlying scientific principles involved will assist in the development of better resistance training programs. The success of any program depends upon the logical development of successive training sessions. This developmental process addresses the basic questions involved in the manipulation of training variables. The major program design components for resistance training are:

- Needs Analysis
- Acute Program Variables
- Chronic Program Manipulations
- Administrative Concerns

Each of these components will be discussed below in the context of resistance training.

Needs Analysis

A *needs analysis* consists of answering some initial questions which affect the other three program design components (see Figure 3.3).

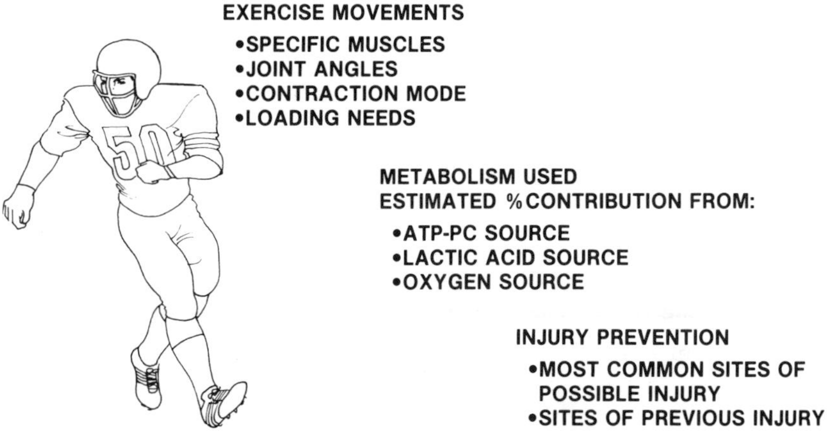

EXERCISE MOVEMENTS
- SPECIFIC MUSCLES
- JOINT ANGLES
- CONTRACTION MODE
- LOADING NEEDS

METABOLISM USED
ESTIMATED % CONTRIBUTION FROM:
- ATP-PC SOURCE
- LACTIC ACID SOURCE
- OXYGEN SOURCE

INJURY PREVENTION
- MOST COMMON SITES OF POSSIBLE INJURY
- SITES OF PREVIOUS INJURY

Figure 3.3   The components of a needs analysis are important when trying to develop questions in the initial stages of program development.

The major questions in a needs analysis are:

1. What muscle groups need to be trained?
2. What are the basic energy sources (e.g., anaerobic, aerobic) which need to be trained?
3. What type of muscle action (e.g., isometric, variable resistance) should be used?
4. What are the primary sites of injury for the particular sport?

Biomechanical Analysis

The first question requires an examination of the muscles and the specific joint angles designated for training. For a sport, this involves a basic analysis of the movements performed and the most common sites of injury. The decisions made at this stage define the acute program variable, choice of exercise. It is important that time be taken to examine these questions. With the proper equipment and a background in basic biomechanics a more definitive approach to this question is possible. With the use of a slow-motion film or videotape, the coach can better evaluate specific aspects of movements and can conduct a quantitative analysis of the muscles, angles, velocities, and forces involved.

Specificity is a major tenet in resistance training. It assumes that muscles show the greatest evidence of strength increase in activities similar to the training exercise in terms of

1. the body joint around which movement occurs,
2. the joint range of motion,
3. the pattern of resistance throughout the range of motion,
4. the pattern of limb velocity throughout the range of motion, and
5. whether the limb movement is concentric, eccentric, or isometric.

Strength training for any sport should include full range of motion exercises around all the major body joints. However, training designed for specific sports movements should also be included in the workout to maximize the contribution of strength training to performance. The best way to select such exercise is to biomechanically analyze, in quantitative terms, a wide range of exercises and physical activites and match them according to the above variables. Little of such analysis has been done to date. Yet biomechanical principles can still be used in a non-quantitative way by an interested athlete or coach to intelligently select exercises. Through the use of slow-motion films or video

tapes, the following steps allow a physical activity to be roughly ana-
lyzed in terms of the variables listed above.[1]

1. View a film or videotape of an athletic performance.
2. Select a movement which appears to involve high-intensity
    physical exertion critical to the performance (e.g., the impact of
    two football linemen; the drive portion of a sprint stride; the
    push-off in a high-jump).
3. Try to identify the body joints around which the most intense
    muscular contraction occurs. Running and jumping, for example,
    involve the most intense contraction around the knee, hip, and
    ankle. Intense exertion doesn't necessarily involve movement.
    Considerable isometric force may have to be applied to keep a
    body joint from flexing or extending under external stress.
4. Determine whether the movement is concentric, isometric or ec-
    centric. While it is tensing, the muscle shortens during a con-
    centric contraction, is held at a constant length by an external
    force during an isometric contraction; and is lengthened by an
    external force during an eccentric contraction.
5. For each joint identified above, determine the range of angular
    motion. To do this, measure the angle between the two body
    segments adjacent to the joint with a protractor. See how the
    joint angle changes through the movement. Record the range
    of motion.
6. Try to determine where in the range of motion around each par-
    ticular body joint the most intense effort occurs. Sometimes, fa-
    cial grimaces or tense muscles seen on film can help identify
    points of peak intensity. Record the joint angle of peak intensity.
7. Estimate the velocity of movement early, middle, and late in the
    range of motion. If using a film or videotape, the time between
    frames in seconds is 1/frame rate. For example, if the rate is 30
    frames per second, the interval time is 1/30 or .033 seconds. In
    a movement segment, the angular velocity equals degrees-
    traveled/total time. For example, if the limb moves 5 degrees in
    3 frame intervals, the movement speed is $5/(3 \times .033) = 50$
    degrees per second.
8. Select exercises to match the limb ranges of motion and angular
    velocities, making sure that the exercises are appropriately con-
    centric, isometric, or eccentric. As an example, in a jump takeoff,
    the supporting leg usually buckles somewhat, allowing elastic
    energy to be stored. Training of this part of the movement could
    be accomplished by lowering a weight too heavy to raise by your-
    self through the prescribed range of motion, and having assis-
    tants help in raising the weight back up. In the jump, after the

[1]These steps are courtesy of Dr. Everett Harman.

knee reaches its smallest angle and the jumper begins to extend the leg for takeoff, high-intensity concentric contraction occurs at slow speed. To train that part of the movement, perform concentric contractions through the specific range of joint motion using heavy weights at slow speed. To train a faster part of the movement, use lighter weights at higher repetition speed for the specific range of motion. Depth jumping from a box, with or without weight, can be used to simulate the complete cycle of muscle stretching and shortening.

9. It is best to make the exercise the most difficult at the point in the range of motion where intensity during the target athletic performance is greatest. This can be accomplished by trial and error, or one can use the principle that during a lifting movement involving little acceleration, the greatest resistance to movement around a body joint occurs when the weight is horizontally farthest from the joint (for example, around the midpoint of an arm curl movement). The most commonly performed weight exercises can be modified to locate peak tension at a desired joint angle. A basic exercise like the arm curl can be done standing or bending over or on a preacher bench to modify the angle of peak tension. To apply additional tension to a muscle at a particular point in the range of angular motion, one can attempt to accelerate the weight as the limb travels through the target angle.

Ideally, this analysis is followed up with appropriate resistance exercises in the weight room that train the specific muscles and joint angles involved. For the individual primarily interested in general fitness and muscular development, the major muscle groups of the shoulders, chest, back, and legs are usually trained. It must be kept in mind that the training stimulus for strength or local muscular endurance will be specific to the angles and velocity of movement of the specific muscles used in the exercise.

Determining the Energy Systems Used in the Activity

Every sport uses a percentage of each of the three energy sources (see chapter 6) to perform an activity. As the exercise intensifies and lessens in duration the anaerobic metabolism becomes more important for energy production (Fox, 1979). Lower exercise intensities and longer durations use primarily aerobic metabolism for production of energy (Fox, 1979). The energy sources to be trained have a major impact on the program design. Resistance training is usually more appropriate for anaerobic energy sources (ATP-PC and Lactic Acid sources) than it is for aerobic metabolism.

Selecting a Resistance Modality

Decisions regarding the use of isometric, dynamic concentric, dynamic eccentric, and isokinetic modalities of exercise are important in the preliminary stages of planning a resistance training program for sport, fitness, or rehabilitation. The basic biomechanical analysis aids in the decision of what muscles to train and in the identification of the type of muscle contraction involved. Most resistance programs use several types of muscle actions. One factor that separates elite power lifters from less competitive power lifters is the rate at which the load is lowered in the squat and bench press. Elite power lifters lower the weight at a slower rate than less competitive lifters even though the former use greater resistances. In this case, some eccentric training may be advantageous for competitive power lifters. Many holds in wrestling involve isometric contractions of muscle groups. Thus, some isometric training may aid in the conditioning of wrestlers.

Program Design

After the needs analysis has been completed a specific workout program is designed which addresses the exact needs of the individual. *Acute program variables* concern the designing of one particular training session. *Chronic program manipulations* concern manipulation of training variables over an entire training period of months or years (cycling or periodization). *Administrative concerns* are factors involved in the implementation of resistance training programs (e.g., for large groups such as classes or athletic teams).

Acute Program Variables

The acute program variables describe all possible single training sessions. By examining each of the variables in Figure 3.4 and making decisions about them, a training session can be designed. The training session is specific to the choices made regarding each variable.

Choice of Exercise

The basis for the choice of exercise has been presented in chapter 2. Every time the angle of an exercise is changed the exercise changes

1. CHOICE OF EXERCISE
   STRUCTURAL
   BODY PART
   CONTRACTION MODE

2. ORDER OF EXERCISE
   LARGE MUSCLE GROUP FIRST
   SMALL MUSCLE GROUP FIRST (PRE-EXHAUST)
   ARM TO LEG OR ARM-ARM, LEG-LEG

3. NUMBER OF SETS

4. REST PERIODS
   SHORT ⟨ 1 MINUTE
   MODERATE   1 TO 3 MINUTES
   LONG ⟩ 3 MINUTES

5. LOAD (INTENSITY)

Figure 3.4   A detailed component model for the acute program variables is presented.

(see chapter 6, Order of Fiber Type Recruitment). The number of possible angles and exercises are almost as limitless as the body's functional movements. Based upon the needs analysis, exercises should be selected which stress the designated muscles and joint angles.

Exercises can also be classified as *structural* or *body-part*. Structural exercises are those lifts which require the coordinated action of many muscle groups. Power cleans, power snatches, deadlifts, and squats are good examples of structural exercises. Exercises which try to isolate a particular muscle group are considered to be body-part exercises. Bicep curls, sit-ups, and leg curls are good examples of body-part exercises. It is especially important to include structural exercises when whole body strength movements are required for a particular sport. This is the case for football, basketball, wrestling, and track and field. In these sports whole body strength movements are the basis of success in blocking, tackling, jumping, executing takedowns, and throwing. Many times, the structural exercises involve advanced-lifting techniques which require additional coaching beyond simple movement patterns (e.g., power cleans, power snatches). Teachers and coaches should have experience with such lifts prior to including them in a training program. For the individual interested in basic fitness, these exercises are advantageous only when there is a limited amount of time and it is necessary to train more than one muscle group at a time. The time economy achieved with structural exercises is an important administrative concern for an individual or team with a limited amount of time per training session.

Order of Exercise

For many years the order of exercise in resistance training programs consisted of performing large muscle group exercises prior to exercising the smaller muscle groups. It has been theorized that by working the larger muscle groups first a maximal stimulus is presented to all of the muscles involved in an exercise. More recently, different types of *pre-exhaustion* methods have been used by East European lifters in their training. These methods reverse the order of the exercises so that the small muscle groups are exercised prior to the larger muscle groups. An example is performing leg extension and flexion exercises followed by squats. Another method of pre-exhaustion involves fatiguing synergistic (or assistance) movers before performing the main exercise movement. An example of this is performing lat pull downs prior to performing the bench press exercise. The advantages of pre-exhaustion methods over the large group/small group ordering (or vice versa) for development of either strength or local muscular endurance remains to be demonstrated.

The ordering of exercises also involves the question of whether one follows a leg exercise with another leg exercise, or whether it is appropriate to proceed to another muscle group. Pre-exhaustion methods are possible with the former of these patterns. Arm-to-leg ordering, on the other hand, allows for some recovery of the arm muscles while the leg muscles are exercised. This concept is also important when designing circuit weight training programs. Beginning students are more likely to be less tolerant of pre-exhaustion and arm-to-arm and leg-to-leg exercise orders. One further consideration is the fitness level of the individual. Training sessions should not be designed which are too stressful for an individual at the onset, therefore not allowing for the staircase effect.

Number of Sets

The number of sets used in a workout is directly related to training results. Typically, three to six sets are used to achieve significant gains in strength. It has been suggested that multiple-set systems work best for development of strength and local muscular endurance (Atha, 1981), and the gains made will be at a faster rate than gains achieved through single-set systems (McDonagh & Davies, 1984). Use of one or two sets of an exercise may be more appropriate for beginners in the initial stages of a base program (first 6 to 12 workouts) or for circuit weight training. The principle idea behind multiple sets is that the muscle will adapt to the given stimulus. Once initial fitness has been achieved, a multiple presentation of the stimulus (three to six sets) with specific rest periods between sets is superior to a single presentation of the stimulus.

Rest Periods

One of the more overlooked variables in exercise prescription is the length of the rest periods between sets and exercises. The amount of time allowed between sets determines the amount of recovery of the anaerobic energy sources allowed prior to the next set (see chapter 6, Repayment of the Anaerobic Energy Sources). Because the ATP-PC energy source is the most powerful, it is required during maximal or near-maximal sets, such as one to three or four RMs (Fox, 1979). When training the ATP-PC energy source, at least two to three minutes of rest are necessary between sets to replenish this energy source (Fox & Mathews, 1974). The amount of rest provided between sets and exercises also dictates the amount of stress placed on the lactic acid energy source. When rest periods are less than one minute long, plasma lactic acid concentrations are extremely high (Noble, Kraemer, Clark, & Culver, 1984). This is also true in circuit weight training where relatively light loads of 40% to 60% of 1 RM are used (Gettman & Pollock, 1981). When rest periods are cut to less than 30 seconds relatively heavy loads are used (70%-85% of 1 RM), lactate levels are very high and not well tolerated except among the most highly conditioned athletes. Lactic acid's involvement in fatigue has been the subject of much controversy. Although it may not cause fatigue it does provide a relative comparison of the stress on the lactic acid energy source. The length of the rest period will determine to a great extent the amount of lactic acid which is produced and removed from the body (see chapter 6, Replenishing the Lactic Acid Energy Source). Figure 3.5 depicts the lactate concentrations consequent to different resistance training exercise sessions.

If a particular needs analysis identifies lactic acid as the primary energy source, the rest periods may be gradually shortened to allow the buildup of plasma lactic acid, thus encouraging an increased tolerance of more acidic conditions. This type of training design (particularly for preseason training) may allow better tolerance for such

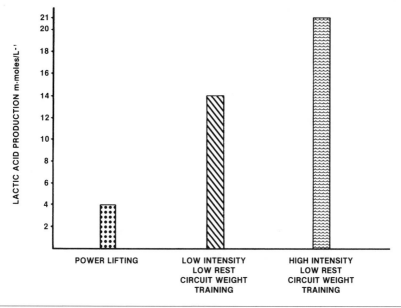

Figure 3.5   The postexercise mean blood lactic acid responses to different types of resistance exercise sessions. *Note.*   From "The Effect of Weight Lifting Exercise on Heart Rate and Metabolism in Experienced Lifters" by J. Keul, G. Haralambei, M. Bruder, and H.J. Gottstein, 1978, *Medicine and Science in Sports,* **10**, pp. 13-15; "Circuit Weight Training: A Critical Review of its Physiological Benefits" by L.R. Gettman and M.L. Pollock, 1981, *The Physician and Sportsmedicine,* **9**, pp. 44-60; and "Stress Response to High Intensity Circuit Weight Training in Experienced Weight Trainers" by B.J. Noble, W.J. Kraemer, M.J. Clark, and B.W. Culver, 1984, *Medicine and Science in Sports and Exercise,* **16**, p. 14. Adapted by permission.

anaerobic athletes as wrestlers, sprinters (100 to 800 m), and basketball players. Other anaerobic athletes, such as baseball players, rely primarily on high energy phosphates for energy production to perform their skills. Consequently, performing resistance training programs which elevate lactic acid concentrations may not be necessary to improve performance of certain sports. Careful manipulation of rest periods is essential to avoid placing inappropriate and needless stresses on the individual during training.

Rest Periods Between Workouts

The amount of rest required between training sessions depends on the recovery ability of the individual. Traditionally, three workouts per week, performed on Monday, Wednesday, and Friday, were found to allow adequate recovery, especially for the novice (Atha, 1981). If loading is not excessive, only moderate amounts of delayed muscular soreness should be experienced one day after the session. The greatest amount of delayed muscular soreness results from eccentric contractions as opposed to isokinetic, dynamic concentric, and isometric contractions (Fleck & Schutt, 1985; Talag, 1973). As one advances and is better able to tolerate resistance exercise sessions the frequency of training can be increased. A recent report has gone so far as to propose that four days in succession may be superior to three alternate days in effecting increases in strength (Hunter, 1985). This suggests that the interaction of stress and recovery may be more complex than previously thought. The onset of perceived discomfort may be masked during consecutive training sessions, and the three-day recovery period may allow for a more complete recovery. Training frequency per week is a function of the training session and the individual's experience and physical condition. Basic guidelines have to be used as guides and not as absolute laws, recognizing that each situation is different.

It is well known that experienced competitive lifters can train six days a week whereas some beginners can tolerate only three days a week. When training is performed on consecutive days it usually involves the use of a split routine (different body parts exercised each day) or a split program (different exercises for the same body part performed each day). It is important to assess the effects of the training on the individual regardless of whether alternate or consecutive workouts are used. If it takes a crane to get the individual out of bed the next morning this may indicate that the exercise stress is too demanding. If this is the case, the workout loads, sets, and rest periods between sets need to be adjusted.

Load (Repetition Maximum Loading)

The amount of resistance (load) used for a specific exercise is probably the most important variable in resistance training (McDonagh & Davies, 1984). Loading in resistance training is most likely the major stimulus related to changes observed in measures of strength and local muscular endurance. When designing a resistance training program a load for each exercise must be chosen. The use of either repetition maximums or a particular load which only allows a specific number of repetitions to be performed is probably the easiest method for determining a load. For example, a load that allows an exercise movement to be performed only six times would be considered a six RM load. Research has supported the basis for a repetition maximum continuum (see Figure 3.6). (Anderson & Kearney, 1982; Atha, 1981; Clark, 1973; McDonagh & Davies, 1984). This continuum simply relates RM loads to the broad training effects derived from their use. It appears that RM loads of six or less have the greatest effect on strength measures or maximal power outputs. RM loads of 20 and above show the greatest effect on muscular endurance measures. This continuum makes it possible to develop a particular feature of muscular performance to varying degrees over a range of loads (RMs).

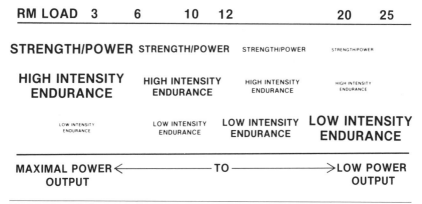

Figure 3.6 A theoretical repetition maximum continuum is presented.

For example, as one moves away from the strength stimulus zone (six RM or less) the gains in strength diminish until they are negligible. The strength gains achieved above the 25 RM load are perhaps more related to enhanced motor performance. A variety of individual responses due to genetic predisposition and training background will affect the training increases observed. As an example, inexperienced individuals who are on the lower end of the training potential curve (Figure 3.1) may experience significant gains in strength in the 15 to 20 RM loading range. Thus, pretraining status must always be considered when evaluating strength improvements.

Another method of loading involves using a percentage of the one RM (i.e., 70%, 80%). If a trainee's one RM for an exercise is 100 lb, an 80% load would be 80 lb . This method requires maximal lifting tests in order to compute the loads used. Generalized charts are available with predicted percentage loads from a known maximal lift. These are used to determine the load for performing a set number of repetitions (see Table 3.1). A person can look at the one RM or 100% load and determine a load that could be done 10 times. Conversely, a person might want to determine the 10 RM or 75% load and predict what could be done for one RM. Thus, this type of chart gives a ballpark estimate of any given training load. Because these charts involve only estimates there is much room for variation. For this reason, it and others like it should be used only as a general guideline. These particular charts are primarily designed for large muscle group lifts such as the bench press, squat, or power clean. The repetition continuum still applies in that an 80% load should allow only a certain number of repetitions depending on the individual's training level. Individual variances make this method less accurate and no less time consuming than the RM method of loading previously described. Percentage loads merely provide another method for determining training loads.

Table 3.1 A Maximum Lift Based on Repetitions

% of 1 RM	100	95	90	85	80	75
REPS	1	2	4	6	8	10
lbs. lifted	700.00	665.00	630.00	595.00	560.00	525.00
	695.00	660.25	625.50	590.75	556.00	521.25
	690.00	655.50	621.00	586.50	552.00	517.50
	685.00	650.75	616.50	582.25	548.00	513.75
	680.00	646.00	612.00	578.00	544.00	510.00
	675.00	641.25	607.50	573.75	540.00	506.25
	670.00	636.50	603.00	569.50	536.00	502.50
	665.00	631.75	598.50	565.25	532.00	498.75
	660.00	627.00	594.00	561.00	528.00	495.00
	655.00	622.25	589.50	556.75	524.00	491.25
	650.00	617.50	585.00	552.50	520.00	487.50
	645.00	612.75	580.50	548.25	516.00	483.75
	640.00	608.00	576.00	544.00	512.00	480.00
	635.00	603.25	571.50	539.75	508.00	476.25
	630.00	598.50	567.00	535.50	504.00	472.50
	625.00	593.75	562.50	531.25	500.00	468.75
	620.00	589.00	558.00	527.00	496.00	465.00
	615.00	584.25	553.50	522.75	492.00	461.25

% of 1 RM	100	95	90	85	80	75
REPS	1	2	4	6	8	10
lbs. lifted	610.00	579.50	549.00	518.50	488.00	457.50
	605.00	574.75	544.50	514.25	484.00	453.75
	600.00	570.00	540.00	510.00	480.00	450.00
	595.00	565.25	535.50	505.75	476.00	446.25
	590.00	560.50	531.00	501.50	472.00	442.50
	585.00	555.75	526.50	497.25	468.00	438.75
	580.00	551.00	522.00	493.00	464.00	435.00
	575.00	546.25	517.50	488.75	460.00	431.25
	570.00	541.50	513.00	484.50	456.00	427.50
	565.00	536.75	508.50	480.25	452.00	423.75
	560.00	532.00	499.50	471.75	444.00	416.25
	555.00	527.25	504.00	476.00	448.00	420.00
	550.00	522.50	495.00	467.50	440.00	412.50
	545.00	517.75	490.50	463.25	436.00	408.75
	540.00	513.00	486.00	459.00	432.00	405.00
	535.00	508.25	481.50	454.75	428.00	401.25
	530.00	503.50	477.00	450.50	424.00	397.50
	525.00	498.75	472.50	466.25	420.00	393.75
	520.00	494.00	468.00	442.00	416.00	390.00
	515.00	489.25	463.50	437.75	412.00	386.25
	510:00	484.50	459.00	433.50	408.00	382.50
	505.00	479.75	454.50	429.25	404.00	378.75
	500.00	475.00	450.00	425.00	400.00	375.00
	495.00	470.25	445.50	420.75	396.00	371.25
	490.00	465.50	441.00	416.50	392.00	367.50
	485.00	460.75	436.50	412.25	388.00	363.75
	480.00	456.00	432.00	408.00	384.00	360.00
	475.00	451.25	427.50	403.75	380.00	356.25
	470.00	446.50	423.00	399.50	376.00	352.50
	465.00	441.75	418.50	395.25	372.00	348.75
	460.00	437.00	414.00	391.00	368.00	345.00
	455.00	432.25	409.50	386.75	364.00	341.25
	450.00	427.50	405.00	382.50	360.00	337.50
	445.00	422.75	400.50	378.25	356.00	333.75
	440.00	418.00	396.00	374.00	352.00	330.00
	435.00	413.25	391.50	369.75	348.00	326.25
	430.00	408.50	387.00	365.50	344.00	322.50
	425.00	403.75	382.50	361.25	340.00	318.75
	420.00	399.00	378.00	357.00	336.00	315.00
	415.00	394.25	373.50	352.75	332.00	311.25

(Cont.)

Table 3.1   (Cont.)

% of 1 RM	100	95	90	85	80	75
REPS	1	2	4	6	8	10
lbs. lifted	410.00	389.50	369.00	348.50	328.00	307.50
	405.00	384.75	364.50	344.25	324.00	303.75
	400.00	380.00	360.00	340.00	320.00	300.00
	395.00	375.25	355.50	335.75	316.00	296.25
	390.00	370.50	351.00	331.50	312.00	292.50
	385.00	365.75	346.50	327.25	308.00	288.75
	380.00	361.00	342.00	323.00	304.00	285.00
	375.00	356.25	337.50	318.75	300.00	281.25
	370.00	351.50	330.00	314.50	296.00	277.50
	365.00	346.75	328.50	310.25	292.00	273.75
	360.00	342.00	324.00	306.00	288.00	270.00
	355.00	337.25	319.50	301.75	284.00	266.25
	350.00	332.50	315.00	297.50	280.00	262.50
	345.00	327.75	310.50	293.25	276.00	258.75
	340.00	323.00	306.00	289.00	272.00	255.00
	335.00	318.25	301.50	284.75	268.00	251.25
	330.00	313.50	297.00	280.50	264.00	247.50
	325.00	308.75	292.50	276.25	260.00	243.75
	320.00	304.00	288.00	272.00	256.00	240.00
	315.00	299.25	283.50	267.75	252.00	236.25
	310.00	294.50	279.00	263.50	248.00	232.50
	305.00	289.75	274.50	259.25	244.00	228.75
	300.00	285.00	270.00	255.00	240.00	225.00
	295.00	280.25	265.50	250.75	236.00	221.25
	290.00	275.50	261.00	246.50	232.00	217.50
	285.00	270.75	256.50	242.25	228.00	213.75
	280.00	266.00	252.00	238.00	224.00	210.00
	275.00	261.25	247.50	233.75	220.00	206.25
	270.00	256.50	243.00	229.50	216.00	202.50
	265.00	251.75	238.50	225.25	212.00	198.75
	260.00	247.00	234.00	221.00	208.00	195.00
	255.00	242.25	229.50	216.75	204.00	191.25
	250.00	237.50	225.00	212.50	200.00	187.50
	245.00	232.75	220.50	208.25	196.00	183.75
	240.00	228.00	216.00	204.00	192.00	180.00
	235.00	223.25	211.50	199.75	188.00	176.25
	230.00	218.50	207.00	195.50	184.00	172.50
	225.00	213.75	202.50	191.25	180.00	168.75

(Cont.)

% of 1 RM	100	95	90	85	80	75
REPS	1	2	4	6	8	10
lbs. lifted	220.00	209.00	198.00	187.00	176.00	165.00
	215.00	204.25	193.50	182.75	172.00	161.25
	210.00	199.50	189.00	178.50	168.00	157.50
	205.00	194.75	184.50	174.25	164.00	153.75
	200.00	190.00	180.00	170.00	160.00	150.00
	195.00	185.25	175.50	165.75	156.00	146.25
	190.00	180.50	171.00	161.50	152.00	142.50
	185.00	175.75	166.50	157.25	148.00	138.75
	180.00	171.00	162.00	153.00	144.00	135.00
	175.00	166.25	157.50	148.75	140.00	131.25
	170.00	161.50	153.00	144.50	136.00	127.50
	165.00	156.75	148.50	140.25	132.00	123.75
	160.00	152.00	144.00	136.00	128.00	120.00
	155.00	147.25	139.50	131.75	124.00	116.25
	150.00	142.50	135.00	127.50	120.00	112.50
	145.00	137.75	130.50	123.25	116.00	108.75
	140.00	133.00	126.00	119.00	112.00	105.00
	135.00	128.25	121.50	114.75	108.00	101.25
	130.00	123.50	117.00	110.50	104.00	97.50
	125.00	118.75	112.50	106.25	100.00	93.75
	120.00	114.00	108.00	102.00	96.00	90.00
	115.00	109.25	103.50	97.75	92.00	86.25
	110.00	104.50	99.00	93.50	88.00	82.50
	105.00	99.75	94.50	89.25	84.00	78.75

Table developed by Mike Clark, Strength and Conditioning Specialist, University of Oregon.

Summary of Acute Program Variables

Any resistance training session can be described by the acute program variables. This helps the individual, coach, or teacher to understand the actual program as well as to allow for specific changes in the program as new needs arise. Due to the great number of acute program variable combinations possible, training sessions should be constantly adjusted in order to be sensitive to the needs of the individual. This constant adjustment of acute program variables over time involves what is called the chronic manipulation of training variables.

Chronic Program Manipulations

Much of the American research concerning resistance training has centered on a search for the optimal combination of sets and repetitions to bring about increases in strength (Anderson & Kearney, 1982; Clarke, 1973; O'Shea, 1966). As already mentioned, this line of research assumes, among other things, that an optimal combination actually exists (see chapter 2). An alternative to this approach is to change the load and the number of sets and repetitions periodically in an attempt to induce optimal strength and power increases. This approach is commonly referred to as *cycling* or *periodization*.

Periodization

Periodization is a popular training regime among Eastern European weight lifters (Matveyev, 1981; Vorobyev, 1978). The underlying concept of periodization is related to *Selye's general adaptation syndrome.* This theory proposes that there are three phases of the body's adaptation when it is confronted with a stress stimulus (in this case, resistance training). The first phase is shock: When confronted with a new training stimulus, soreness develops and performance actually decreases. The second phase is adaptation to the stimulus: The body adapts to the new training stimulus and performance increases. The third phase is staleness: The body has already adapted to the new stimulus and adaptations are no longer taking place. Performance during this last phase may actually decrease unless the stimulus is changed. Periodization is used, therefore, to avoid staleness and to keep the exercise stimulus/response effective. A key factor to continuous gains in strength is variation in the exercise stimulus.

Periodization consists of four phases in each training cycle, not including active rest. This type of training program is characterized by initiating training with a large volume of exercise (i.e., sets and repetitions) of a low intensity (i.e., small amount of resistance) as depicted in Table 3.2. During the training cycle the volume of exercise is decreased and the intensity is increased. The objective is to change the training stimulus so that staleness does not develop; in this way the body continues to adapt to the training stimulus.

The initial phase of the training cycle is the hypertrophy phase, which is characterized by high-volume, low-intensity exercise. The major goal of this phase is to increase muscle mass. During the next three phases, volume of training is gradually decreased while intensity is increased.

Table 3.2   Periodization Training for a Strength/Power Sport

	Hypertrophy	Strength	Power	Peaking	Active Rest
Sets	3-5	3-5	3-5	1-3	Physical
Reps	8-20	2-6	2-3	1-3	activity
Intensity	low	high	high	very high	not necessarily resistance training.

Note. From "A Hypothetical Model for Strength Training" by M.H. Stone, H. O'Bryant, and J. Garhammer, 1981, *Journal of Sports Medicine, 21,* p. 344. Adapted by permission.

The major goal of the strength and power phases is to bring about increases in maximal strength. The goal of the peaking phase is to peak strength for a particular competition. This gradual decrease in volume and increase in intensity allow the individual to psychologically prepare for greater training resistances and allow for physiological adaptations. An example of the latter is inhibiting the protective function of the golgi tendon organs (see chapter 6, Proprioceptors). The active rest phase consists of either light resistance training or some physical activity other than resistance training. The goal of this phase is to allow the body to completely recover from the training cycle both physically and psychologically, but to still be at a higher strength level prior to the next training cycle. The entire periodization cycle is then repeated.

Weight lifters originally developed periodization. One periodization cycle was performed over the course of a year, with the peaking phase occurring right before the major competitions of the year. Each training phase was two to three months in duration. It has been observed that performance of two or three cycles per year resulted in gains in strength as great as or greater than the gains in one cycle per year. Some Olympic-style lifters have cut each phase to as little as two weeks in duration. Empirical evidence suggests that gains in strength are greater with the use of shorter cycles.

Table 3.2 depicts the number of sets and repetitions for strength sports such as weight lifting and shot putting. Periodization can also be used for endurance sports such as endurance swimming. The concept of gradually reducing volume while gradually increasing intensity is maintained, but the number of repetitions and sets of the exercise is changed to accommodate the nature of the activity. An example of periodization of endurance training would be: a hypertrophy phase of 4 to 6 sets of 40 to 50 repetitions; a strength phase of 4 to 6 sets of 25 to 35 repetitions; a power phase of 4 to 6 sets of 15 to 25 repetitions; and the peaking phase of 3 to 5 sets of 10 to 15 repetitions. The performance of the peaking phase as classically defined (i.e., very low-volume and very high-intensity exercise) may not be performed at all in the training cycle by an endurance athlete.

A major point to be noticed in the above example of periodization is that the volume and intensity of resistance training is determined by the nature of the activity. Using the concept of periodization and basic knowledge of the nature of an activity, it is possible to tailor a resistance training program to the needs of any sports activity.

Please note that the number of sets and repetitions in each phase are guidelines. In other words, by varying the sets and repetitions within the guidelines for each phase, it is possible to have difficult, moderate, and light days of training. Variation of the volume and intensity within a phase may in fact be more productive in terms of strength gains (Matveyev, 1981). For example, within the hypertrophy phase the number of sets and repetitions during three training sessions might consist of 5 and 10, 5 and 20, and 4 and 15, respectively. Using this concept it is possible to vary the training volume and intensity within each phase of the training cycle.

Not all exercises in a training program need to be cycled. A common practice among competitive lifters is to cycle major exercises (such as bench press, squat, or power cleans) and not to cycle assistive exercises (lat pulls and curls). The advantages or disadvantages of this practice in terms of gains in strength remain to be proven scientifically.

Periodization Training Effects

One cycle of periodization has been compared with the traditional three-sets-of-six-repetitions training program (Stone et al., 1981). High school football players formed two groups, one using periodization training and the second using the traditional program. The athletes trained three times per week for six weeks, performing the same resistance exercises: squat, leg curl, bench press, behind-neck press, and clean pull from the floor and mid-thigh. At the conclusion of training the group performing periodization training demonstrated gains significantly greater than the traditionally trained group in both squatting ability and squat per kilogram of body weight. Both groups increased significantly in vertical jumping ability but the difference between these increases was not significant. Leg power during vertical jumping, however, was significantly greater in the periodization group. Though neither group changed significantly in body weight, only the periodization group exhibited an increase in lean body mass and a significant decrease in percent body fat.

Periodization has also been observed to cause significantly greater improvement in the lifting ability of Olympic-style lifters than the Norwegian system, which is largely based on two to three repetitions per set with little variation in the volume of training. The Olympic lifters who used periodization demonstrated significantly greater gains in maximal weight lifted during the Olympic lifts (on an absolute and per kilogram of body weight basis) than the group utilizing the Norwegian system. Unfortunately this study involved a limited number of weight lifters. The evidence to date indicates that periodization programs are superior to several common combinations of sets and repetitions.

Administrative Concerns

Once the optimal program has been designed the administrative concerns are addressed. These concerns have a potentially major impact on the program design. Administrative considerations that severely limit the use of the optimal program should be remedied if possible. This usually involves acquiring more equipment and/or space. In any case, the ideal training program should always be kept in mind even when compromises have to be made. This is precisely why the program is written first, and then followed by any changes which may be necessary due to administrative limitations. The major administrative concerns are the following:

- Availability of equipment
- Number of individuals in
  training
- Availability of space
- Availability of time

Availability of Equipment

The major problem faced by most people trying to develop a resistance training program is equipment availability. Although sophisticated equipment is not required to develop a resistance training program, the proper development of a weight room allows more flexibility and diversity when designing a resistance training program (Rieger, 1985).

For people who are training alone with simply an interest in basic strength/endurance fitness, many types of equipment for the home exist which are safe and effective. The safety aspects of home equipment should be evaluated prior to purchase. Purchasers should consider whether the construction of the equipment can withstand daily use and whether it is stable when in use. In addition, many facilities exist for training outside the home (e.g., health clubs, recreation centers, and school facilities). Formal exercise programs should be evaluated prior to joining according to the basic consumer guidelines given in Table 3.3.

Table 3.3 Basic Consumer Guideline Questions

Consumer Exercise Protection Checklist

1. Is the instructor certified by a professional organization?
2. Is the instructor certified to perform cardiopulmonary resuscitation?
3. Is the exercise individually prescribed?
4. Is the exercise monitored with a physiological variable (e.g., heart rate)?
5. Have you been screened for possible disease prior to exercise?
6. Have you been pre-tested to determine your initial level of physical fitness?
7. Is there a medical or scientific advisory board?
8. Is there a medical emergency plan in case of injury?

Developed by Dr. Bruce Noble, University of Wyoming, Laramie, WY.

The problem of equipment availability is most often faced by coaches who must train large groups of athletes and by fitness directors who must establish programs for large numbers of people. The development of a resistance training facility (referred to as a weight room) is the primary goal for the coach or fitness director who wants to provide a safe and effective environment for training.

The basic needs analysis and program design dictate the exercise movements which will be trained in different programs. The specific exercise movements must now be matched with the equipment available in the present situation.

If the equipment availability is minimal, viable substitutes must be found for each exercise. In school situations shop classes can help in this area, but safety must never be compromised when developing homemade equipment. It is possible to substitute other forms of exercise, such as plyometrics (e.g., depth jumping), paired-partner exercises, and dynamic drills (e.g., stair running) in situations where no resistance training equipment is available.

A specific planning list should be created for the necessary equipment. Goals for the weight room should be established as to when to purchase specific pieces of equipment. This is an exciting phase of program development. Prioritize each piece of necessary equipment. High priority is usually given to equipment which exercises large muscle groups and offers a wide variety of exercise movements. Low priority is given to specialized pieces of equipment which exercise only small muscle groups and can only be used for one exercise.

Next, examine all budget planning resources and develop prospective money raising events, either in the form of budget requests, fund raisers, or donations. It is important that while the facility is in use, perspective is kept with regard to what can be accomplished with the present equipment as well as what the future goals of the program are. Organization is the key to good program development.

Number of Individuals in Training

Frequently the existing facility has the proper equipment but is inadequate due to the large numbers of individuals using it. The first step required in such situations is to better organize the flow of people into and out of the facility. This task is hampered by individual schedules, individual training time preferences, and the use of the facility by several athletic teams.

To overcome these obstacles, first document the use of the facility to determine the number of individuals who train there. Before determining schedules establish how many people use the facility at various times of the day. The heaviest volume usually occurs at noon and late afternoon when athletic teams are most likely to train. When working with athletic teams obtain a list of preferred and alternate times from each team. Inform the coaches they should indicate their preferences based upon the class schedules of their atheltes. Being aware of the fluctuation of use throughout the day aids in allocating training schedules that satisfy most parties using the facility. Accurate statistical information regarding the facility's use also provides strong support for budget requests.

Organization of the population flow in the training facility also involves the use patterns of the equipment. In other words, it is necessary to determine how people use particular exercises in their training programs. This information is used to adjust the exercise order of the various training programs in order to eliminate lines of people waiting to use one or several pieces of equipment. This is especially important when timed exercise workouts (i.e., one minute rest periods) are critical to the effectiveness of the exercise stimulus. Efficient patterned population movement in the facility is accomplished by four basic steps:

- Use predetermined exercise progressions
- Make sure individuals who are involved in a particular exercise flow pattern have the same rest period needs
- Group those individuals with identical training regimes together when possible
- Carefully plan those training schedules which involve more than one exercise flow pattern during the same time period

Patterns of movement are accomplished by training flow charts which specify the sequence of exercises and rest periods. Innovative techniques include taperecorded exercise sequences for use either on a facility-wide audio system or on personal cassette recorders, and color-coded, taped floor movement patterns and workout sheets with a flow chart. Whichever method is chosen, it is important that it be appropriate to the facility. Although these specific organization methods may be mandatory when there is an extreme number of people using the facility, some of these ideas might be used simply to stress the proper sequence of exercise and adherence to rest periods.

Availability of Space

The availability of space for training refers to the amount of room available for exercise equipment. Until recently university and high school weight rooms were given low priority areas in the basement, the boiler room, the men's locker room, or a storage shed. This led to problems of access (e.g., women being unable to train because the weight room was in the men's locker room), temperature control, ventilation problems, and inadequate space to place certain pieces of equipment in the room. Basic remodeling or relocation of the resistance training facility solves many of these problems. No equipment purchases should be made without prior measurements of the space available within the facility. A basic floor plan should be made prior to developing a new facility or area. Placement of equipment in the facility that best allows for population flow is vital, as is the provision of space to house new equipment. The facility should have easy accessibility, good ventilation, cleanliness, and a comfortable temperature. These qualities must be taken into account when selecting the location of the facility and developing a floor plan. Future equipment purchases and the acquisition of additional floor space must be closely linked if the training facility is to be a safe and desirable place in which to train.

Availability of Time

The amount of training time available can cause problems if the designed training programs do not match the projected training time. The length of a training session should be calculated immediately after the session is planned. The session must consider the individual's as well as the facility's schedule. Though individuals should use the best training program possible, there are cases, such as multisport athletes and individuals with demanding personal schedules, in which time is so limited that the training session has to be modified. Any modifications due to time limitations should be done carefully. Large muscle group exercises and low rest periods are acute variable choices which can provide time economy but should only be prescribed in appropriate situations. Only a sufficient amount of small muscle group exercises should be eliminated to allow the training session to fit into the time available. Also, short rest periods (less than one minute) should only be used when higher lactate levels are desired.

Summary of Administrative Concerns

In the real world administrative concerns most likely play the biggest role in limiting resistance training effectiveness. Everything possible should be done to minimize the detrimental effects of these limitations on the exercise stimulus. Instead of becoming a slave to administrative concerns, deal with them directly to overcome their negative effects on the resistance training program. An example of how one can become a slave to administrative concerns is the coach who eliminates an exercise from a training session because it does not fit on the workout card. Use proper organizational procedures to make the program more effective, avoid excessive paper work, and keep only that information which supports the program's existence and helps to evaluate its effectiveness. Although there is a great deal of organization involved in the management of individuals in a resistance training facility, remember that the first responsibility is to provide the best exercise stimulus possible.

Case Study Exercise Prescriptions

The following are some case studies which demonstrate the different manipulations of acute and chronic program variables. Because every situation is unique the basic information in this chapter should be viewed as guidelines for the development of a resistance exercise program.

Photo courtesy of the University of Oregon, photographer David Weintraub.

CASE STUDY ONE

John just took a job at Wilmont Senior High School as the head wrestling coach and physical education teacher. He was an avid weight trainer in college and felt it played a large role in his athletic career. John's undergraduate courses in exercise science stimulated an interest in strength training. On the basis of his interest, previous experience, and certification he was appointed head of the high school's strength and conditioning program. John decided first to develop a workout program for his wrestling team.

John started with a needs analysis for the sport and determined that the movements and angles involved with wrestling were varied, but primarily involved the large muscles of the hip, leg and back. Dynamic contractions were the most common although there were a certain amount of isometric contractions taking place during various wrestling moves. The energy was derived primarily from the lactic acid energy source: Wrestling entailed intense activity extended over 6 minutes with a limited amount of rest. John designed the following needs analysis for the wrestling team:

Muscle Groups to be Trained: This sport requires overall physical training, but the large muscle groups of the back, hip and legs are especially important for the performance of most moves. Wrestling requires a great deal of dynamic strength and local muscular endurance.

Injury Sites: The main injury sites are the neck, shoulder, ankle, and knee.

Muscle Action: The dynamic concentric contraction is the primary one involved. Isometric contractions are used to a lesser extent.

Energy Systems: The lactic acid source is the major contributor of energy during a match. The remainder derive from the ATP-PC source and oxygen source.

John now examined the acute program variables of a basic workout design for the sport and designed the following workout for his wrestlers.

OFF SEASON

M-W-F Body-Part Workout (High Lactic Acid)

Bench Press —10ı10ı10ı
Upright Row—10ı10ı10ı
         *   *   *

Lat Pull Down—10ı10ı10ı
Seated Row   —10ı10ı10ı
         *   *   *

Leg Extensions—10ı10ı10ı
Leg Flexions   —10ı10ı10ı
         *   *   *

Squats   —10/ 5/ 5/ 5/ 5
                 → → → →

Sit-ups   —50ǀ50ǀ
Knee-ups   —25ǀ25ǀ
                   *   *

Arm Curls   —10 * 10 * 10 *
                 → → →

Calf Raisers   —10 * 10 * 10 *
                 → → →

Four-way neck isometrics
/ = 2-5 min rest
* = 1 min rest period
→ Indicates order of exercises
NOTE: All repetitions listed are RM loads.

The M-W-F program is designed to strengthen the various body parts of the wrestler using primarily body part exercises with one structural exercise (squat). Exercises are ordered within a group to exercise the same body part at different angles. This exercise order stresses the lactic acid energy source and calls for mainly one-minute rest periods between both sets and exercises. This type of workout helps the wrestler to adapt to the high concentrations of lactic acid encountered during a wrestling match. In order to address the structural strength needs of the wrestler, a T-Th training session is also developed. This is used at the onset of the program and is subject to chronic program manipulations.

T-TH Structural Workout
  Deadlift—8 / 8 / 8 / 8 / 8 /
            → → → → →

  Hang Cleans—10 / 10 / 10 / 10 / 10 /
              → → → → →

  Sit-ups—4 × 25

  Split Squats—10 / 10 / 10 / 10 /
              ǀ → → → →

  High Pulls—8 / 8 / 8 / 8 /
             → → → →

Note: All repetitions listed are RM loads.

This workout is designed to develop explosive power in the legs, hips, and back. Structural exercises are chosen to accomplish this goal. Adequate rest is given between sets and exercises to allow the wrestler to handle the high-intensity loading factor and to promote primarily strength fitness.

Chronic Manipulations

Chronic manipulations of the above workouts include several possibilities. As the season approaches, the number of repetitions can be decreased to five or six, and even two or three repetitions for the structural exercises on MWF and T-Th workouts. The rest periods between sets and exercises can be gradually decreased to 20 seconds for the body-part workouts (MWF). These two manipulations help to peak strength levels while maintaining a high amount of stress on the lactic acid energy source. In addition, to create variations in daily training one might include one or two additional sets or one or two fewer sets at a higher intensity. This causes increases and/or decreases in the volume and intensity of the daily workouts; subsequently the training stimulus is altered, preventing the staleness portion of the general adaptation syndrome. One might also wish to use two- or three-week cycles where the intensity (RM) is changed on the T-TH workouts (e.g., 10, 5, 3) and the rest is altered on the MWF workouts (e.g., 60 s, 45 s, 20 s). As the season approaches it becomes necessary to focus training on the practice of actual wrestling skills. One way to decrease the time spent in the weight room is to decrease the number of sets and repetitions along with decreasing the rest periods between them. Another way to accomplish this is to increase the number of structural workouts at the expense of the body-part workouts; the goal is to eventually stop performance of the body-part workouts altogether and perform only three structural workouts per week. Structural exercises stress several muscle groups at once whereby all major muscle groups are stressed in a shorter period of time (as opposed to body-part workouts).

Individual Considerations

John realized that all of his wrestlers did not have the same level of experience with resistance training and physical conditioning. He therefore made individual modifications in the beginning loads and rest periods until each of his wrestlers could tolerate the basic body-part and structural sessions. He also ran teaching sessions in the weight room to instruct his athletes on the basic techniques of the lifts. One of his wrestlers had a chronic shoulder problem from the previous season. In this case, John added a few more exercises for the shoulder area to improve the athlete's overall shoulder strength. Some of the heavier wrestlers had very low aerobic fitness. For these John developed some basic aerobic fitness programs for use during the off-season program. All of his wrestlers were on aerobic fitness programs to facilitate better recovery between rounds and between matches (especially during tournaments). Finally, John stressed off-season weight control.

Photo courtesy of the University of Oregon, photographer David Zahn.

CASE STUDY TWO

Kathy was primarily interested in a personal fitness program. She was actively involved in an aerobic running program and was ready to include a resistance training program to balance her conditioning activities, improve her basic upper body strength, and prevent lower limb injury during her aerobic exercise. Her basic needs analysis indicated additional upper body strength along with quadricep, hamstring, and calf exercises to aid in her injury prevention maintenance program. The acute workout design variables produced the following beginning workout:

Chest Exercise:	Bench Press	12, 10, 10
Back Exercise:	Lat Pull Down	10, 10, 10
Abdomen Exercises:	Bent Leg	
	Sit-ups	15, 15
	Knee-ups	15, 15
Arms/Shoulder Exercises:	Military Press	12, 10, 10
	Arm Curls	12, 10, 10
Leg Exercises:	Leg Extensions	15, 15, 15
	Leg Flexions	15, 15, 15
	Toe Raisers	15, 15

This program is designed to achieve moderate strength gains in the upper body musculature. Two minutes of rest were allowed between both sets and exercises. Higher maximum repetition loadings are used in this workout so that the strength training does not interfere with aerobic metabolism development. All of the above exercises are standard for the various body parts. Due to the allowance of long rest periods the training session can be performed in multiple-set fashion (complete each exercise) or can be done in a circuit format (exercise to exercise). Initially Kathy performs only one exercise per body part and one or two sets of each exercise until tolerance to the workouts improves.

Chronic Changes

Kathy is not a competitive athlete and therefore is not attempting to prepare for a particular competition or season. She is interested in general fitness, and the purpose of her resistance training is to increase upper body strength and improve in lower body strength development to prevent injury. The major goals of chronic manipulations (periodization) are to prepare the individual for a particular season or competition and to insure continued gains in fitness and strength. Because these are not the goals of Kathy's program a great deal of chronic manipulation is unnecessary.

Kathy may, however, consider two chronic manipulations of her program. One is to periodically substitute different exercises that stress the same muscle group for exercises already in her program. Examples of this are substituting the leg press for leg extensions and leg flexions, the inclined press for the military press, and bent over rowing for lat pull downs. This will help to keep the program from becoming tedious. Finally, Kathy should continually try to shorten her rest periods. This decreases the amount of time necessary to complete a workout and improves Kathy's local muscular endurance.

Photo courtesy of the University of Oregon, photographer David Zahn.

CASE STUDY THREE

Spike is a women's collegiate volleyball coach. Due to a rather poor season last year he decided to initiate an off-season resistance training program to improve his team's performance. Spike had ideas as to what the goals of a resistance training program for women's volleyball should be. To make these goals more specific, he conducted a literature search concerning women's volleyball and discovered that several training factors have been found to improve performance, including vertical jumping ability (Fleck, Case, Puhl, & Van Handle, 1985; Gladden & Colacino, 1978; Spence, Disch, Fred, & Coleman, 1980), upper body and arm strength (Morrow, Jackson, Hosler, & Kachurick, 1979), and low percentage of body fat (Morrow et al., 1979; Fleck et al., 1985). The goals of Spike's program were to increase vertical jumping ability and upper body strength and to decrease percentage of body fat. The exercises chosen to fulfill the needs were as follows:

	Sets	Repetitions
Incline Press	3	10
Squats	3	10
Lat pull down	3	10
Sit-ups	3	20
Toe raises	3	10
Wrist curls	3	10
Back hyperextensions	3	10
Leg extensions	3	10
Leg curls	3	10

Due to the arrangement of the weight room and available time, Spike decided to run the program as a timed circuit allowing 30 seconds to perform the exercise and one minute rest between exercises. He placed the athletes in groups of three, which provided spotters for each exercise and assistance in changing the resistance needed for each exercise. The athletes would begin training using a 10 RM; when they could complete all three circuits of an individual exercise the resistance would be increased. Resistance training was performed on Monday, Wednesday, and Friday. Spike also had team meetings in which proper diet and caloric balance were discussed. The aim of these meetings was to educate his players in the role these factors play in weight control and athletic performance.

Chronic Manipulations

Spike decided to start the resistance training program nine weeks prior to the onset of the volleyball season. He decided to incorporate the concept of periodization: For the first four weeks the original workout was performed; weeks five, six, and seven called for exercises at 8 RMs; and for the last two weeks the athletes performed at five RMs. The rest periods diminished from 50 seconds to 40 seconds and finally to 30 seconds during the last two weeks of the program. In addition, for the last five weeks of the program plyometric jumping exercises were performed on Tuesday, Thursday and Saturday.

Using the concepts of a needs analysis, acute program design, chronic program design, and consideration of administrative factors results in the optimal program for your situation. It is then up to you to be creative and search out ways to improve the design of the program and your resistance training facility. The next chapter discusses various resistance training systems (i.e., sets and repetitions) for your consideration for inclusion in programs you design.

Chapter 4

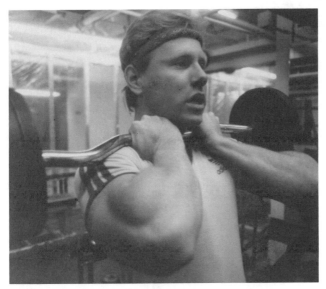

Systems of Resistance Training

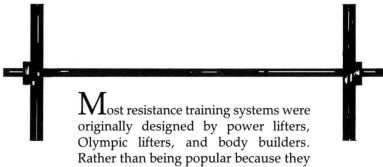

Most resistance training systems were originally designed by power lifters, Olympic lifters, and body builders. Rather than being popular because they have scientifically demonstrated superiority over other programs in bringing about increases in strength, resistance training systems are popular because they effect increases in strength and or hypertrophy for practitioners, or because the system has been marketed by an individual or company. More research is needed concerning all of the training systems described within this chapter. Knowledge of these various systems are of value to a practitioner. The fact that a system has been used by enough individuals to have name recognition indicates that it has a good success rate in producing gains in strength or hypertrophy. In this context the system may be worth trying.

Knowledge of the various systems is also of value in manipulating training variables to bring about optimal gains in strength or hypertrophy. Many resistance trainers adapt one system of training and then attempt to apply it to all individuals and muscle groups. This will inevitably lead to less than optimal gains in some muscle groups as well as in many individuals. The indefinite use of one program also leads to plateaus in progress and overtraining. Manipulation of the acute and chronic training variables as described in chapter 3 must be used to avoid these problems. Optimal gains in strength or muscular hypertrophy are achieved by mixing the various training programs and manipulating the training variables appropriately.

Several common mistakes are made by novice resistance trainers when examining the various resistance training programs. One mistake is to assume that the system used by a champion body builder, power lifter, or Olympic lifter is the best for the novice. Programs used by competitive weight lifters and body builders many times are too intense for the novice resistance trainer. It has taken years of training for the competitive athlete to achieve the fitness level necessary to tolerate the program he or she is presently using. Although all individuals realize gains in strength in a resistance training program, the champion weight lifter or body builder has also a genetic potential for superior strength and muscle size. The genetics of these athletes allows them to tolerate very intense programs and exhibit gains in strength.

A training record is invaluable for determining which training system works best for each individual. Without a record, a program which is found to be successful in effecting strength or muscular hypertrophy will most likely not be remembered exactly so that it can be repeated. A training record answers many questions concerning an individual's response to a particular program; it can also be used to compare programs to identify which of them leads to the greatest gains in strength or muscular hypertrophy for the individual. Finally, training logs are a useful motivational tool; athletes can see their own progress over the course of a specific training period.

Single Set System

The single set system, the performance of each exercise for one set, is one of the oldest resistance training programs. First published in 1925 (Liederman, 1925), the single set program consisted of using heavy weights and few repetitions with a five-minute rest between exercises. This system experienced great popularity throughout the first 40 years of the twentieth century.

A single set of each exercise (8 to 12 repetitions) is still quite popular and recommended by one of the leading manufacturers of resistance training equipment. Significant gains in strength by a single set system have been demonstrated (Hurley et al., 1984a; Peterson, 1975; Stone, et al., 1979; Stowers et al., 1983). However, it has also been demonstrated that a single set system of one set of ten repetitions (one times ten) resulted in a significantly smaller strength gain than either a multiple set system of three times ten or a periodization program involving light, moderate, and heavy training days (Stowers et al., 1983). All three groups in this study trained three times per week for seven weeks. This study clearly demonstrates the superiority of multiple set programs over a single set program in producing strength gains. Even though a single set system many not be the best overall program it may be a viable program for an individual who has very little time to dedicate to resistance training. A professional person might be such an individual.

Multiple Set System

The multiple set system of training consists of two to three warm-up sets of increasing resistance; this is followed by several sets at the same resistance. This system of training became popular in the 1940s (Darden, 1973) and was the forerunner of the multiple set and repetition systems of today.

The optimal resistance and number of repetitions for strength development using a multiple set system has undergone considerable research (see chapter 2, Dynamic Constant Resistance). A five to six RM performed for a minimum of three sets appears to be the optimal resistance and number of repetitions to cause optimal increases in strength. A multiple set system can, however, be performed at any desired resistance, for any number of repetitions and sets to be consistent with the desired goals of a resistance training program. The majority of training systems are some variation of a multiple set system.

Bulk System

The bulk system refers specifically to a multiple set system of three sets of five to six repetitions per exercise. A comparative study of ten resistance training systems resulted in some very interesting conclusions (Leighton, Holmes, Benson, Wooten, & Schmerer, 1967). This study trained college students two times per week for eight weeks. Twenty to twenty-nine subjects were in each group. All groups performed two-arm arm curls, two-arm arm presses, lat pull downs, half squats, sit-ups, side bends, leg presses, leg curls, toe raises, and bench presses. Static strength using cable tensiometry was determined both before and after the eight-week training period for all groups. The bulk system turned out to be one of the most effective of those compared in bringing about increases in static strength of the back and legs (see Table 4.1) and therefore may be a valuable system for increasing general leg and back strength.

Light-to-Heavy System

As the name implies the light-to-heavy system entails progressing from light to heavy resistances. This system became popular in the 1930s and 1940s among Olympic lifters (Hatfield & Krotee, 1978). It consists of performing a set of three to five repetitions with a relatively light resistance. Five pounds are then added to the bar and another set of three to five repetitions are performed. This is continued until only one repetition can be performed.

The DeLorme regimen of three sets of ten repetitions with the resistance progressing from 50% to 66% to 100% of a ten RM is a light-to-heavy system. The DeLorme system does cause significant increases in strength over short training periods (DeLorme & Watkins, 1948; DeLorme, Ferris, & Gallager, 1952; Leighton, 1967). The DeLorme training group in the study depicted in Table 4.1 demonstrated a significant increase in static elbow strength but no significant increases in static elbow extension and back and leg strength. A second light-to-heavy system (descending half triangle or descending half pyramid—see Triangle Programs for complete definition) also demonstrated significant increases in all three static strength tests. This appears to be one of the more effective ways of increasing back and leg static strength.

Heavy-to-Light System

The heavy-to-light system is a reversal of the light-to-heavy system. In this system, after a brief warm-up, the heaviest set is performed first and for each succeeding set the resistance is lowered. The Oxford technique is a heavy-to-light system and is merely a reversal of the sets performed for the DeLorme system. Significant gains in strength have been achieved with the Oxford technique (Leighton et al., 1967; McMorris & Elkins, 1954; Zinovieff, 1951).

Comparisons reveal that the heavy-to-light and light-to-heavy systems are equivocal but tend to favor the heavy-to-light system. One study found the heavy-to-light system to be superior to the light-to-heavy system in strength gains, but indicated that further research is necessary (McMorris & Elkins, 1954). A second study (see Table 4.1) found little difference between the two in increasing elbow flexion, but clearly favors the heavy-to-light system in increasing elbow extension and back and leg strength. The research to date, though sparse, favors a heavy-to-light system over a light-to-heavy system in producing strength gains.

Table 4.1 Comparison of Ten Resistance Training Systems

	Descending half triangle	Super set	Cheating	Bulk	Tri-set	Double progressive	Heavy-light[a] training days	DeLorme	Oxford	Isometric[b]
Elbow flexion	11*	12*	23*	8*	25*	7	3	9*	7*	0
Elbow extension	9**	9	66**	9	30**	25*	34**	16	28**	35*
Back and leg Strength	24*	21*	27*	24**	17*	13	19*	0	11	– 5

** = significant increase pre- to post-training at 0.01 level of significance

* = significant increase pre- to post-training at 0.05 level of significance

Values given are percent change pre- to post-training

a = heavy-light refers to maximal resistance being used during only one training session per week, 2/3 maximal used during the second session

b = training consisted of one maximal contraction

Note. From "A Study of the Effectiveness of Ten Different Methods of Progressive Resistance Exercise on the Development of Strength, Flexibility, Girth and Body Weight" by J.R. Leighton, D. Holmes, J. Benson, B. Wooten, and R. Schmerer, 1967, *Journal of the Association for Physical and Mental Rehabilitation,* **21,** p. 79. Copyright 1967 by the American Corrective Therapy Association. Adapted by permission.

Triangle Programs

Triangle or pyramid programs are used by many power lifters. A complete triangle program starts with a set at a light resistance of 10 to 12 repetitions. The resistance is then increased over several sets so that fewer and fewer repetitions can be performed until only a one repetition maximum is performed. Then, over several sets the resistance is decreased in the reverse manner it was increased; the session finishes with a set of 10 to 12 repetitions (see Figure 4.1).

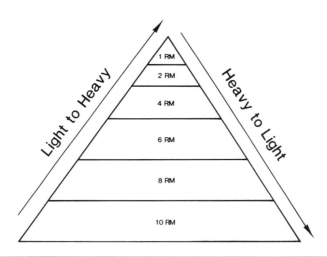

Figure 4.1 A light-to-heavy or ascending pyramid system consists of performing sets progressing from light to heavy resistance. In a heavy-to-light or descending pyramid system sets are performed starting with heavy and progressing to light resistances. A full pyramid consists of both the ascending and descending portions of the pyramid.

Two variations of the complete triangle program you are already familiar with. The light-to-heavy system is an ascending half pyramid (or ascending half triangle) consisting of only the increasing resistance portion of a complete pyramid. The heavy-to-light system is a descending half pyramid (or descending half triangle) consisting of only the decreasing resistance portion of a complete triangle program.

Super Set System

Super setting has evolved into two distinct but similar types of programs. One program uses several sets of two exercises for the same body part but two groups of antagonistic muscles. Examples of this type of super setting would be arm curls immediately followed by tricep extensions or leg extensions immediately followed by leg curls. Significant increases in strength due to this type of super setting have been reported (Table 4.1). The super set system is one of the most effective systems of the ten compared for increasing back and leg static strength.

The second type of super setting uses one set of several exercises in rapid succession for the same muscle group or body part. An example of this type of super setting is one set of each of the following: lat pull-down, seated rowing, and bent-over rowing. Both types of super setting involve sets of eight to ten repetitions with little or no rest between sets and or exercises. Super setting is a popular program among body builders, suggesting its benefits for muscular hypertrophy. If the goal of a training program is to produce increases in muscular hypertrophy super setting warrants consideration.

Circuit Program

Circuit programs consist of a series of resistance training exercises that are performed one after the other with minimal rest (15-30 seconds) between exercises. Approximately 10 to 15 repetitions of each exercise are performed per circuit at a resistance of 40% to 60% of a one RM. If desired, several circuits of the exercise can be performed. The circuit can be designed to include exercises which meet the specific goals of the training program. This type of program is very time efficient when large numbers of individuals are involved because each piece of equipment is virtually kept in constant use.

One major goal of a circuit program is to improve cardiovascular conditioning. Circuit programs of short-term training (8-20 weeks) increase maximal oxygen consumption approximately 4% and 8% in men and women, respectively (Gettman & Pollock, 1981). This, however, is substantially less than the 15% to 20% increase in maximal oxygen consumption due to running programs over the same time period. If one goal of a program is to increase cardiovascular endurance, circuit training is the program of choice. Circuit training with its short rest periods is very time efficient and therefore is ideal for an individual with limited time to dedicate to resistance training.

Peripheral Heart Action System

The peripheral heart action system is a variation of circuit training. A training session using this system is divided into several sequences (Gajda, 1965). A sequence is a group of five or six exercises, each for a different body part. A training session consists of four to six sequences, all of which contain different exercises for each body part being trained. The number of repetitions per set of each exercise in a sequence varies with the goals of the program, but normally 8 to 12 repetitions per set are performed. One training session consists of performing all the exercises in the first sequence three times in a circuit fashion. The remaining sequences are then performed one after the other in the same fashion as the first sequence. An example of the exercises in a peripheral heart action training session is given in Table 4.2.

The aim of the peripheral heart action system is to keep blood moving from one body part to the next, not allowing the blood to pool in any particular part of the body for a long period of time (Gajda, 1965). This system is extremely fatiguing. Heart rate should be kept at 140 beats per minute or higher. The short rest periods and maintenance

Table 4.2 Example of a Four-Sequence Peripheral Heart Action Training Session

	Sequence			
Body part	1	2	3	4
Chest	bench press	incline press	declines	flys
Back	lat pull-down	seated row	bent-over rows	T-bar row
Shoulders	military press	upright row	lateral raise	front raise
Leg	squat	leg extension	Back squat	split squat
Abdomen	sit-ups	leg raise	Roman chair sit-ups	V-ups

of a relatively high heart rate make this program very similar to normal circuit training. The peripheral heart action system is therefore also an ideal program if a major goal is to increase cardiovascular endurance.

Tri-Set System

The tri-set system is similar to the peripheral heart action system in that it incorporates groups of exercises. As the name implies it consists of groups of three exercises for the same body part. The exercises can include different muscle groups. The exercises are performed with little or no rest between exercises and sets. Normally three sets of each exercise are performed. An example of three exercises comprising a tri-set is arm curls, tricep extensions, and military presses. Tri-setting is one of the most effective systems for increasing static strength of the systems compared in Table 4.1. The short rest periods and the use of three exercises in series for a particular body part make this a good system to increase local muscular endurance.

Multi-Poundage Systems

The multi-poundage system requires one or two spotters to assist in the training session. The trainee performs four or five repetitions at a four or five RM resistance. The spotters then remove 20 to 40 lbs from the bar. The trainee then performs another four or five repetitions. This procedure is continued for several sets (Poole, 1964). The number of sets possible depends upon the original resistance used and the goals of the program. The potential for the performance of several sets of an exercise in rapid succession makes this a good system for increasing local muscular endurance.

Cheat System

The cheat system is quite popular among body builders; as the name implies, it involves cheating or breaking strict form of the exercise (Weider, 1954). As an example, in the performance of standing barbell curls, rather than maintaining an erect upper body the trainee utilizes a slight body swing to start the barbell moving. The body swing is not grossly exaggerated but is sufficient to allow the trainee to lift 10 to 20 more lb of resistance than he is capable of lifting in a strict form fashion.

In the barbell curl the weakest position is when the arms are fully extended and the strongest position is when the elbow joint is at approximately a 90-degree angle. When barbell curls are performed in a strict form fashion the maximal amount of resistance that can be lifted is dependent upon the resistance that can be moved from the weakest or fully extended position. The muscles involved in flexing the elbow therefore are not maximally contracting in the stronger portions of the movement. The object of cheating is to allow the use of heavier weights which will cause the muscle(s) to contract with a force closer to maximal through a greater range of the movement and thus enhance strength gains. Care must be exercised when using the cheat system. The use of the heavier resistances and the use of a cheating movement to start the resistance moving increases the chance of injury. As an example the use of a swinging movement of the hips and lower back when performing arm curls in a cheating fashion places additional stress on the lower back.

Comparisons of strength gains due to the cheat system versus various other training systems indicate that this system is quite effective (Table 4.1). The cheating system appears to be one of the most effective systems in increasing both arm and back and leg static strength. The cheating system can be used in conjunction with virtually all other training systems (e.g., cheating during a full pyramid system).

Split Routine System

Many body builders use a split routine system. Body builders must perform many exercises for the same body part to cause muscular hypertrophy of all muscles in that body part. Because this is a time-consuming process, not all parts of the body can be exercised in a single training session. Solving this predicament has lead to the split routine system: Various body parts are trained on alternate days. A typical split routine system entails the training of arms, legs, and abdomen on Monday, Wednesday, and Friday, and chest, shoulders, and back on Tuesday, Thursday, and Saturday. This system solves the predicament concerning time per session but it means that training is performed six days of the week.

Variations of a split routine system can be developed so that training sessions take place four or five days per week. Even though training sessions are quite frequent sufficient recovery of muscle groups between training sessions is possible because body parts are not trained on successive days. The split routine system allows the intensity of the training on a particular body part or group of exercises to be maintained at a higher level than would be possible if the four to six training sessions were combined into two or three long sessions. The maintenance of a higher intensity (heavier resistances) should result in greater gains in strength.

Blitz Program

The blitz program is a variation of the split routine system. Rather than training several body parts during each training session, only one body part is trained per training session. The duration of the training session is not reduced. An example of a blitz program is to perform all arm, chest, leg, trunk, back, and shoulder exercises on Monday, Tuesday, Wednesday, Thursday, Friday, and Saturday, respectively. This type of program is performed by many body builders in preparation for a contest. A short-term blitz-type program may also be appropriate if an athlete's performance is being limited by strength of a particular muscle group or groups. A long jumper might perform a blitz program for the legs immediately prior to the start of a season.

Isolated Exercise System

The isolated exercise system devotes an entire training session to a single exercise (Horvath, 1959). Exercises for different training days are selected that affect different body parts. An example of exercises for four different training sessions would be bench press, squat, arm curls, and upright rows. On Monday only the bench press is performed, Tuesday—the squat, Thursday—arm curls, and Friday—upright rows. Other exercises can be added to acheive as many training days per week as desired. A resistance is selected that allows eight to ten repetitions to be performed. The trainee then performs set after set of that day's exercise for as many repetitions as possible for one and one half hours. A one-minute rest is allowed between sets. This system places a great deal of stress on the muscles involved in each exercise; it is recommended that it not be used for more than six consecutive weeks (Horvath, 1959). As with the blitz program a short-term isolated exercise system may be appropriate for an athlete whose performance is limited by one particular muscle group.

Exhaustion Set System

Sets to exhaustion can be incorporated into virtually any training system. Body builders especially use sets to exhaustion in their training programs. Advocates of this system believe more motor units will be recruited and therefore receive a training stimulus with sets to exhaustion than when sets are not performed to exhaustion. It has been reported that one set to exhaustion of ten repetitions causes significant gains in squatting ability, but that three sets of ten repetitions, two sets of which were to exhaustion, cause significantly greater increases in squatting ability (Stowers et al., 1983). Training in this study was conducted twice weekly for seven weeks. This same study also demonstrated that a group trained with periodization (cycling) had significantly greater increases in squatting ability than either of the set-to-exhaustion groups. However, no significant difference among the three groups in bench press ability was demonstrated.

Burn System

The burn system is an extension of the exhaustion set system. The burn system can be incorporated into any of the other training systems. After a set has been performed to exhaustion half or partial repetitions are performed. Normally five to six partial repetitions are performed which causes an aching or burning sensation, thus the name resulted (Richford, 1966). Advocates of this system claim it is especially effective when training the calves and arms.

Forced Repetition System

Forced repetitions are also an extension of the exhaustion set system and are employed by many power lifters. After a set to exhaustion has been performed training partners assist the trainee by lifting the resistance just enough to allow the trainee to force out three to four additional repetitions. This system can be easily performed with most exercises after a set to exhaustion has been performed. Forced repetitions are appropriate when the goal of a program is to increase local muscular endurance; this system forces the muscle to continue to produce force when it is partially fatigued.

Super Pump System

Proponents of the super pump system believe that advanced body builders need to perform 15 to 18 sets for each body part per training session in order to achieve the muscular development desired (Page, 1966). To achieve this high number of sets, anywhere from one to three exercises per muscle group are performed per training session. Advocates of this system recommend 15 second rest periods between sets of five to six repetitions (Page, 1966). The repetitions must all be performed with strict adherence to correct form, and each muscle group must be trained two to three times per week. The super pump system appears to be the most effective for training the arms, chest, and shoulders. This system is too fatiguing to use in training the large muscles of the legs and back (Darden, 1973). This system is appropriate for advanced lifters who desire greater muscular hypertrophy of the arms, chest, and shoulders.

Functional Isometrics

The functional isometrics system of training attempts to take advantage of the joint angle specificity of gains in strength due to isometric training (see chapter 2, Isometrics). Functional isometrics entail performing a dynamic contraction for four to six inches of a movement; at that point the resistance hits the pins in a power rack. The trainee continues to attempt to lift the resistance with maximal effort for five to seven seconds. The pins in the power rack are normally placed at the sticking point of the exercise being performed.

The objective of this system is to use isometrics' joint angle specificity to cause increases in strength at the weakest point within the range of motion. The maximal amount of resistance that can be lifted in any exercise is determined by the amount of resistance that can be moved through the sticking point or weakest point in that movement. An example of functional isometrics in the bench press is presented in Figure 4.2. The use of functional isometrics in conjunction with normal dynamic constant resistance training has been shown to cause significantly greater increases in 1-RM bench press strength than dynamic constant resistance training alone (Jackson, Jackson, Hnatek & West, 1985). The system is appropriate in cases where the major goal of the program is to increase 1-RM capabilities of a particular lift or exercise.

Figure 4.2   The use of functional isometrics at the sticking point in a bench press is depicted.

Double Progressive System

The intensity of the training in the double progressive system is varied by changes in both the number of repetitions and the resistance lifted. Initially the resistance is held constant while the number of repetitions per set is increased until a specified number of repetitions is reached. The resistance is then increased and the number of repetitions is decreased until the number of repetitions performed is back to the initial number. This process is then repeated. An example of this system is given in Table 4.3. Of the systems compared in Table 4.1 the double progressive system appears to be one of the least effective. Although the research is sparse it does indicate that use of the double progressive system is unwarranted.

Table 4.3 Example of the Double Progressive System

Sets	Repetitions	Resistance (lb)
1	4	120
2	6	120
3	8	120
4	10	120
5	12	120
6	10	140
7	8	160
8	6	175
9	4	185

Comparison of Various Systems

All of the aforementioned systems were designed to address specific training goals. Each system can be described in terms of its acute program variables (see Table 4.4). Some systems are extensions of other systems (e.g., forced repetitions, burns). In some systems acute program variables are not specifically defined. This may explain why training responses to a system may vary considerably.

With manipulation of acute program variables it is easy to design many distinctly different systems. The resistance system designed should address the needs of the individual and/or the event for which the individual is being trained. Popular or fad training systems should be described and evaluated in terms of their acute program variables and their ability to address the needs of an individual or sport.

The choice of which training system or systems to use depends upon the goals of the program, time constraints, and how the goals of the resistance training program relate to the goals of the entire fitness program. This last consideration is discussed in chapter 5.

Table 4.4   Acute Program Variables of Resistance Training Systems

Acute Program Variables:	Load	Choice of Exercise	Order of Exercise	Rest	Sets
Resistance Training Systems					
Single Set	10 RM	NS	NS	5 min	1
Multiple Set	5-6 RM	NS	NS	NS	3
Bulk System	5-6 RM	NS	NS	NS	3-5
Light-to-Heavy	Light-to-Heavy	NS	NS	NS	NS
Heavy-to-Light	Heavy-to-Light	NS	NS	NS	NS
Triangle	Light-to-Heavy Heavy-to-Light	NS	NS	NS	Several
Super Set	8-10 RM	Opposing muscle group	Agonist to antagonist	None	Several
Circuit	40%-60% 1 RM	NS	NS	15-30 seconds	1-several
Peripheral Heart Action	NS	Sequence of 5 or 6 exercises each for different body part	NS	None or little	4-6
Tri-set system	NS	3 exercises per body part	NS	NS	3
Multi-poundage	4-5 RM starting, load reduced 20-40 lb to allow 4-5 more repetitions	NS	NS	None	Several
Cheat System	Greater than 1 RM	NS	NS	1 s	Several

Split Routine	NS	Different muscle groups each training session	NS	NS	NS
Blitz	8-10 RM	One muscle group/day	NS	NS	NS
Isolated Exercise	8-10 RM	One exercise	NS	NS	As many as can be performed in 1-1 1/2 hours
Exhaustion	To failure	NS	NS	NS	NS
Burn	After movement failure continued for 1/2 or partial movements to 5 or 6 times	NS	NS	NS	NS
Forced Repetitions	After set to exhaustion assisted repetitions for 3-4 more repetitions	Exercise where load movement can be assisted	NS	NS	NS
Super Pump	5-6 RM	1-3 exercises	NS	15 s	15-18
Functional Isometrics	5-7 seconds >1 RM. Weak part in range of motion	NS	NS	NS	NS
Double Progressive	Constant with increasing number of reps, then increased load with decreasing number of reps	NS	NS	NS	NS

NS = not specified

Chapter 5

Resistance Training's Relationship to Other Fitness Components

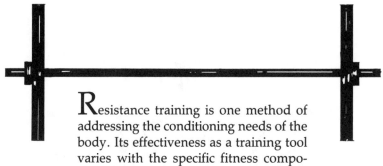

Resistance training is one method of addressing the conditioning needs of the body. Its effectiveness as a training tool varies with the specific fitness component desired to be enhanced (see Figure 5.1). For example, resistance training normally increases the strength component to a greater extent than it does cardiovascular endurance. Resistance training can make a significant contribution to increasing physical fitness. The level of fitness desired for each component depends upon the specific needs and goals of the individual and the sport. Resistance training is just

FITNESS COMPONENTS

- **•STRENGTH/POWER**
- **• FLEXIBILITY**
- **•CARDIOVASCULAR ENDURANCE**
- **•LOCAL MUSCULAR ENDURANCE**

Figure 5.1   The major components which make up physical fitness.

one form of conditioning modality within a total program. It is important to understand the basic guidelines for exercise prescription in other training modalities so that resistance training programs can be designed to meet the specific needs of the individual within a total conditioning program.

Aerobic Training and Exercise Prescription

Photo courtesy of the University of Oregon, photographer Sam Gloss.

A great deal of information exists regarding the effects and prescription of endurance exercise. The knowledge base spans from cardiac rehabilitation to elite distance racing (Froelicher, 1983). The ability to prescribe aerobic exercise is necessary to address the cardiovascular endurance needs of a conditioning program.

Prior to an endurance training program it is recommended to have both proper medical evaluation and exercise testing. This aids in the screening of individuals with coronary heart disease risk factors and possible cardiovascular or pulmonary disease. According to the American College of Sports Medicine (1980), "persons of any age may significantly increase their habitual levels of physical activity safely if there are no contraindications to exercise and a rational program is developed." It is very important that each individual is prescribed the proper intensity, duration, and frequency of exercise in a progressive manner.

The prescription of exercise intensity is individualized from exercise test data. Results of treadmill testing is a direct method of individualized exercise prescription (see Figure 5.2). From this information the

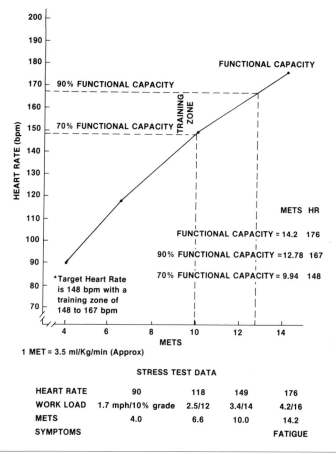

Figure 5.2 Exercise intensity is derived from treadmill stress test results.

intensity of the exercise can be related to a heart rate value. A training heart rate zone is typically prescribed which produces the aerobic exercise stimulus. An individual then performs steady state exercise within the training zone. Energy demands are expressed in *METs*. One MET is equivalent to resting oxygen consumption, which is approximately 3.5 ml/kg minute. For example ten METs represent an exercise intensity approximately ten times the resting metabolic rate. An individual with a ten MET functional capacity would have a maximal oxygen consumption value of approximately 35 ml/kg/min (10 × 3.5). High MET values, which reflect high maximal oxygen consumption values, are associated with the functional capacities of individuals who possess good cardiovascular endurance.

Many individuals do not have the resources available to obtain a laboratory stress test, most notably coaches who are prescribing exercise for hundreds of athletes. Yet an individual prescription for exercise should be given. Thus, for healthy individuals a training zone can be calculated using the Karvonen formula (see Figure 5.3). Coaches and individuals must realize that for basic aerobic fitness, endurance training doesn't have to hurt to be effective. This is quite different from the competitive endurance racer who has to use a much higher training intensity to prepare for a race.

KARVONEN FORMULA

% max $\dot{V}O_2$ (max HR - resting HR) + resting HR
220-20 = 200 bpm predicted max HR*

70% $\dot{V}O_2$max HR = 70% x (200-60) + 60
158 = 98 + 60

90% $\dot{V}O_2$max   HR = 90% x (200-60) + 60
186 = 126 + 60

Target HR = 158   Training Zone = 158 to 186

***A conservative estimate of max heart rate can be**
calculated 220-age = max heart rate

Figure 5.3   Karvonen formula is presented for calculation of training heart rates. *Note.*   Modified from Sharkey, 1984.

The duration and frequency of exercise also needs to be progressively increased as the individual becomes more tolerant of exercise stress. For basic cardiovascular endurance fitness the duration of exercise should last 20 to 60 minutes and be performed three to five days per week (Pollock, Wilmore, & Fox, 1978). Running, bicycling, and swimming are the best cardiovascular conditioners. Table 5.1 gives a basic summary of endurance training ranges. Improvement of aerobic capacity can be accomplished through interval training. Because the intensity is higher this should only be used with individuals who already have a good endurance base (Fardy, 1977).

An endurance exercise training session has a warm-up, a training period, and a cool-down (see Figure 5.4). The heart rate is checked and the pace of the exercise adjusted so that an individual is exercising within his or her training zone. The heart rate is manipulated by

Table 5.1   Basic Guidelines for Intensity, Frequency, and Duration of Endurance Exercise

Fitness level	Intensity	Frequency	Duration
Endurance athletes	85%-90%	5-7 days	1-2 hours
Healthy individuals	70%-90%	3-5 days	15-60 minutes

Note.   From "Training for Aerobic Power" by P.S. Fardy, in *Toward an Understanding of Human Performance*, E.J. Burke (Ed.), 1977, Ithaca: Movement Press. Copyright 1977 by Movement Press. Adapted by permission.

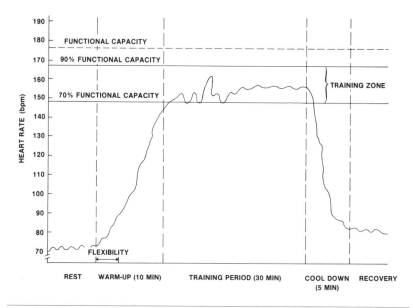

Figure 5.4   Heart rate response to warm-up, training period, and cooldown during endurance training session. *Note.*   Adapted from Sharkey, 1984.

the pace at which one exercises. A ten-second pulse rate can be taken after a steady state exercise duration is achieved (usually three to five minutes). One should conduct such a pace test over a number of training sessions. When running or bicycling, the pace tests should be performed on flat terrain. Also, as fitness levels improve it is important to check this pace to the heart rate response relationship. In Figure 5.5 a one-mile run is used but shorter distances (e.g., one-half mile)

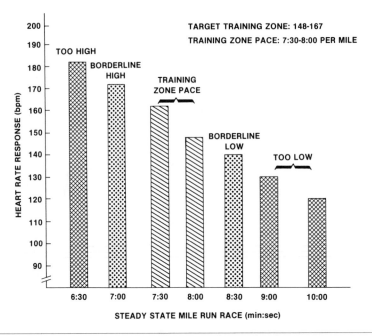

Figure 5.5 An individual should determine his or her heart rate response to differently paced endurance steady state exercise.

can also be used to evaluate this relationship. A less-conditioned individual usually requires shorter pace distances to evaluate a training pace. It is important to insure that steady state exercise is achieved at the selected distance (three-five minutes of exercise duration after warm-up).

Compatibility of Endurance Training

Training is specific: The adaptations of the body's physiological systems are specific to the exercise stimulus presented (see chapter 7). A topic which has gained increasing interest is the compatibility of resistance training and aerobic training performed during the same conditioning period.

Hickson (1980) compared three groups: one underwent both resistance and aerobic training; the second only resistance training; and the third only aerobic training. He observed decrements in leg strength in the group training simultaneously for strength (5 RMs) and high-intensity aerobic fitness during the last 2 weeks of a 10-week conditioning program, as compared to the group that trained only for strength. This study demonstrates that the development of dynamic strength may be compromised by performance of both resistance training and high-intensity endurance training. This study lasted eight weeks, so whether this reduction of strength development would continue over a longer training period is unknown. Because no periodization of either the resistance or the endurance training was used, the possibility exists that overtraining occurred in the group that performed both types of training simultaneously. Conversely, improvement of the aerobic capacity of the group training for strength and endurance was not compromised compared to the group performing only endurance training.

Dudley and Djamil (1985) found only decrements in the magnitude of increase in angle-specific peak torque at fast velocities (160-278 degrees/second) of contraction of a group simultaneously trained for strength and endurance as compared to a group trained only for strength. No decrements in angle-specific peak torque were observed for slow velocities (48-96 degrees/s) of contraction in the group simultaneously trained for strength and endurance. Aerobic power of the combination training group was not compromised compared to a group trained for endurance only. Both of the aforementioned studies indicate that simultaneous training for strength and endurance does compromise increases in strength, but not in aerobic power, in short-term training. Based on limited data, a third study indicates that concurrent training for strength and endurance results in compromised endurance capabilities (Nelson, Conlee, Arnall, Loy, & Silvester, 1984). Only limited cellular data is available to explain such a paradox. It has been demonstrated that mitochondrial volume density in the triceps muscle decreased following a high intensity strength training program (MacDougall et al., 1979). Because mitochondria are the site of aerobic energy production, any decrease in the volume density of motochondria would decrease the oxidative capacity of the muscle. This offers an explanation of a compromised improvement in endurance capabilities when simultaneously training for strength and endurance. A cellular explanation, however, of how concurrent training for strength and endurance diminishes strength gains is as yet unknown.

Many distance runners do not perform resistance training fearing it will compromise their endurance capabilities. A decrease in mitochondrial density due to resistance training would appear to support this belief. Many distance runners have overreacted to the information concerning mitochondrial density by eliminating resistance exercise from their training regimens. They fail to recognize, however, that resistance training offers other benefits such as injury prevention. Thus, resistance training programs which use moderate intensities (12-15 RM) and emphasize injury prevention may be more appropriate for distance runners and not affect endurance performance. Common sense dictates that distance runners not perform heavy squats as a regular part of their training; it is not part of the needs analysis of this sport. At present, the majority of limited data indicates that resistance training does not compromise development of aerobic power (Dudley & Djamil, 1985; Hickson, 1980).

It is possible that, in a sport that depends almost exclusively on one of the three energy sources, training of a second energy source may retard the development of the primary energy source. For example, distance runners depend heavily on the oxygen energy source and training of the adenosine triphosphate phosphocreatine energy source utilizing resistance training may compromise the development of the oxygen energy source over long training periods (years). For the same reason weight lifters may not wish to heavily train the oxygen energy source. Whether this is due to overtraining resulting from the high volume and intensity necessary to train simultaneously for endurance and strength, or to some underlying physiological mechanism is still unknown. It should be pointed out that many sports are not dependent on only one energy source (Fox & Mathews, 1981). The needs analysis of these individuals will dictate a demand for training of multiple energy sources. In this case, the compatibility question may be a moot point and research should center on what mixture of strength and endurance training will cause the greatest possible gains in both parameters, when simultaneous training must be performed.

Flexibility and Resistance Training

Photo courtesy of Boston College Sports Information.

Flexibility is an important component of physical fitness and needs to be addressed in the context of a resistance training program. Stretching can be performed in both warm-up and cool-down phases of a training session. There are four basic types of stretching techniques (Moore & Hutton, 1980).

1. Static stretching
2. Dynamic or ballistic stretching
3. Slow movements
4. Proprioceptive neuromuscular facilitation (PNF) techniques

Deciding which technique to employ in a program depends on the amount of time available for stretching, the effectiveness of the flexibility technique, and the availability of a training partner (Anderson et al., 1984).

Static Stretch

The most common type of stretching technique used over the past 10 years has been the static stretching technique. Use of this form of stretching involves a voluntary passive relaxation of the muscle while it is being elongated. This technique has become popular because it is easy to learn, effective, and accompanied by minimal incidence of soreness or injury (Moore & Hutton, 1980).

Static stretching is still one of the most effective and desirable techniques to use when comfort and limited training time are major factors in the implementation of a stretching program (Moore & Hutton, 1980). This technique involves holding the muscle in a static position at the greatest muscle length possible. Many variations of this technique have been proposed with stretch time ranging up to 60 seconds. Typically a muscle is stretched four to six seconds and repeated two to three times. An example of this technique would be the toe touch. In the exercise one bends over and tries to touch their toes while keeping the knees straight. The movement is held where minimal discomfort is experienced and repeated two to three times. It is important that stretching be performed progressively. Each time the individual tries to reach further to extend the range of movement and holds the stretch at that point in the range of movement where only minimal discomfort is experienced. Subsequent stretching continues to improve the range of motion.

Ballistic Stretching

Ballistic stretching involves a bouncing or bobbing movement during the stretch; the final position in the movement is not held. Ballistic stretching acquired unpopularity due to the increased amount of delayed muscle soreness and the possibility of injury during the stretching exercise (DeVries, 1980). This type of exercise might be more appropriate to use as part of a dynamic warm-up after a static-type of stretch has been performed. The exact value of using ballistic stretching techniques prior to activity remains unclear and caution must be taken to eliminate delayed muscle soreness and the possibility of injury.

Slow Movements

Slow movements of a muscle(s) such as neck rotations, arm rotations, and trunk rotations are also used as a type of stretching activity. The value of using this type of stretching technique may be more important to warm-up activities than to achieving increases in flexibility. Compared to ballistic stretching it might provide a better dynamic technique to be used in warm-up activites.

Proprioceptive Neuromuscular Facilitation (PNF) Techniques

PNF stretching techniques have increased in popularity over the last 10 years as a method of improving flexibility (Cornelius, 1985; Shellock & Prentice, 1985). A number of different procedures have been proposed including contract-relax and contract-relax/agonist contraction (Moore & Hutton, 1980). The theoretical basis of these techniques is that the voluntary contraction of the agonist muscle will provide neural activation resulting in reciprocal inhibition of the antagonist muscle thus allowing greater range of motion. There are three different types of PNF stretching techniques (Shellock & Prentice, 1985).

1. Slow-reversal-hold
2. Contract-relax
3. Hold-relax

Using the hamstring stretch as an example, Shellock and Prentice (1985) describe the slow-reversal-hold technique as follows:

"With the individual lying on his/her back, with the knee extended and the ankle flexed to 90°, a partner passively flexes the leg at the hip joint to the point where slight discomfort is felt in the muscle. At this point, the individual pushes against the partner's resistance by contracting the hamstring muscle. After pushing for ten seconds, the hamstring muscles are relaxed and the agonist quadriceps muscle is contracted while the partner applies passive pressure to further stretch the antagonist quadriceps. This should move the leg so that there is increased hip joint flexion. The relaxation phase lasts for 10 seconds, at which time the individual again pushes against the partner's resistance beginning at this new joint angle. This push-relax sequence is typically repeated at least three times. (p. 273)

The other two PNF techniques commonly used are similar to the slow-reversal-hold method. The contract-relax technique involves a dynamic concentric contraction prior to the relaxation/stretch phase. In the above example the hamstrings are contracted so the leg moves toward the floor. The hold-relax technique uses an isometric contraction prior to the relaxation/stretch phase.

The different PNF techniques have been studied by Moore and Hutton (1980). PNF has not proved to be superior to static stretching. Each technique is capable of improving flexibility. Except for the hold-relax technique, the other PNF methods require a partner. Furthermore, there is a period of time required for individuals both to teach and to learn such techniques. Moore and Hutton suggested that, unless an individual is willing to tolerate the greater discomfort associated with PNF training, the use of static stretching is more appropriate. Individuals must be well motivated and have the time to perform PNF stretching.

Resistance Training and Flexibility

There is a great deal of individual variation regarding joint looseness. Joint looseness has been observed to be a function of the particular joint and individual characteristics (Marshall et al., 1980). Thus, one should not expect all joints of individuals to possess the same amount of flexibility. A properly developed and consistently performed program of stretching will allow relative flexibility gains to be made.

The concept of being muscle-bound is often associated with resistance training. Some individuals and coaches believe that resistance training results in a decrease in flexibility. Little scientific or empirical evidence supports this contention (Tood, 1985). As early as 1956 Massey and Chaudet demonstrated that heavy resistance training does not cause a decrease in flexibility.

Typically, heavy resistance training results in either an improvement or no change in flexibility (Massey & Chaudet, 1956). Competitive weight lifters possess average or above-average flexibility in most joints (Leighton, 1955, 1957b). Olympic weight lifters in a descriptive study of several groups of athletes were observed to be second only to gymnasts in a composite flexibility score (Jensen & Fisher, 1979). It appears that resistance training does not have to result in a loss of flexibility. Care should be taken, however, to stress the full range of motion of both the agonist and antagonist muscle groups, and to choose exercises which exercise the agonists and antagonists of each joint to insure an adequate strength balance between both sides of the joint. Following these guidelines, one can eliminate any loss in flexibility.

Anaerobic Sprint and Interval Training

Photo courtesy of Boston College Sports Information.

Anaerobic training describes many activities from resistance training to sprint running. Many sports have a large anaerobic component involved with their performance. Athletic performance also usually entails a large motor skill component. An individual, therefore, has to address both the skill component and the conditioning component in order to be successful. We discuss training adaptations associated with resistance exercise in chapter 7. In this chapter we address other anaerobic training guidelines.

In addition to resistance training other anaerobic training which is more sport specific may be necessary. Some examples are sprinting for football and sprint swimming for waterpolo. This type of training enhances the motor skill component needed for performance in a particular sport. Thus, in order to improve sport performance, sport-specific movement needs to be performed in addition to resistance training. Anaerobic training adaptations are similar to those observed for resistance training (Howald, 1982); they are discussed in chapter 7.

Sprinting and Interval Training

In order to sprint well a skill component is necessary. Coaches must teach the skills involved with running, swimming, skiing, and cycling. Once the skill of the activity is taught, it is improved with mass practice and conditioning (Wilt, 1968).

Conditioning is the second component necessary to enhance speed or anaerobic endurance. Sprint activites of a few seconds require a higher power output than longer duration sprints of one to two minutes (Brooks & Fahey, 1984). Training needs to be related to both the distance and the duration of the activity used in the particular sport. For a football lineman, 5- to 20-yard sprints (one to three seconds) are appropriate, whereas a receiver may want to train using sprint distance ranging from 10 to 60 yards. An 800-m sprinter would need to train at distances and paces equivalent to the distance and pace needed in a race (Wilt, 1968). This last program involves more interval-type training, which also emphasizes the aerobic component of the sport activity.

Sprint Workouts

Sprint workouts should be performed one to five days per week depending upon the sport (i.e., soccer vs. track sprinting) and the training cycle. A sprint workout includes

1. flexibility exercise,
2. form running drills,
3. start drills, and
4. a conditioning phase.

Shorter sprint training involves more all-out exercise intensity. As the duration of the activity increases to longer sprint distances (e.g., 800 m), pace becomes important and can be learned through interval training. Interval training can also be designed to address the aerobic metabolic needs necessary to perform longer sprints (e.g., 800 m) (Fox & Mathews, 1974). Figure 5.6 demonstrates interval and power unit workouts. The power unit workout is a symmetrical form of interval train-

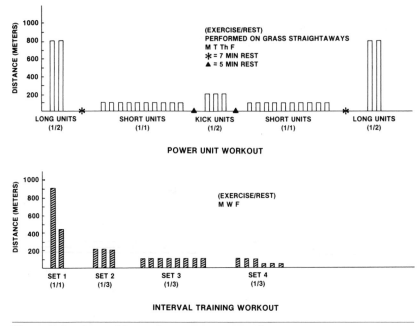

Figure 5.6   Anaerobic workouts are presented.

ing. It consists of long units (distances longer than the race itself), short units (40 to 60 m) and kick units (approximate distances used for a kick in a race). Track coaches use the power unit workout to promote the development of race speed. The long units develop endurance at the race distance and the short units help to develop leg speed. This program is typically performed during the pre-season as well as in season on grass straight-aways. One must make sure that an adequate endurance conditioning base is attained before initiating such high-intensity workouts.

The importance of tolerating the high lactate levels associated with different sport activities (e.g., longer duration sprinting and wrestling) necessitates training which increases lactate production and in turn enhances lactate removal pathways (Brooks & Fahey, 1984). Exercise intervals shorter than 20 seconds do not result in anaerobic energy source depletion when used with a recovery interval of a similar duration (Lamb, 1978). This allows repeating of short sprints at a near maximal velocity. This means that recovery time between sprint distances must be carefully controlled (see Table 5.2). For example, a sprint workout for basketball might include a five-second duration of exercise. From Table 5.2 it is clear that each sprint has to be run at 100% intensity and that only a five-second recovery period between sprints is allowed.

Table 5.2   General Guidelines for Interval Training

Exercise duration (min:s)	Intensity %	Recovery (min:s)	Number of intervals	Sessions per week
0:05	100	0:05	20-30	2-4
0:10	100	0:10	20-30	2-4
0:20	100	0:15	10-20	2-4
0:30	100	1:00-2:00	8-18	2-4
1:00	95-100	3:00-5:00	5-15	2-4
2:00	90-100	5:00-15:00	4-10	2-4
3:00	80-90	5:00-15:00	3-8	2-4

Note. From *Physiology of Exercise: Responses and Adaptations* (p. 167) by D.R. Lamb, 1978, New York: Macmillan. Copyright 1978 by Macmillan. Adapted by permission.

Twenty to 30 intervals are required two to four times per week. This table can be used as a general guideline when developing an interval workout for different sports. Many combinations of exercise-recovery ratios are possible to use in interval training. Rest and exercise intensity should be manipulated in response to the individual's fitness level, periodization of training, and bioenergetic sport needs (Fox & Mathews, 1981). Both common sense and good judgment, which is based on a solid understanding of basic training principles, must be used when designing each training session. It is important to understand the needs of the individual, being sensitive to exercise tolerance in both the acute and the chronic time frames.

Integrating the Fitness Components

Muscular strength, flexibility, cardiovascular endurance, and local muscular endurance all play varying roles in health fitness and sports performance. Training for sports performance is considerably different from training for health and fitness. Also, better sports performance is not always associated with better health as one grows older (Sheehan, 1985). This might be especially true as performances progress toward an elite level and risk of injury is high due to the training volume and intensity.

Developing an overall conditioning program that addresses each fitness component is necessary for balance. The needs analysis (chapter 3) facilitates the determination of the extent of time and effort spent on a specific fitness component. Although certain data suggest that some incompatibility exists between different fitness components, proper modification of the exercise program makes it possible to address each component. The shot-put champion may not spend a great deal of time performing cardiovascular endurance exercises, but that person may train three days a week for 20-30 min of cardiovascular conditioning to assist anaerobic recovery and/or maintain remedial aerobic fitness levels. Conversely, the champion cross-country runner may not perform a lot of resistance training but may work out in the weight room twice a week for 20-30 minutes to perform resistance exercise (12-15 RM) for the ankles, quadriceps, hamstrings, shoulder, and back. These exercises help to prevent injury and improve postural muscle strength.

The art and science of successful exercise prescription involves understanding all of the following:

- The goals and objectives of training (needs analysis)
- The fitness levels of the individual (exercise testing)
- The variables involved with prescription and stimulus/effect relationships of the exercise stimuli
- The training adaptations associated with different exercise stimuli
- The psychological ability to perform the exercise (interaction and training observations)

Proper exercise prescription can result in the successful design of exercise programs which address the specific component(s) of physical fitness needed by the individual for health, fitness, and performance.

The program emphasis will shift according to the specific needs of the individual. It is important to understand, however, that no one form of training (e.g., resistance training) can produce all the required training effects for every sport or individual. By understanding basic muscle physiology (chapter 6) and training adaptation (chapter 7) one can begin to appreciate the specificity of the exercise stimulus and the functional changes occurring with training. By knowing how to prescribe exercise for the various conditioning needs, one can succeed in designing exercise programs for a total conditioning program.

Chapter 6

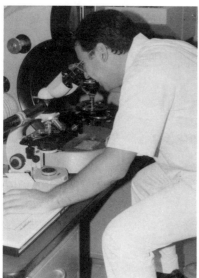

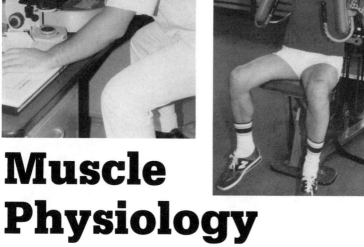

Muscle
Physiology

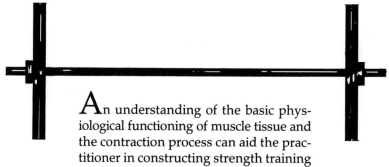

An understanding of the basic physiological functioning of muscle tissue and the contraction process can aid the practitioner in constructing strength training programs that are based on fact rather than myth or hearsay. For example, knowledge of the order of recruitment of muscle fiber types gives the practitioner insight into which fiber types may be recruited and therefore trained during a particular type of strength training program. Information concerning the three major sources of energy for muscular contraction assist the coach or athlete in determining which energy source is used in the performance of a particular sport. With this information it is possible to construct a strength training program to best develop that energy source. In short, basic physiological knowledge allows the construction of scientifically sound strength training programs.

Neuromuscular Considerations

To completely understand how a muscle functions it is necessary to understand not only the muscle itself but also its innervation. A muscle and its nerves are collectively considered by the term neuromuscular.

Nerve Cell Anatomy

Figure 6.1 is a schematic of a typical alpha (α) motor nerve cell (neuron). Typically a motor neuron consists of a cell body (soma), numerous short projections (dendrites) that carry impulses towards the soma, and a long projection (axon) that carries impulses away from the soma toward the skeletal muscle. The terminal ending of a motor neuron's axon on

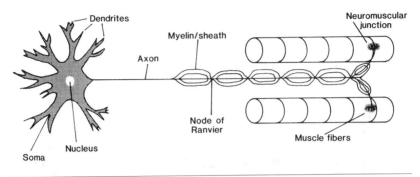

Figure 6.1   A motor neuron and the muscle fibers it innervates are called a motor unit.

skeletal muscle is termed the motor end plate or neuromuscular junction.

Human as well as many mammalian axons are covered with a white substance high in lipid (fat) content called the myelin sheath. Nerve fibers possessing a myelin sheath are referred to as medullated. Fibers devoid of the myelin sheath are called nonmedullated fibers. Schwann cells surround the axon and are responsible for the presence of the myelin sheath. The myelin sheath serves several functions. A nerve is composed of many nerve fibers. One function of the myelin sheath is to insulate the impulse in one axon from the impulses in other axons and dendrites traveling in the same nerve. This prevents impulses meant for one muscle from inadvertently reaching a different muscle. The myelin sheath does not run continuously along the length of the fiber but is laid down in segments with small spaces between segments. These small spaces are known as the nodes of Ranvier (see Figure 6.1).

Nervous Impulse Transmission

A nervous impulse is transmitted in the form of electrical energy. When no impulse is being transmitted by a neuron the inside of the neuron has a net negative electrical charge, as compared to the outside of the neuron which has a net positive charge. This arrangement of electrical charges is termed the resting membrane potential. It is attributed to the distribution of molecules with electrical charges or ions and the impermeability of the cell membrane at rest to these ions. Basically, sodium ions with plus charges (Na^+) are predominantly located outside the neuron. Potassium ions also with plus charges (K^+) are predominantly located inside the neuron. There are, however, relatively more Na^+ ouside than K^+ inside the neuron giving the inside a less positive or net negative charge as compared to the outside of the neuron.

When an impulse is being transmitted down an axon or dendrite the cell membrane of the neuron becomes very permeable to both Na⁺ and K⁺. Ions tend to move from areas where they are highly concentrated to areas where they are less concentrated. So Na⁺ moves into the neuron and K⁺ moves out of the neuron giving the inside a plus charge compared to the outside of the neuron. This reversal of electrical charges is called an action potential. This reversal of electrical charges, however, lasts only a very brief (milliseconds) time period. The membrane quickly becomes impermeable to the ions again. An active pumping system removes Na⁺ from the inside of the neuron and brings K⁺ back into the neuron. This quickly restores the neuron to its original state of a net negative charge on the inside. This process is repeated each time a nervous impulse or action potential is conducted by a neuron.

In a nonmedullated axon the action potential must travel the entire length of the axon. In myelinated axons the nodes of Ranvier make possible a fast type of impulse conduction called saltatory conduction. As depicted in Figure 6.2 the nodes of Ranvier allow the action potential to jump from one node of Ranvier to the next. This is possible because the nodes of Ranvier are low resistance areas to ionic current on the axon. In a large myelinated axon where saltatory conduction can take place the velocity of impulse conduction is 60-100 m per second. Whereas the velocity of impulse conduction in a large nonmedullated axon is only six-ten meters per second.

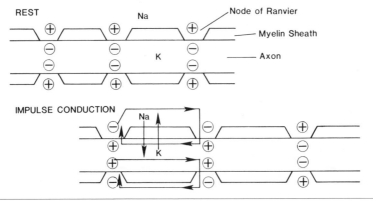

Figure 6.2 At rest K⁺⁺ is concentrated inside the axon and Na⁺⁺ outside the axon, giving the interior of the axon a net negative charge as compared to the exterior. During impulse conduction, movement of K and Na result in the interior of the axon's having a net positive charge compared to the exterior.

Diameter of Neurons

The diameter of a neuron determines in large part the velocity at which an impulse will travel. The greater the diameter of the neuron the faster the velocity of the impulse; this is true for both medullated and non-medullated fibers. Medullated fibers due to saltatory conduction have a faster conductance velocity than nonmedullated fibers of the same diameter. Large medullated fibers, such as those that innervate skeletal muscle, have a conduction velocity approximately 10 times that of a nonmedullated fiber of the same diameter. In addition, it takes less of a stimulus to initiate an impulse in a small diameter axon versus a large diameter axon. In general fast-twitch muscle fibers are innervated by larger diameter axons than slow-twitch muscle fibers. In general, slow-twitch muscle fibers due to the smaller size of their axon will be stimulated to contract prior to fast-twitch muscle fibers. This is discussed in more detail in "Order of Fiber Type Recruitment."

Sensory and Motor Neurons

Sensory neurons convey impulses from receptor sites to the central nervous systems (brain and the spinal cord). Examples of sensory neurons are those excited by sound, pain, and light. Motor neurons are those that when stimulated cause muscular contraction.

Motor neuron's cell bodies are located in the spinal cord. Sensory neuron's cell bodies are located outside the spinal cord in the dorsal root ganglion. A motor neuron has relatively short dendrites and a long axon that carries impulses from the central nervous system to the neuromuscular junction. A sensory neuron has a relatively short axon and long dendrites that carry impulses from the periphery to the central nervous system.

The alpha motor neuron is a relatively large myelinated neuron (9-20 μm in diameter) and therefore has a very fast conduction velocity of 100 to 120 m per second. Sensory neurons vary a great deal in diameter (.5 to 20 μm) and can be myelinated or unmyelinated. Therefore, the conduction velocity of sensory neurons can vary from very slow (.5 m/second) to among the fastest conduction velocities (120 meters/second).

Neuromuscular Junction

The connection or junction where two cells that are capable of conducting an ionic current meet is called a synapse (see Figure 6.3). The synapse formed by an axon from a motor neuron and a muscle fiber is called the motor end plate or neuromuscular junction. When an ionic

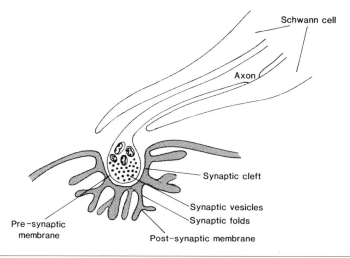

Figure 6.3 The neuromuscular junction in cross section.

impulse reaches the neuron portion or pre-synaptic side of the neuromuscular junction it causes the release of a neurotransmitter. Acetylcholine (ACh) is the neurotransmitter at a neuromuscular junction and is stored within synaptic vesicles in the end of the axon. The ACh diffuses from the pre-synaptic membrane through the synaptic cleft or space between the pre- and post-synaptic membranes to the post-synaptic membrane.

On the post-synaptic side of the neuromuscular junction the ACh is attached or bound to a receptor on the post-synaptic membrane. The ACh causes the permeability to sodium and potassium ions of the membrane around the muscle fiber to increase. If enough ACh is bound to the post-synaptic membrane the permeability of the membrane will increase enough to start a conducted ionic current similar to that found within a neuron. This post-synaptic ionic current will initiate the contraction process of the muscle fiber. The muscle fiber will continue to contract as long as a sufficient amount of ACh is bound by the post-synaptic membrane.

The ACh will eventually be destroyed by the enzyme acetylcholinesterase found within the synaptic cleft, thus terminating the stimulus for contraction of the muscle fiber. Portions of the destroyed ACh are actively taken up by the pre-synaptic membrane and utilized in the production of more ACh that is once again stored in synaptic vesicles.

Why is a neurotransmitter needed at the neuromuscular junction? Why can't the ionic current of the neuron simply be conducted to the membrane surrounding a muscle fiber and thus initiate contraction?

The neuron is very small in size compared to a muscle fiber. Therefore, the size of the ionic current conducted by the neuron is of insufficient strength to be directly transferred to the muscle fiber's membrane and stimulate the fiber to contract. The ACh is necessary to cause an ionic current of sufficient strength to be conducted by the muscle fiber's membrane and initiate contraction of the muscle fiber.

Motor Unit

A motor unit consists of an alpha (α) motor neuron and all the muscle fibers (cells) it innervates. Motor units (Figure 6.1) are the functional units of muscular activity under neural control. Each muscle fiber is innervated by at least one α motor neuron. The smaller the number of muscle fibers in a motor unit the smaller the amount of force the motor unit will produce when stimulated to contract. The number of muscle fibers within a motor unit depends upon the amount of fine control necessary for a muscle to perform its function. The motor units of the muscles of the eye, for example, contain only ten muscle fibers whereas motor units of a muscle such as the gastrocnemius contain as many as 1000 muscle fibers. Normally the muscle fibers of a particular motor unit are all of the same type (i.e., fast- and/or slow-twitch fibers).

All-or-None Law

The fact that either all of the muscle fibers within a motor unit contract or none of them contract is referred to as the all-or-none law. While this law holds true for individual motor units, whole muscles such as the biceps are not governed by the all-or-none law. If whole muscles followed the all-or-none law, this would mean that either the entire biceps contracts or none of the biceps contracts. In the latter case there would be very little control of the amount of force the muscle generates and therefore little control of body movement.

Gradations of Strength

The fact that motor units follow the all-or-none law makes possible one method in which variations in the force a muscle produces can be achieved. The more motor units within a muscle that are stimulated to contract, the greater the amount of force that is developed. In other words, if one motor unit contracts a very small amount of force is developed. If several motor units contract more force is developed; if all the motor units in a muscle contract maximal force is developed.

This method of varying the force produced by a muscle is called multiple motor unit summation.

Graduations of force can also be achieved by controlling the force produced by one motor unit: This is called wave summation. A motor unit responds to a single impulse conducted by an axon by producing a twitch. A twitch (Figure 6.4) is a brief period of contraction producing tension, which is followed by relaxation of the motor unit. When

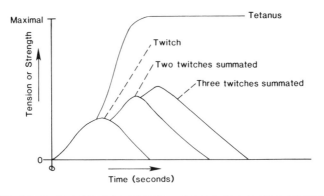

Figure 6.4 Gradations in strength caused by wave summation.

two impulses conducted by an axon proximately reach the neuromuscular junction the motor unit responds with two twitches. The second twitch, however, occurs prior to complete relaxation from the first twitch: The second twitch summates with the force of the first twitch producing more total tension. This wave (twitch) summation can continue until the impulses occur at a high enough frequency that the twitches are completely summated. This complete summation is called tetanus and is the maximal force a motor unit can develop.

Sliding Filament Theory

The major function of skeletal muscle is to shorten and thus develop tension to move the joints of the body. The Huxley sliding filament theory is an explanation of how muscle fibers shorten and so develop tension. To understand the sliding filament theory of muscular contraction, it is first necessary to know the structural arrangement of skeletal muscle. Skeletal muscles are called striated muscle because the arrangement of protein molecules in the muscle give it a striped or striated appearance under a microscope. A sarcomere is the smallest functional unit that can undergo contraction. Muscle fibers are composed of sarcomeres stacked one on top of the other. At rest there are several distinct light and dark areas creating striations within each sarcomere. These light and dark areas are due to the arrangement of the actin and myosin filaments, the major proteins involved in the contractile process. In the contracted state there are still striations of the muscle tissue, but they have a different pattern. This change in the pattern of the striations occurs due to the sliding of the myosin and actin protein filaments one over another (see Figure 6.5).

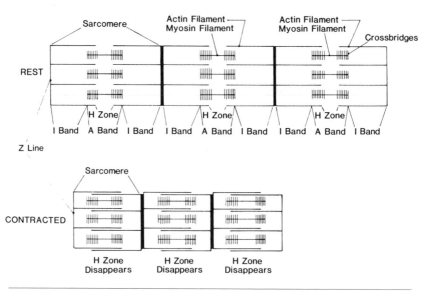

Figure 6.5 Sarcomeres demonstrating the sliding filament theory. As the actin and myosin filaments slide over each other the entire sarcomere shortens, but the length of the individual filaments does not change.

A sarcomere runs from one Z-line to the next Z-line and is the smallest functional unit that undergoes contraction. At rest there are two distinct light areas in each sarcomere: the H zone, which contains no actin and only a small amount of myosin; and the I bands located at the ends of the sarcomere which contain only actin filaments. These two areas appear light in comparison to the A band, which contains actin and myosin filaments.

As the sarcomere shortens during contraction, the actin filaments slide over the myosin filaments. This causes the H zone to seem to disappear as actin filaments slide into it and give it a dark appearance. The I bands become shorter as the Z-lines come closer to the ends of the myosin filaments. When the sarcomere relaxes and returns to its original length, the H zone and I bands return to their original size and appearance.

Phases of Contraction

Since Huxley originally proposed the sliding filament theory a great deal more has been discovered about how the sliding takes place. At rest the projections or crossbridges of the myosin filaments are not in contact with the actin filament. The actin filament has active sites upon which the crossbridges make contact with the actin. At rest, however, the active sites are covered by troponin and tropomyosin, two other proteins that compose part of the actin filament (see Figure 6.6).

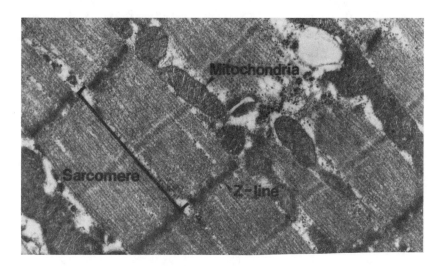

Figure 6.6 A human muscle micrograph demonstrating the striated appearance of skeletal muscle and some of the structures present in muscle (courtesy of D. Billings).

When ACh causes an ionic current within the membrane surrounding the muscle fiber it triggers the release of calcium ions (CA^{++}) from the sarcoplasmic reticulum. The sarcoplasmic reticulum is a membranous structure that surrounds each muscle fiber. The released CA^{++} is bound to the troponin molecule and triggers a change in the troponin and tropomyosin that exposes the active sites on the actin (Cohen, 1975). The crossbridges now can make contact with the active sites and do so. This is called the *excitation-coupling* phase of the contraction process.

Contraction or shortening of the sarcomere can now take place. The attachment of the crossbridge to the active site activates an enzyme (myosin ATPase) that breaks down an ATP molecule located on the crossbridge and in so doing releases energy. ATP (adenosine triphosphate) is an energy source for many cellular activities including muscle contraction. The released energy is used to cause the crossbridge to swivel to a new angle (Huxley, 1969) or to collapse (Davies, 1966). The result of either of these two actions is to pull the actin over the myosin causing the sarcomere to shorten.

For more shortening to occur the crossbridge must break with the active site with which it is in contact and bind to another active site on the actin filament closer to the Z-line. This is accomplished by reloading the crossbridge with an ATP molecule. Once the crossbridge is reloaded it breaks the bond with the active site with which it is in contact and binds to a new active site closer to the Z-line. The process of breaking contact with one active site and binding to another is termed *recharging*. A new ATP molecule is broken down causing further shortening of the sarcomere; this process is repeated until either the sarcomere has shortened as much as possible or relaxation of the muscle takes place.

Relaxation of the muscle occurs when the impulse from the motor axon ends. This triggers the active pumping of the CA⁺⁺ back into

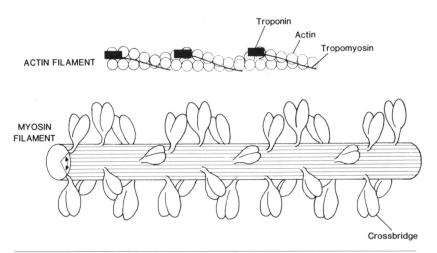

Figure 6.7 Schematic of a myosin and actin filament. The active sites are located on the actin underneath the troponin and tropomyosin molecules. From ''The Cooperation Action of Muscle Protein'' by J. Murray and A. Weber, 1974, *Scientific American,* **230,** p. 60. Copyright 1974 by Scientific American, Inc. Adapted by permission.

storage within the sarcoplasmic reticulum. The troponin and tropomyosin assume their original position covering the active sites. The crossbridges now have no place at which to contact the actin and pull it over the myosin, so the sarcomere returns to its original length.

Length Tension Curve

The length tension curve (see Figure 6.8) demonstrates that there is an optimal length at which the muscle fibers generate their maximal force. At the optimal length there is the potential for maximal crossbridge formation and thus maximal tension. Below this optimal length

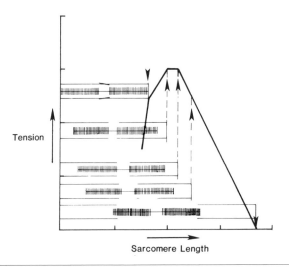

Sarcomere Length

Figure 6.8 There is an optimal length at which a sarcomere develops maximal tension. At lengths less than or greater than optimal, less tension is developed. Data from "The Variation in Isometric Tension With Sarcomere Length in Vertebrate Muscle Fibers" by A.M. Gordon, A.F. Huxley, and F.J. Jullian, 1966, *Journal of Physiology, 7*, pp. 170-192.

less tension is developed during contraction, because with excessive shortening there is an overlap of actin filaments such that the actin filaments interfere with each other's ability to contact the myosin crossbridges. Less crossbridge contact with actin results in a smaller potential to develop tension.

At lengths greater than optimal there is less and less overlap of the actin and myosin filaments: This results in less of a potential for crossbridge contact with the actin. The total amount of tension developed depends upon the total number of crossbridges in contact with the actin. Thus as the sarcomere is stretched past its optimal length less and less tension can be developed.

The length tension curve demonstrates that some prestretch of the muscle prior to initiation of a contraction will increase the amount of force generated. Too much prestretch will, however, actually decrease the total amount of tension developed.

Force Velocity Curve

As the velocity of contraction of a muscle increases the force that is developed decreases (Figure 6.9). This is empirically true: If you are asked to bench press the maximal amount of weight possible the weight will

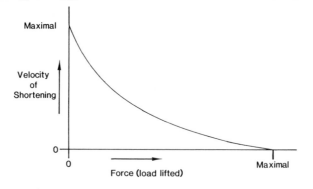

Figure 6.9 The force velocity curve demonstrates that the maximal velocity of shortening of a muscle fiber occurs when no load is being lifted and maximal force is generated at zero velocity of shortening.

move very slowly. If you bench press half your maximal amount of weight you can move the bar at a faster velocity. Maximal velocity of shortening occurs when no resistance (weight) is being moved or lifted. It is determined by the maximal rate at which crossbridges can be formed and broken between the actin and myosin filaments. The force velocity curve is important when examining various forms of weight training, such as isokinetic training where the velocity of the movement is controlled and not the resistance as is done in other types of training (e.g. isometric, variable resistance).

Bioenergenics

Bioenergenics concerns the sources of energy for muscular contraction. Such words as aerobic (energy production with oxygen) and anaerobic (energy production without oxygen) training have become popular among coaches and athletes. There are two major anaerobic sources of energy (ATP-PC and lactic acid) and one source of aerobic energy (Kreb's cycle and electron transport). Knowledge of these energy sources and their interactions with each other is necessary to successfully plan a resistance training program that will optimally condition an individual for a particular sport or activity.

ATP, the Energy Molecule

The final source of energy for muscular contraction is the adenosine triphosphate molecule or ATP. The chemical makeup of ATP is quite complex. The main functional components of ATP, however, are a sugar molecule called adenosine and three phosphate groups. When ATP is broken down to adenosine diphosphate (two phosphates) and a free phosphate molecule, energy is released. This energy is used to cause the myosin crossbridges to pull the actin filaments across the myosin filaments causing shortening of the muscle (see Figure 6.10).

$$ATP \rightleftharpoons ADP + P_i + energy$$
$$ATP = adenosine\ triphosphate$$
$$ADP = adenosine\ diphosphate$$
$$P_i = phosphate$$

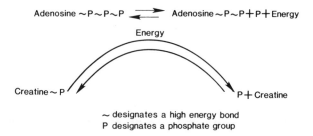

~ designates a high energy bond
P designates a phosphate group

Figure 6.10 When ATP breaks down to ADP the energy derived can be used to perform muscular contractions. The energy obtained from the breakdown of phosphocreatine is used to recombine ADP plus P into ATP.

Although ATP is the immediate source of energy for muscular contraction there are three sources of ATP in the cell. Two of these sources, the adenosine triphosphate-phosphocreatine source (ATP-PC) and the formation of lactic acid (LA), require no oxygen to provide ATP and are called anaerobic. The third source requires oxygen to provide ATP and is referred to as aerobic.

ATP-PC Energy Source

Stored within muscle and ready for immediate use to supply energy to the cell are two compounds. One of these compounds is ATP. The other compound, phosphocreatine (PC), is similar to ATP in that it also has a phosphate group and a high energy bond. In PC the phosphate group is bound to a creatine molecule.

When ATP is broken down, ADP, P_i, and energy result and this energy is used to cause muscular contractions. However, when PC is broken down to creatine, P_i, and energy, the resulting energy is used to recombine ADP and P_i back into ATP. The rebuilt ATP can then be broken down again to ADP, P_i and the energy released is used to perform more muscular contractions.

ATP and PC are stored within the muscle and oxygen is not required to release the energy stored within these two compounds. This is an anaerobic source of energy. There is, however, only a limited amount of ATP and PC stored within the muscle; this limits the amount of energy that the ATP-PC source can produce. In fact, in an all-out workbout the energy available from the ATP-PC source will be exhausted in 30 seconds or less (Goldspink, Larson, & Davies, 1970; Meyer & Terjung, 1979). One advantage of this energy source is that the energy is immediately available for use. A second advantage is that the ATP-PC source has a large power capacity; this source is capable of giving the muscle a large amount of energy per unit of time.

Because of the characteristics of the ATP-PC energy source, it is the primary source of energy for short-duration high-power events. It supplies the major portion of energy to the muscles for such activites as a maximal lift, the shot put, the high jump, and the 40-yard dash. One of the reasons for continued heavy breathing after the completion of an intense short-duration work bout is that the muscular stores of ATP and PC must be restored if the ATP-PC energy source is to be used again at a later time. This is discussed in greater detail in "Repayment of the Anaerobic Energy Sources."

Lactic Acid Energy Source

The needles-and-pins feeling in the fingers and toes after a long, hard set is in part due to the buildup of a waste product from this energy system. The waste product is lactic acid, the compound from which this energy source takes its name.

Stored within the muscle is a carbohydrate called glycogen. Glycogen is composed of a long string of a sugar molecule called glucose. The energy necessary to make ATP is derived by splitting glucose molecules in half yielding a compound called pyruvate and releasing energy. The energy released from splitting each glucose molecule produces a net gain of two ATP. The pyruvate is then transformed into lactic acid. No oxygen is required in order for this process to take place, so this energy system is anaerobic. The entire process of splitting glucose in half and yielding ATP and lactic acid is called anaerobic glycolysis.

The buildup of lactic acid in the blood and muscle has several side effects. One of these effects occurs when the concentration of lactic acid is high enough to affect nerve endings, causing pain. Also, as the concentration of lactic acid increases, the interior of the muscle cells becomes more acidic. This can interfere with the chemical processes of the cell, including the processes of producing more ATP (Trivedi & Danforth, 1966), and the binding of Ca^+ to troponin (Nakumura & Schwartz, 1972). The amount of energy that can be obtained from the lactic acid system is therefore limited due to the side effects of the buildup of lactic acid.

Despite the side effects of lactic acid this energy source can produce a larger amount of energy than the ATP-PC source. The lactic acid energy source, however, cannot supply the muscle with as much energy per unit of time as the ATP-PC source and therefore is not as powerful as the ATP-PC source.

The lactic acid energy source is a major supplier of ATP in all-out work bouts lasting from appoximately 1 to 3 min. Such exercise bouts include long sets to failure, sets with short rest periods between them, and the 400-m run. Heavy breathing continues after completion of these types of work bouts. This is in part due to the need to remove the accumulated lactic acid from the body. This process is discussed in "Repayment of the Anaerobic Energy Sources."

Oxygen Energy Source

The oxygen energy source has, over the last several years, received a lot of attention. The major goal of jogging, swimming, and aerobic dancing is to improve cardiovascular fitness, which is analogous to improving the oxygen energy source. This energy source utilizes oxygen in the production of ATP and is therefore an aerobic energy source.

The oxygen system metabolizes carbohydrates (sugar) and fats. Significant amounts of protein are normally not metabolized, but during long-term starvation and long intense exercise bouts significant amounts of protein can be metabolized (Dohm, Williams, Kasperek, & Van, 1982; Lemon & Mullin, 1980). Normally, the body at rest derives one-third of the needed ATP from metabolizing carbohydrates and two-thirds from fats. During physical work there is a gradual change to metabolizing more and more carbohydrates and less and less fats as the intensity of the work is increased. During maximal physical work the muscle is metabolizing nearly 100% carbohydrates if sufficient carbohydrates are available.

Aerobic metabolism of the carbohydrate glycogen begins in the same manner as it does in anaerobic glycolysis. Here, however, due to the presence of sufficient oxygen, the pyruvate is not converted into lactic acid, but enters into two long series of chemical reactions called Kreb's cycle and electron transport. These series of reactions eventually produce carbon dioxide, which is expired through the lungs, and water. The water is produced by combining hydrogen molecules with the oxygen that was originally taken into the body through the lungs. Up to 39 ATP can be produced by aerobically metabolizing one glycogen molecule. The aerobic metabolism of fats does not start with glycolysis. Fats go through a series of reactions called beta oxidation and then enter directly into Kreb's cycle. The end products of fat metabolization are similarly water, carbon dioxide, and ATP.

The maximal amount of energy that can be produced via aerobic metabolism is dependent upon how much oxygen the body can obtain and utilize. Maximal aerobic power is the maximal amount of oxygen the body can obtain and utilize per unit of time ($\dot{V}O_2$max). It is usually expressed either in liters of oxygen per minute (L O_2/min), or milliliters of oxygen per kilogram (2.2 lb) of body weight per minute (ml O_2/Kg-min^{-1}). $\dot{V}O_2$max in L O_2/min does not take into account body weight. A heavy individual is expected to be able to use more oxygen per minute solely due to his or her body size. Expressing $\dot{V}O_2$max in ml O_2/Kg-min^{-1} places everyone on a scale relative to body weight. In this manner, comparisons can be made between individuals of different body weights.

In relation to the two anaerobic energy sources the oxygen energy source is the least powerful. The aerobic energy source cannot produce enough ATP per unit of time to allow the performance of maximal intensity work, such as a one-RM lift or a 40-yard sprint. On the other hand, the aerobic energy source, due to the abundance of glycogen and fats and the lack of production of toxic waste products, can supply virtually an unlimited amount of ATP over a long period of time. The oxygen energy source is, therefore, the energy source for long-duration, low-intensity activities. Such activities include extremely long sets of an exercise at a low intensity (load) and marathoning.

Repayment of the Anaerobic Energy Sources

Following an intense work bout the anaerobic energy sources must be replenished if they are to be utilized again at a later time. The anaerobic energy sources are replenished by the aerobic energy source. After cessation of an anaerobic activity heavy breathing continues for a period of time, even though physical activity is no longer taking place. The oxygen taken into the body, above what is normally used at rest, is used to replenish the two anaerobic energy sources. This extra oxygen taken into the body after cessation of physical activity is referred to as an oxygen debt.

Replenishing the ATP-PC Energy Source

Immediately after an intense exercise bout there is a several-minute period of very heavy rapid breathing. The oxygen taken into the body above normal resting oxygen consumption is used to aerobically produce ATP in excess of what is required during rest. Part of this excess ATP is immediately broken down to ADP and P_i; the energy released is utilized to combine P_i and creatine back into PC. Part of the excess ATP is simply stored as intramuscular ATP. This rebuilding of the ATP and PC stores is accomplished in several minutes (Hultman, Bergstrom, & McLennan, 1967; Karolsson, Bonde-Peterson, Hendriksson, & Knuttgen, 1975; Lemon & Mullin, 1980). This part of the oxygen debt is referred to as the alactacid portion.

The half-life of the alactacid portion of the oxygen debt is approximately 20 seconds (DiPrampero & Margaria, 1978; Meyer & Terjung, 1979). This means that within 20 seconds 50% of the depleted ATP and PC is replenished; in 40 seconds 75% is replenished; and in 60 seconds 87% is replenished. Thus, within approximately three to four minutes the majority of the depleted ATP and PC intramuscular stores are replenished.

If activity is performed during the alactacid portion of the oxygen debt the rebuilding of the ATP-PC system will take longer. This is because part of the ATP generated via the aerobic system has to be used to provide energy to perform the activity and is therefore not available to rebuild the PC stores or become part of the ATP stores. An understanding both of the alactacid portion of the oxygen debt and of the rebuilding of the ATP-PC energy source is important in the planning of a training program which involves short-duration, high-intensity work, such as heavy sets of an exercise. The ATP-PC energy source is the most powerful energy source and is therefore the major source of energy for maximal lifts and heavy sets. Several minutes of rest must be allowed between heavy sets and maximal lifts to replenish the ATP and PC intramuscular stores; otherwise, they will not be available for use in the next heavy set. If sufficient recovery time is not allowed between heavy sets and/or maximal lifts, the lift or set either will not be completed or will not be completed with the desired speed or form.

Replenishing the Lactic Acid Energy Source

The replenishment of the lactic acid energy source entails removing from the blood and muscle the lactic acid accumulated during activity. After several minutes of very rapid, heavy breathing following an intense exercise bout, a longer period of gradual return to normal breathing occurs. This more gradual return to normal breathing is called the lactacid portion of the oxygen debt. The excess oxygen, taken in above normal resting oxygen needs, is used to aerobically metabolize accumulated lactic acid.

Many tissues of the body can aerobically metabolize lactic acid, including skeletal muscle (Gasser & Brooks, 1979; Hermansen et al., 1976), cardiac muscle (Spitzer, 1974), kidney (Yudkin & Cohen, 1974), liver (Rowell et al., 1966), and the brain (Nemoto, Hoff, & Sereringhaus, 1974). Sixty percent of the accumulated lactic acid is aerobically metabolized (Gasser & Brooks, 1979). Portions of the remaining 40% are converted to glucose and protein, and a small portion is excreted in the urine and sweat (Ingjer, 1979). The half-life of the lactacid portion of the oxygen debt is approximately 25 minutes (Hermansen et al., 1976). Thus, approximately 95% of the accumulated lactic acid is removed in one hour and 15 minutes.

If light activity (walking, stretching) is performed after a workout the accumulated lactic acid is removed more quickly than if complete rest follows the workout (Hermansen et al., 1976). When light activity is performed following the activity, a portion of the accumulated lactic acid is aerobically metabolized to supply some of the needed ATP to perform the light activity. Because of this it is recommended that the rest period between sets in which lactic acid is accumulated consist of light activity rather than complete rest. The practice of performing light activity after an exercise bout in which lactic acid is built up is most likely to be of practical value only when the rest periods are at least several minutes in length.

Interaction of the Energy Sources

Although one energy source may be the predominant energy source for a particular activity (e.g., ATP-PC for a maximal lift, aerobic for running a marathon), all three sources supply a portion of the ATP needed by the body at all times. Thus the ATP-PC energy source is operating even when the body is at rest and the aerobic energy source is operating during a maximal lift.

All three energy sources supply some portion of the ATP necessary for any activity. At one end of the spectrum are activites such as a maximal lift, the shot put, and a 40-yard sprint. The ATP-PC energy source supplies the vast majority of energy for these activites. The lactic acid energy source supplies the majority of the necessary energy for activities such as sets of 20 to 25 repetitions and sprints of 440 yards. The aerobic energy source supplies the majority of the needed ATP for extremely long sets and five-mile runs.

The more intense and consequently the shorter the duration of the activity, the more ATP the anaerobic energy sources supply. Activities of longer duration and lower intensity derive the majority of the necessary energy from the lactic acid energy source; as the duration of the activity further increases it is derived from the aerobic energy source. There is no exact point at which one energy source ceases to provide the majority of the necessary ATP for an activity. Rather, there is a gradual transition from one energy source to another as the major supplier of ATP for an activity.

Muscle Fiber Types

Skeletal muscle is a heterogeneous mixture of several types of muscle fibers. The biochemical and physical characteristics of the different muscle fibers has lead to the development of several classificatory systems dividing the fibers into fast-twitch (white, Type II) and slow-twitch (red, Type I) fibers. Fast-twitch fibers (FT) are better adapted to perform anaerobic work, whereas slow-twitch fibers (ST) are better adapted to perform aerobic work.

Fast-Twitch Fibers

FT fibers are suited to the performance of high-intensity, short-duration work bouts as evidenced by their biochemical and physical characteristics. Such work bouts include a 40-yard sprint, a one-RM lift, and short sets (2-4 repetitions) of an exercise.

These type of fibers have a high activity of myofibrillar ATPase, the enzyme that breaks down ATP and releases the energy to cause fiber shortening. FT fibers are able to shorten with a high contraction speed and have a quick relaxation time. Possessing these characteristics allows these fibers to develop a large amount of force per cross-sectional area in a short period of time (see Table 6.1).

FT fibers rely predominantly upon anaerobic sources to supply the energy necessary for muscle contraction. This is evidenced by their high levels of ATP and PC intramuscular stores, as well as their high glycolytic enzyme activity. FT fibers have a low aerobic capability as evidenced by their low intramuscular stores of triglyceride, low capillary density, low mitochondrial density, and low aerobic enzyme activity. The fact that FT fibers rely predominantly on anaerobic sources of ATP and have low capabilities to supply ATP aerobically makes them highly susceptible to fatigue. They are consequently suited to perform work where a large amount of force is necessary and the activity is of short duration.

Several subtypes of FT fibers have been demonstrated. Type IIA fibers possess good aerobic and anaerobic characteristics, whereas Type IIB fibers possess good anaerobic characteristics but poor aerobic characteristics (Essen, Jansson, Henriksson, Taylor, & Saltin, 1975; Staron, Hikida, & Hagerman, 1983). Type IIC fibers are very rare in humans and fall between Types IIA and IIB fibers in several biochemical characteristics.

The subtypes of the Type II fibers represent a continuum in aerobic and anaerobic capabilities. The Type IIA, B, and C fibers may play a role in fiber type transformation among FT subtype fibers due to physi-

Table 6.1 Characteristics of Slow- and Fast-Twitch Muscle Fibers

Characteristic	Slow-Twitch Fiber	Fast-Twitch Fiber
Force per cross-sectional area	low	high
Myofibrillar ATPase activity (ph 9.4)	low	high
Intramuscular ATP stores	low	high
Intramuscular PC stores	low	high
Contraction speed	slow	fast
Relaxation time	slow	fast
Glycolytic enzyme activity	low	high
Endurance	high	low
Intramuscular glycogen stores	no difference	no difference
Intramuscular triglyceride stores	high	low
Myoglobin content	high	low
Aerobic enzyme activity	high	low
Capillary density	high	low
Mitochondrial density	high	low

cal training (Ingjer, 1979; Staron, Hikida, & Hagerman, 1983) and possibly between FT and ST fibers (Haggmark, Jansson, & Eriksson, 1982; Howald, 1982). For example, anaerobic training may cause Type IIA fibers to transform into Type IIB fibers.

Slow Twitch Fibers

ST fibers are suited to the performance of endurance (aerobic) activity. To a lesser extent than FT fibers, they possess characteristics needed for short-term, high-intensity work such as intramuscular ATP and PC stores, contraction speed, and glycolytic enzyme activity. ST fibers have these characteristics: high aerobic enzyme activity, capillary density, mitochondrial density, intramuscular triglyceride stores, and low fatigability. ST fibers are ideal for the performance of low-intensity, long-duration (endurance) activities. Such activities include long distance running and swimming, and long sets of an exercise (20 repetitions and up).

Order of Fiber Type Recruitment

The order in which motor units are recruited or activated to contract during an activity or specific movement is in most cases relatively constant (Desmedt & Godaux, 1977). Motor units in humans are homogeneous in their fiber type composition (i.e., either all ST or all FT). During an activity or contraction, therefore, the order in which ST and FT fibers are recruited is relatively constant and depends upon the motor units activated.

According to the size principle of motor neurons, the larger the motor neuron the more difficult it is to initiate a propagated action potential in that motor neuron. FT motor units have very large motor neurons in comparison to ST motor units. Consequently, FT motor units are the last motor units activated in a muscular contraction. For example, if a light weight is being lifted slowly, predominantly ST motor units are recruited to perform this movement. If the weight is increased, or if it is moved at a faster velocity, FT (Type IIA) motor units, in addition to the ST units, are recruited. In both of the above instances more total force is needed either to lift the heavier weight or to move the weight at a faster velocity. If the weight is increased again or moved at a still faster velocity, FT (Type IIA and Type IIB) motor units are recruited. Thus, the order of recruitment would be ST, and then FT (Type IIA and then Type IIB) motor units. The determining factor of whether to recruit FT motor units is the total amount of force necessary to perform the muscular contraction. If a large amount of force is necessary either to move a heavy weight slowly, or to move a light weight at a fast velocity, FT motor units are recruited.

This order of recruitment ensures that ST motor units are predominantly recruited to perform low-intensity, long-duration (endurance) activites. FT motor units are not recruited unless high-intensity (anaerobic) activity is performed. Notice that the order of recruitment holds the FT motor units in reserve, which are highly fatigable, until the ST motor units can no longer perform the particular muscular contraction.

Recruitment order is important from a practical standpoint for several reasons. First, in order to recruit the FT fibers and attain a training effect, the exercise must be of an intense nature. Secondly, the order of recruitment is fixed for a specific movement (Desmedt & Godaux, 1977). If the body position is changed, however, the order of recruitment can also change (Grimby & Hannerz, 1977). The order of recruitment can also change for multifunctional muscles from one movement to another (Grimby & Hannerz, 1977; Harr Romeny, Denier Van Der Gon, & Gielen, 1982). Recruitment order in the quadriceps is different for the performance of a leg extension from the performance of a squat. The variation in the recruitment order may be one of the factors responsible when strength gains are specific to the exercise even though the same muscle groups are involved. The variation in recruitment order provides some evidence to support the belief held by many strength coaches that in order to completely develop a particular muscle it must be exercised through several different movements.

Proprioceptors

Specialized sensory receptors located within muscles and tendons continually monitor their length and tension. The length and tension of the muscles of a joint determine the joint's position; in this manner joint position is monitored. These specialized receptors are called proprioceptors. The information these propriceptors gather is constantly relayed to conscious and subconscious portions of the brain. By this relay of information the brain is constantly informed of the progress of a movement or series of movements.

Muscle Spindles

The main functions of muscle spindles are to monitor stretch or length of the muscle in which they are embedded, and to initiate a contraction to reduce the stretch in the muscle. The knee-jerk or stretch reflex is attributed to the response of muscle spindles.

Spindles (see Figure 6.11) are parallel to the normal muscle fibers or extrafusal fibers. The modified muscle fibers containing spindles are called intrafusal fibers. These intrafusal fibers are composed of a stretch-sensitive central area or sensory area, and portions at ends of the sensory area which are capable of contraction. If a muscle is stretched, as in tapping the patellar tendon to initiate the knee-jerk reflex or adding an external weight, the spindles are also stretched. The sensory nerve of the spindle carries an impulse to the spinal cord; here the sensory neuron synapses with alpha motor neurons. The alpha motor neurons cause contraction of the stretched muscle and its agonists, or muscles that cause the same joint movement. In addition, other neurons inhibit contraction of antagonistic muscles, or muscles that cause the opposite joint motion to the stretched muscle. The stretched muscle shortens and the stretch on the spindle is relieved. Performing strength training exercises from a prestretched position takes advantage of this stretch reflex. This reflex is one explanation for a stronger contraction from the prestretched position.

Gamma motor neurons innervate the end portions of the intrafusal fibers capable of contraction. Stimulation of these end portions by the brain regulates the length and therefore the sensitivity of the spindles to changes in length of the extrafusal fibers. Adjustments of the spindles in this fashion enable the spindle to continuously monitor the length of the muscles in which they are embedded.

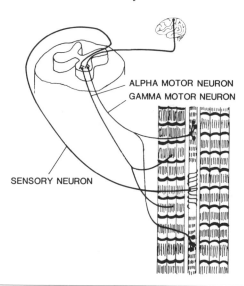

Figure 6.11 A muscle spindle and its neuronal connections.

Golgi Tendon Organs

Golgi tendon organs' main functions are to respond to tension within the tendon and, if it becomes excessive, to relieve the tension. These proprioceptors are located within the tendons of muscles and are consequently in a good location to monitor tension developed by a muscle.

The sensory neuron of a golgi tendon organ travels to the spinal cord. In the spinal cord it synapses with the alpha motor neurons both of the muscle whose tension it is monitoring and of the antagonistic muscles. As a muscle contracts and develops tension, the tension within the tendon of the muscle increases and is monitored by the tendon organs. If the tension becomes great enough that damage to the muscle or tendon is possible, inhibition of the contracting muscle occurs and contraction of the antagonists of the contracting muscle is initiated. The tension within the muscle is alleviated and damage to the muscle or tendon avoided.

This protective function is not foolproof. It may be possible through resistance training to learn to disinhibit the effects of the golgi tendon organs. The ability to disinhibit this protective function may in part be responsible for injuries that occur in maximal lifts by highly resistance trained athletes.

Basic physiological knowledge concerning how the muscular and nervous systems work together to control contraction aids in developing scientifically based resistance training programs. This knowledge is also important in understanding the adaptations due to the performance of resistance training as presented in the next chapter.

Selected Readings

Armstrong, R.B., Marum, P., Saubert, C.W., Seeherman, J.J., & Taylor, C.R. (1977). Muscle fiber activity as a function of speed and gait. *Journal of Applied Physiology: Respiratory, Environmental and Exercise Physiology*, **43**, 672-677.

Boyd, I.A. (1981). The muscle spindle controversy. *Scientific Progress* (Oxford), **47**, 205-221.

Donaldson, S.K.B., & Hermansen, L. (1986). Differential, direct effects of H^+ on CA^{++} activated force of skinned fibers from the soleus, cardiac and adductor magnus muscles of rabbits. *Pflugers Archives*, **376**, 55-65.

Edgerton, V.R., Roy, R.R., Gregor, R.J., Hager, C.L., & Wickiewicz, T. (1983). Muscle fiber activation and recruitment. In H.G. Knuttgen, J.A. Vogel, & S. Poortmans (Eds.), *Biochemistry of exercise* (pp. 31-49). Champaign, IL: Human Kinetics.

Garett, W.E., Mumma, M., & Lucaveche, C.L. (1985). Ultrastructural differences in human skeletal muscle fiber types. In G.G. Weiker (Ed.), *Clinics in sports medicine* (Vol. 4, pp. 189-201). Philadelphia: W.B. Saunders.

Gordon, A.M., Huxley, A.F., & Julian, F.J. (1966). The variation in isometric tension with sarcomere length in vertebrate muscle fibers. *Journal of Physiology* (London), **184**, 170-192.

Murray, J., & Weber, A. (1974). The cooperative action of muscle proteins. *Scientific American*, **230**, 58-71.

Sullivan, T.E., & Armstrong, R.B. (1978). Rat locomotory muscle fiber activity during trotting and galloping. *Journal of Applied Physiology: Respiratory, Environmental and Exercise Physiology*, **4**, 358-363.

Urbova, G. (1979). Influence of activity on some characteristic properties of slow and fast mammalian muscles. In R.J. Hutton & D.I. Miller (Eds.), *Exercise and sport science reviews* (pp. 181-212). Franklin Institute.

Chapter 7

Training Adaptations

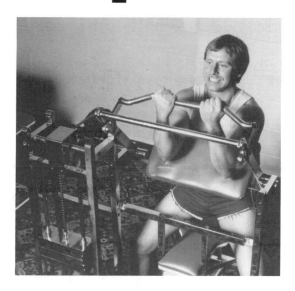

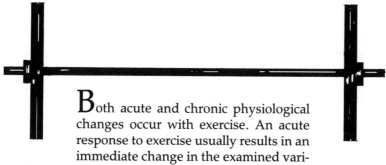

Both acute and chronic physiological changes occur with exercise. An acute response to exercise usually results in an immediate change in the examined variable. For example, when heart rate increases in response to an 80% of maximal oxygen consumption ($\dot{V}O_2$max) exercise intensity, this is called an acute response. Chronic change has to do with the body's response to an exercise stimulus over the course of the training period. The physiological process by which the body adapts to the exercise is called training adaptation (i.e., chronic response): For example, the heart rate response to an 80% $\dot{V}O_2$max exercise intensity decreases over time. Though the body responds acutely to a given exercise stress (by increasing heart rate) repeated exposure to the exercise stimulus by means of training in this case reduces the acute response (lower heart rate). It is important to be familiar with both the acute and the chronic changes which occur with exercise; this knowledge facilitates exercise prescription as well as program design.

Muscle Enlargement

Various athletic groups exhibit enlargement of muscles due to strength training. Sport scientists, athletes, and coaches all agree that a properly designed and implemented strength training program leads to muscle growth. There are two schools of thought, however, concerning how enlargement of the total muscle takes place. The first school holds that hypertrophy is responsible: An increased cross-sectional area of existing muscle fibers accounts for enlargement of the whole muscle. The second school of thought believes that hyperplasia is also a process by which muscle growth occurs: Fibers split leading to an increase in the total number of muscle fibers present.

In laboratory animals, muscle growth has occurred due to hyper-trophy alone (Bass, Mackova, & Vitek, 1973; Goldberg, Eltinger, Gold-spink, & Jablecki, 1975; Gollnick, Timson, Moore, & Riedy, 1981; Timson, Bowlin, Dudenhoeffer, & George, 1985). Increased muscle size in strength-trained athletes has also been attributed to hypertrophy of existing muscle fibers (Prince, Hikida, & Hagerman, 1976; Hagg-mark, Jansson, & Svane, 1978; Gollnick, Parsons, Riedy, & Moore, 1983). This increase in the cross-sectional area of existing muscle fibers is attributed to increased size and number of the actin and myosin fila-ments and addition of sarcomeres within existing muscle fibers (Gordon, 1967; MacDougall et al., 1979).

Hyperplasia has been implicated in contributing to muscle enlarge-ment in laboratory animals (Gonyea, 1980; Ho et al., 1980). Criticism of these studies has claimed that damage to the muscle samples as well as degenerating muscle fibers account for the observed hyperplasia. Several studies comparing body builders and power lifters concluded that the cross-sectional area of the body builders' individual muscle fibers was not significantly larger than normal; yet these athletes pos-sessed larger muscles than normal (MacDougall et al., 1982; Tesch & Larsson, 1982). This indicates that these athletes have a greater total number of muscle fibers than the control group: Hyperplasia may ac-count for this increase. Yet another study using body builders concludes that, on the contrary, they possess the same number of muscle fibers as the control group but possess much larger muscles (MacDougall et al., 1984). This study suggests that the large muscle size of body builders is due to hypertrophy of existing muscle fibers rather than hyperplasia. Another study of hyperplasia in laboratory animals has indicated that in order for hyperplasia to occur in cats the exercise in-tensity must be sufficient to recruit FT fibers (Type IIB) (Gonyea, 1980). It is possible that only high-intensity resistance training can effect hyperplasia. Though no concrete evidence supports the relationship, there are indications that hyperplasia occurs due to resistance train-ing. Due to these conflicting results, this topic remains controversial; further research on elite competitive lifters may help to resolve the con-troversy.

Conventional weight training in humans (Gonyea & Sale, 1982) and animals (Edgerton, 1978) appears to hypertrophy, selectively, the FT fibers to a greater degree than the ST fibers. Studies do, however, in-dicate that it may be possible to selectively hypertrophy either the FT or the ST fibers depending on the training regimen. Power lifters who train predominantly with high intensity (i.e., heavy resistances) and low volume (i.e., small number of sets and repetitions) have been shown to have FT fibers with a mean fiber area of 79 $\mu m^2 \cdot 100$ in the vastus lateralis (Tesch, Thorsson, & Kaiser, 1984). Conversely, body builders who train predominantly with a lower intensity but a higher volume have been shown to have FT fibers with a mean fiber area of 62 $\mu m^2 \cdot 100$ in the same muscle (Tesch et al., 1984). This study indicates that the high-intensity/low-volume training of Olympic and power lifters and the low-intensity/high-volume training of body builders may selectively hypertrophy the FT fibers and ST fibers, respectively.

An increase in the number of capillaries in a muscle may also enlarge the entire muscle. As with the selective hypertrophy of FT fibers, the increase of capillaries appears to be linked to the intensity and volume of strength training. It has been shown that power lifters and weight lifters exhibit no change in the number of capillaries per muscle fiber; due to hypertrophy of the fibers those same athletes showed a decrease in capillary density (i.e., the number of capillaries per cross-sectional area of tissue) when compared to nonathletic individuals (Tesch et al., 1984). It has also been proposed that the training performed by body builders induces increased capillarization (Schantz, 1982). Thus, high-intensity/low-volume strength training actually decreases capillary density whereas low-intensity/high-volume strength training has the opposite effect of increasing capillary density. An increase in capillary density may facilitate the performance of low-intensity weight training by increasing the blood supply to the active muscle. The short rest periods used by body builders during their workouts result in large increases in blood lactate levels (Noble et al., 1984); increased capillary density might aid in lactate clearance.

Physical activity also increases the size and strength of ligaments and tendons (Fahey, Akka, & Rolph, 1975). The increased size of these structures may cause in part the apparent enlargement of a muscle due to weight training. As the skeletal muscles become able to develop more tension through training, damage to ligaments and tendons is more likely to occur. Increased strength of the ligaments and tendons is a necessary adaptation to aid in preventing possible damage to these structures caused by the muscle's ability to lift heavier weights and develop more tension.

Body Compositional Changes

Body compositional changes do occur in short-term resistance training programs (6 to 24 weeks). Table 7.1 depicts the changes in body composition due to various training programs. Normally the body is divided into two compartments when examining body composition.

Lean body mass (LBM) is what the individual's body would weigh if no fat were present. Fat weight is the weight of fat contained in the body. Total body weight equals LBM plus fat weight. For the purpose of comparison fat weight is frequently expressed in percentage of total body weight: percentage of body fat (% fat). For example, if a 100-kg athlete is 15% fat his LBM, fat weight, and total body weight are related as follows:

Fat Weight $=$ .15 $\times$ 100 kg.
$\qquad\qquad$ $=$ 15 kg

LBM $\qquad$ $=$ total body weight − fat weight
$\qquad\qquad$ $=$ 100 kg − 15 kg
$\qquad\qquad$ $=$ 85 kg

Ideally a strength training program should increase LBM and decrease fat weight and % fat. Increases in LBM are viewed normally as mirroring increases in muscle tissue weight. Table 7.1 indicates that strength training induces decreases in % fat and increases in LBM. Total body weight, for the most part, experiences small increases over short training periods. This occurs in both males and females using dynamic constant resistance, variable resistance, and isokinetic training along with programs involving a variety of combinations of exercises, sets, and repetitions. Because of the variation in the numbers of sets, repetitions, and exercises and relatively small body compositional changes, it is impossible to reach concrete conclusions concerning which program is optimal for decreasing % fat and increasing LBM.

The largest increases in LBM are a little greater than three kilograms (6.6 lb) in 10 weeks of training. This translates into an LBM increase of 0.66 pounds per week. Though some coaches desire huge gains in body weight for their athletes during the off-season, this is impossible if that added body weight is going to be muscle mass.

Table 7.2 summarizes the results of studies investigating % fat of body builders and Olympic and power lifters. Mean % fat of these highly weight-trained males ranged from 8.3% to 12.2%, whereas female body builders demonstrated a mean % fat of 13.2%. All of these values are lower than the average % fat of college-aged males and females of 14% to 16% and 20% to 24%, respectively. Highly weight-trained athletes are therefore leaner than average individuals.

It should be noted, however, that the mean % fat of all the depicted groups of male athletes are above the essential fat levels of 6% (Sinning, 1974). Essential fat is the fat stores necessary to allow the body to function normally. It is not possible to have zero-percent fat. Fat stores are needed to pad the heart, kidneys, and other vital organs; they also serve as structural components of membranes and as fuel

Table 7.1 Changes in Body Composition

Reference	Sex	Type of Training	Length of training (weeks)	Days of training/ week	Sets and repetitions	Number of exercises	Total weight	LBM	% Fat
Brown & Wilmore, 1974	F	IT	24	3	8 wk = 1 × 10,8,7,6,5,4 16 wk = 1 × 10,6,5,4,3	4	-0.4	+1.0	-2.1
Mayhew & Gross, 1974	F	IT	9	3	2 × 10	11	+0.4	+1.5	-1.3
Wilmore et al., 1978	F	IT	10	2	2 × 7-16	8	-0.1	+1.1	-1.9
Withers, 1970	F	IT	10	3	40%-55% 1 RM for 30 seconds	10	+0.1	+1.3	-1.8
Hunter, 1985	F	IT	7	3	3 × 7-10	7	-0.9	+0.3	-1.5
Hunter, 1985	F	IT	7	4	2 × 7-10	7	+0.7	+0.7	-0.5
Fahey & Brown, 1973	M	IT	9	3	2 exercises 5 × 5 2 exercises 3 × 5 1 exercise 5 × 1-2	5	+0.5	+1.4	-1.0
Misner et al., 1974	M	IT	8	3	1 × 3-8	10	+1.0	+3.1	-2.9
Wilmore et al., 1978	M	IT	10	2	2 × 7-16	8	+0.3	+1.2	-1.3
Withers, 1970	M	IT	10	3	40%-55% 1 RM for 30 seconds	10	+0.7	+1.7	-1.5
Gettman et al., 1979	M	IT	20	3	50% 1 RM, 6 wk = 2 × 10-20 14 wk = 2 × 15	10	+0.5	+1.8	-1.7

(Cont.)

Table 7.1 (Cont.)

Reference	Sex	Type of Training	Length of training (weeks)	Days of training/week	Sets and repetitions	Number of exercises	Changes in Body Composition		
							Total weight	LBM	% Fat
Coleman, 1977	M	IT	10	3	2 × 8-10 RM	11	+1.7	+2.4	-9.1
Coleman, 1977	M	VR	10	3	1 × 10-12 RM	11	+1.8	+2.0	-9.3
Peterson, 1975	M	VR	6	3	1 × 10-12	20	–	-0.8	+0.6
Gettman, Culter, & Strathman, 1980	M	VR	20	3	2 × 12	9	-0.1	+1.6	-1.9
Gettman & Ayres, 1978	M	IK (60°/second)	10	3	3 × 10-15	7	-1.9	+3.2	-2.5
Gettman & Ayres, 1978	M	IK (120°/seconds)	10	3	3 × 10-15	7	+0.3	+1.0	-0.9
Gettman, Ayres, & Pollock, 1979	M	IK	8	3	4 wk = 1 × 10 at 60°/second 4 wk = 1 × 15 at 90°/second	9	+0.3	+1.0	-0.9
Gettman, Cutler, & Strathman, 1980	M	IK (60°/second)	20	3	2 × 12	10	-0.6	+2.1	-2.8
Hunter, 1985	M	IT	7	3	3 × 7-10	7	+0.6	+0.5	-0.2
Hunter, 1985	M	IT	7	4	2 × 7-10	7	0.0	+0.5	-0.9
Hurley et al., 1984	M	VR	16	3-4	1 × 8-12 RM	14	+1.6	+1.9	-0.8

Table 7.2 Percent Fat of Extremely Strength-Trained Athletes

Reference	Caliber of athletes	% fat
	Men	
Fahey, Akka, & Rolph, 1975	OL-national & international	12.2
Tanner, 1964	OL-national & international	10.0
Sprynarova & Parizkova, 1971	OL-national	9.8
Fahey, Akka, & Rolph, 1975	PL-national & international	15.6
Katch, Katch, Moffat, & Gittleson, 1980	OL & PL-national & international	9.7
Katch, Katch, Moffat, & Gittleson, 1980	BB-national	9.3
Zruback, 1972	BB-national	6.6
Fahey, Akka, & Rolph, 1975	BB-national & international	8.4
Pipes, 1979	BB-national & international	8.3
	Women	
Freedson, Michevic, Loucks, & Birandola, 1983	BB-national	13.2

OL — Olympic lifters
PL — power lifters
BB — body builders

stores for energy. The female body builders mean % fat of 13.2% is very close to the lower limit of female essential fat levels of 13% to 22% (Frish & McArthur, 1974). (See chapter 9, Menstrual Cycle Irregularities.) Females' essential fat levels may need to be higher than males in order to ensure normal functioning of the reproductive cycle (Frish & McArthur, 1974). Many individuals as they approach essential fat levels become lethargic and moody. Essential fat levels, therefore, are not to be viewed as ideal fat levels for physical activity.

Neural Factors

The initial quick gains in strength during the first few weeks of a weight training program along with no noticeable increase in muscle mass suggests that other factors besides muscle mass are involved in muscular force production. Following a resistance training program there are weak relationships between increases in strength and changes in limb circumference (Moritani & De Vries, 1979, 1980), muscle fiber cross-sectional area (Costill, Coyle, Fink, Lesmes, & Witzmann, 1979), and muscle fiber type (MacDougall et al., 1980), indicating other factors are responsible for gains in strength. In one study isometric training produced a 92% increase in maximal static strength but only a 23% increase in muscle cross-sectional area (Ikai & Fukunaga, 1970). On the basis of this kind of evidence researchers have concluded that some neural factors have a profound influence on muscular force production. Such neural factors are related to the following processes: increased neural drive to the muscle, increased synchronization of the motor units, increased activation of the contractile apparatus, and inhibition of the protective mechanisms of the muscle (i.e., golgi tendon organs). In young males (20–30 years) it is believed that neural factors are the predominant cause of strength increase during the first three to five weeks of training (Moritani & DeVries, 1980). After this period hypertrophy of the muscle becomes the predominant factor in strength increases.

Researchers have investigated neural drive to a muscle using integrated electromyogram (EMG) techniques (Hakkinen & Komi, 1983; Kamen, Kroll, & Zigon, 1984; Moritani & DeVries, 1980; Sale, McDougall, Upton, & McComas, 1983; Thorstensson, Karlsson, Viitasalso, Luhtanen, & Komi, 1976). EMG techniques measure the electrical activity within the muscle and nerves and indicate the amount of neural drive to a muscle. In one of these studies, 8-weeks of dynamic constant resistance weight training shifted the EMG activity to muscular force ratio to a lower level (Moritani & DeVries, 1980). Because the muscle produced more force with a lower amount of EMG activity, more force production was realized with less neural drive. Calculations predicted a 9% strength increase due to training-induced hypertrophy; in actuality, however, strength increased 30%. It is believed that this increase in strength beyond that expected from hypertrophy resulted from the combination of the shift in the EMG-to-force ratio and the 12% increase in maximal EMG activity. This and other research support the idea that an increase in maximal neural drive to a muscle increases strength. The studies reveal that less neural drive is required to produce any particular submaximal force after training; consequently there is either an improved activation of the muscle or a more efficient recruitment pattern of the muscle fibers. Because it has been demonstrated that improved activation of the muscle does not occur after training (McDonagh et al., 1983) it follows that a more efficient recruitment order is responsible for the increased force produced.

A second neural factor that could cause increased force production is increased synchronization of motor unit firing. The greater the synchronization the greater the number of motor units firing at any one time. Increased synchronization of motor units has been observed after strength training (Milner-Brown, Stein, & Yemin, 1973). During submaximal force production, however, increased synchronization of motor units is actually less effective in producing force than asynchronous activation of motor units (Lind & Petrofsky, 1978; Rack & Westbury, 1969). Thus, it is unclear whether greater synchronization of motor units produces greater force or not.

Training has been shown to increase the period of time that all motor units can be tonically active from several to 20 seconds (Grimby, Hannerz, & Hedman, 1981). An adaptation of this type may not cause an increase in maximal force but does aid in maintaining it for a longer period of time. It has also been observed that during maximal voluntary contractions the high threshold FT motor units normally do not reach stimulation rates required for complete tetany to occur (DeLuca, LeFever, McCue, & Xenakis, 1982). If the stimulation rate to these high threshold motor units were increased, so also would be the actual force production.

Sale et al. (1983) have investigated the possibility that following strength training additional motor units can be recruited. As a mechanism to increase force production, this process assumes that an individual is not able to simultaneously activate all motor units in a muscle prior to training. Belanger and McComas (1981) found that this is true for some muscles but not for others. All possible forms of neural adaptation to strength training require further research before concrete conclusions can be reached.

Inhibitory Mechanisms

Inhibition of muscle contraction by reflex protective mechanisms such as the golgi tendon organs has been hypothesized to limit muscular force production (Caiozzo et al., 1981; Wickiewicz et al., 1984). The effect of these inhibitory mechanisms can be partially removed by hypnosis. Ikai and Steinhaus (1961) found that force developed during forearm flexion by non-resistance-trained individuals increased 17% under hypnosis. In the same study force developed by a highly resistance trained individual under hypnosis was not significantly different from force developed in the normal conscious state. The researchers concluded that resistance training may cause voluntary inhibition of these protective mechanisms. These protective mechanisms appear to be especially active when large amounts of force are developed, such as maximal contractions at slow speeds of movement (Caiozzo et al., 1981; Wickiewicz et al., 1984).

Several practical applications derive from information concerning protective mechanisms that limit muscular contraction. Many resistance training exercises involve contraction of the same muscle groups of both limbs simultaneously or of bilateral contractions. The force developed during bilateral contractions is less than the sum of the force developed by each limb independently (Ohtsuki, 1981; Secher, Rorsgaard, & Secher, 1978). The difference between the force developed during bilateral contraction and the sum of the force developed by each limb independently is called bilateral deficit. This bilateral deficit is associated with reduced motor unit stimulation (Vandervoot, Sale, & Moroz, 1984). The reduced motor unit stimulation could be due to inhibition of contraction by the protective mechanisms and subsequently less force production. Training with bilateral contractions reduces bilateral deficit (Secher, 1975) by bringing bilateral force production closer to the sum of unilateral force production. Although bilateral exercise reduces the bilateral deficit, the performance of unilateral exercises may be important to maintain the deficit in, for example, sports where force production of one limb independently is required. Unilateral exercises can be performed using dumbbells and some types of weight training equipment.

Knowledge of the neural protective mechanisms is also useful in understanding the expression of maximal strength. Neural protective mechanisms appear to have their greatest effect in slow-velocity/high-resistance movements (Caiozzo et al., 1981; Wickiewicz et al., 1984). A resistance training program in which the antagonists are contracted immediately prior to performance of the exercise is more effective in increasing strength at low velocities than a program in which precontraction of the antagonists is not performed (Caiozzo, Laird, Chow, Prietto, & McMaster, 1983). The precontraction in some way partially inhibits the neural self-protective mechanisms, thus allowing a more forceful contraction. Precontraction of the antagonists can be used as a method both to enhance the training effect and to inhibit the neural protective mechanisms during a maximal lift. For example, immediately prior to a maximal bench press attempt, forceful contractions of the arm flexors and muscles that adduct the scapula (i.e., pull the scapula toward the spine) should make possible a heavier maximal bench press than no precontraction of the antagonists.

Force Velocity Curve

With strength training, ideally, the skeletal muscle force velocity curve moves up and to the left. (See Figure 6.9.) After training, the muscle is stronger at all velocities of movement from an isometric contraction to a contraction performed at maximal speed. There is disagreement, however, regarding the optimal velocity of movement at which resistance training exercises should be performed. Some coaches and researchers feel that in order to be strong at a fast velocity of movement one must train at a fast velocity of movement. Others feel slow velocities of movement during resistance training are most beneficial.

Throughout the 1970s research indicated that in order to increase strength at a fast velocity of movement one must use fast training speeds (Moffroid & Whipple, 1970; Pipes, 1975). These studies trained individuals at very slow velocities (24 and 36 degrees/seconds, respectively) and intermediate velocities (108 and 136 degrees/seconds, respectively) of movement. The results indicated that training at a particular velocity of movement increased force (torque) production at and below the training velocity. Training at a slow velocity increases strength at slow velocities only; training at intermediate velocities increases strength at both intermediate and slow velocities.

Research has revealed that the training effect of velocity of movement on force production is more complex than previous studies indicate. The research performed in the 1970s measured peak force without regard to the joint angle at which the force was generated. Joint angle determines the length of the muscle, and muscle length has a large effect on force production (see Figure 10.7). Joint angle specific torque is a better test criterion than maximal torque irrelevant of the joint angle. A project (Caiozzo et al., 1981) in which individuals trained at either an intermediate velocity (96 degrees/seconds) or a fast velocity (239 degrees/seconds), also determined force at a particular joint angle and therefore particular muscle length. The findings conflicted with those of earlier projects. Caiozzo et al., using joint angle specific torque, demonstrated that the intermediate training speed (96 degrees/seconds) increased force production both below and above the training velocity (0 to 239 degrees/seconds) and that the fast training speed (239 degrees/seconds) increased force production only below the training velocity (143 to 239 degrees/seconds). The individuals in this project trained, however, for only four weeks. Consequently, the majority of the training effect would be neural in nature with muscle hypertrophy's having only a small effect on the results. A second study (Dudley & Djamil, 1985) trained individuals at 239 degrees per second for 7 weeks and used joint angle specific torque as a testing criterion. Dudley and Djamil determined that at fast training speeds muscular force production increases at and below the training velocity (0 to 239 degrees/seconds). Due to the longer training period both neural factors and muscular hypertrophy contributed to the force production.

Another study (Kanehisa & Miyashita, 1983) revealed that groups trained at 60 (slow) and 179 (intermediate) degrees per second both increased force production from 60 to 299 degrees per second. This study determined peak force irrelevant of joint angle. The intermediate-speed trainees, however, showed greater increases at the faster velocities (179 to 299 degrees/seconds) than the slow-speed group. The slow-speed trainees demonstrated greater gains at the slower velocities (60 to 119 degrees/seconds) than the intermediate-speed group. A third group in this study trained at 299 (fast) degrees per second; this fast speed group showed increases in force production at only the fast velocities (239 to 299 degrees/seconds). The intermediate-speed trainees, however, demonstrated greater gains than the fast-speed trainees at the fast velocities (239 to 299 degrees/seconds).

All of these studies point to three important conclusions. First, if the training program prescribes the use of only one velocity of movement it should be an intermediate speed. Second, any training velocity increases strength within a range above and below the training velocity. Third, further research is needed to distinguish between the effects of neural factors and muscle hypertrophy on the force velocity curve.

Oxygen Consumption

Maximal oxygen consumption ($\dot{V}O_2$max) determined in a treadmill test is normally considered to be the best indicator of cardiovascular fitness. Circuit weight training for a duration of 8 to 20 weeks has been shown to elicit an increase of $\dot{V}O_2$max of 5% in men and 8% in women (Gettman & Pollock, 1981). Circuit weight training consists of a series of exercises performed for 12 to 15 repetitions of each exercise with a resistance of 40% to 60% of one RM, with a short rest period of approximately 30 seconds between exercises. Studies in which a typical resistance training regimen (i.e., high loads and long rest periods) was followed for eight to nine weeks actually demonstrated a decrease in $\dot{V}O_2$max of 0.5% to 9% (Gettman & Pollock, 1981). A recent study, however, demonstrated an increase of $\dot{V}O_2$max of 5.5% following an eight-week Olympic-style resistance training program (Stone, Wilson, Blessing, & Rozenek, 1983). The program included several common resistance exercises, snatch and clean pull exercises, and vertical jumping exercises. All of these results, however, are significantly lower than the 20% increase normally associated with running endurance training programs of the same duration.

Maximum oxygen consumption values of highly weight-trained males, including competitive body builders and Olympic and power lifters, range from 41.5 to 55 ml/O^2/Kg • min^{-1} (Saltin & Astrand, 1967). The majority of highly weight-trained individuals perform little or no aerobic conditioning. One can conclude from the above data that it is possible to increase $\dot{V}O_2$max with resistance training. These values are, however, significantly lower than $\dot{V}O_2$max of values of 70–80 ml/O$_2$/Kg • min^{-1} reported for endurance-trained athletes.

In order to elicit maximal increases in $\dot{V}O_2$ max, heart rate must be maintained at a minimum of 70% of maximal for a minimum of 15 minutes (American College of Sports Medicine, 1978). Circuit weight training and traditional resistance training programs allow heart rate to decrease below 70% of maximal during the rest periods between sets of exercises. This is the major reason why resistance training does not increase $\dot{V}O_2$ max to the same degree as traditional endurance running programs. If cardiovascular fitness is the major goal of a fitness program, resistance training is not the optimal method of training.

Fuel Availability to the Energy Sources

One adaptation that can lead to increased physical performance is an increase in the fuel available to the three energy sources. The intramuscular stores of the phosphates ATP and PC can increase significantly due to resistance training. In humans it has been demonstrated that after 5 months of strength training the resting intramuscular concentrations of PC and ATP are elevated 22% and 18%, respectively (MacDougall et al., 1977). In this same study, intramuscular stores of glycogen were elevated 66%. Blood glucose levels did not change significantly during one hour of resistance training (Keul et al., 1978). Research in this area supports the idea that anaerobic fuel sources are increased with resistance training; and at least for one training session fuel availability to the lactic acid energy source is not a limiting factor to performance.

The aerobic energy source uses glycogen (carbohydrates), triglycerides (fats), and some protein to produce ATP. It has already been stated that intramuscular glycogen stores can be increased due to strength training. Yet unknown is what happens to the concentration of intramuscular stores of triglycerides due to strength training. Both because most resistance training programs are anaerobic and because triglycerides are only metabolized aerobically, it is likely that resistance training has little or no effect upon intramuscular stores of triglycerides.

Enzymatic Changes

Increases in the activities of the enzymes of an energy source can lead to more ATP production and utilization per unit of time. This could lead to increases in physical performance. Enzyme activity of the ATP-PC energy source (e.g., creatine phosphokinase and myokinase) have been shown to increase in humans due to isokinetic training (Costill et al., 1979) and in rats due to isometric training (Exner, Staudte, & Pette, 1973). Costill et al. used two training regimes for the legs in their isokinetic study. The leg extensors of one leg performed 10 6-second all out bouts at 180 degrees per second. The leg extensors of the opposite leg performed 30-second bouts of exercise at 180 degrees per second until the total work performed equaled that performed during the 10 6-second bouts. The enzymes associated with the ATP-PC energy source showed significant increases of approximately 12% in the leg trained with 30 second bouts and insignificant changes in the leg trained with 6-second bouts. According to these findings, enzymatic changes associated with the ATP-PC energy source are linked to the duration of the exercise bouts; the changes do not take place with exercise bouts of six seconds or less.

Costill et al. (1979) also demonstrated a significant increase of one enzyme (phosphofructokinase) associated with the lactic acid energy source of 7% and 18%, respectively, in the 6-second and 30 second-trained legs. Neither leg showed a significant increase in a second enzyme (lactate dehydrogenase) associated with the lactic acid energy source. It is clear that, similar to the ATP-PC energy source, enzymatic changes that occur in the lactic acid energy source are dependent on the duration of the sets in a given resistance training session.

Increases in the activity of enzymes associated with aerobic metabolism have been reported with isokinetic training in humans (Costill et al., 1979) isometric training in humans (Grimby et al., 1973), and isometric training in rats (Exner et al., 1973). Enzymatic changes associated with the aerobic energy source may also be dependent upon the duration of individual exercise bouts (Costill et al., 1979).

Enzymatic changes which are associated with any of the three energy sources are dependent upon the duration of individual sets rather than the total amount of work performed. For practical application, a training program which calls for resistances that are tolerable for at least 30 seconds will most likely effect increases in the activity of enzymes.

Hormonal Responses

The endocrine system aids an organism in adapting to its environment. This is very important to both the acute response and the chronic adaptations associated with physical training. A specific stimulus causes the release of a chemical messenger or hormone, targeted for specific tissue cells, into the blood. One example of hormonal action is the basic endocrine reflex: a feedback system which maintains a specific homeostatic level. For example, blood glucose levels are maintained by a negative feedback system. Elevation of blood glucose levels after eating a candy bar stimulates the pancreas to secrete the hormone insulin. Insulin causes the cells to increase the uptake of glucose from the blood resulting in a decrease of blood glucose levels. The lower blood glucose levels produce a negative feedback on the cells of the pancreas, that is, cause the pancreas to reduce the amount of insulin secreted. Over time this feedback system brings the blood glucose levels back to normal (see Figure 7.1).

Both the actions and the mechanisms of action of the various hormones are diverse (Norris, 1980). Hormones can affect almost every

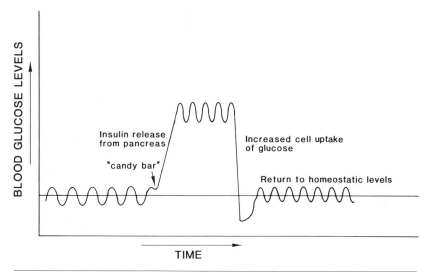

Figure 7.1 Blood glucose levels fluctuate within tightly controlled homeostatic levels. Ingestion of a candy bar causes a dramatic insulin response which helps return blood glucose to normal homeostatic levels.

physiological function in the body. Cellular transport, enzyme synthesis, cell growth, protein synthesis, cell metabolism, and reproductive function are just a few physiological events which are mediated, in part, by hormonal actions. The close association of hormones to the nervous system make the neural-endocrine system potentially one of the most important physiological systems related to training adaptations.

General understanding of the hormonal response to resistance training is limited. This is because the relationship between various hormones and resistance exercise has only been partially explored. Hormonal responses to physical training have been generally linked to metabolic function and cellular growth. The majority of hormonal research in this area has been directed toward the responses of testosterone and growth hormone and their relationship to changes in muscular hypertrophy and gains in strength.

Weiss, Cureton, and Thompson (1983) examined the male hormone testosterone with a three-set, four-exercise training session: 80% of 1 RM for the lat pull, bench press, arm curl, and leg press. Men demonstrated greater absolute testosterone response than women to resistance exercise. Although not solely responsible for exercise-induced muscle hypertrophy (Goldberg, 1971), greater testosterone increases in men may help to explain observed differences between sexes in resistance training adaptations.

Testosterone increases have been observed following activities besides resistance training (Sutton, Coleman, & Casey, 1973); its effects on muscle tissue growth may require the synergistic action of other neural and hormonal stimuli specific to resistance training. A recent study observed that resting testosterone levels are suppressed by aerobic training and increased by resistance training (Stone, Byrd, & Johnson, 1984). More research is needed to understand the physiological role of testosterone in strength development and exercise-induced muscle hypertrophy.

Growth hormone is another hormone with potentially significant anabolic effects on muscle (Goldberg, 1971; Goldberg & Goodman, 1969). Vanhelder, Redonski, and Goode (1984) demonstrated that growth hormone is sensitive both to rest periods and to intensity when performing a leg press exercise. This finding is significant to the examination of the training effects produced by different resistance training programs. In addition, it is known that growth hormone stimulates the release of somatomedians, mediating important growth properties related to muscle tissue growth, bone development, and collagen metabolism (Phillips & Vassilopoulou-Sellin, 1980; Tepperman, 1980).

Table 7.3 Selected Hormones of the Endocrine System and Their Actions

Endocrine Gland	Hormone	Some Actions
Testes	Testosterone	Stimulates development and maintenance of male sex characteristics, growth, and increased protein anabolism
Anterior Pituitary	Growth Hormone	Stimulates somatomedins, protein synthesis, growth, and organic metabolism
	Adrenocorticotropin (ACTH)	Stimulates glucocorticoids in adrenal cortex
	Thyroid-stimulating hormone (TSH)	Stimulates thyroid hormone synthesis and secretion
	Follicle-stimulating hormone (FSH)	Stimulates growth of follicles in ovary and seminiferous tubules in testes, ovum, and sperm production
	Luteinizing hormone (LH)	Stimulates ovulation and secretion of sex hormones in ovaries and testes
	Prolactin (LTH)	Stimulates milk production in mammary glands; maintains corpora lutea and secretion of progesterone
	Melanocyte-stimulating hormone	Stimulates melanocytes, which contain the dark pigment melanin
Posterior pituitary	Antidiuretic hormone (ADH)	Increases contraction of smooth muscle and reabsorption of water by kidneys
	Oxytocin	Stimulates uterine contractions and release of milk by mammary glands

(Cont.)

Table 7.3 (Cont.)

Endocrine Gland	Hormone	Some Actions
Adrenal cortex	Glucocorticoids (cortisol, cortisone, etc.)	Inhibits or retards amino acid incorporation into proteins; stimulates conversion of proteins into carbohydrates; maintains normal blood sugar level; conserves glucose; promotes use of fat
	Mineralcorticoids (aldosterone, deoxycorticosterone, etc.)	Sodium-potassium metabolism increases body fluid
Adrenal medulla	Epinephrine	Increases cardiac output; increases blood sugar, glycogen breakdown, and fat mobilization
	Norepinephrine (some)	Similar to epinephrine plus constriction of blood vessels
Thyroid	Thyroxine	Stimulates oxidative metabolism in mitochondria and cell growth
	Calcitonin	Reduces blood calcium phosphate levels
Pancreas	Insulin	Stores glycogen and; absorbs glucose
	Glucagon	Increases blood glucose levels
Ovaries	Estrogens	Develops female sex characteristics
	Progesterone	Develops female sex characteristics; maintains pregnancy; develops mammary glands
Parathyroids	Parathormone	Increases blood calcium; decreases blood phosphate

Besides the anabolic function of hormones, many help to meet the metabolic demands of strenuous exercise. Regulation of blood glucose levels, glycogen storage, and mineral metabolism are all mediated via hormonal actions. Table 7.3 provides a summary of the major hormones and their actions. At this point the effects of resistance training on acute and chronic hormonal responses requires a more detailed analysis. The challenge is to link physiological responses to chronic adaptations such as muscle hypertrophy and strength.

Cardiovascular Adaptations

The stress of resistance training on the heart and circulatory system demands various adaptations of these structures. Morganroth, Maron, Henry, and Epstein (1975) were among the first to demonstrate that adaptations of the heart are different to endurance training than they are to resistance training. The data demonstrated that the hearts of endurance-trained athletes had normal wall thickness but greater than normal ventricular cavity size, whereas, resistance-trained athletes had greater than normal heart wall thickness and normal ventricular cavity size. Morganroth et al. hypothesized that in endurance training a large amount of blood had to be pumped at a relatively low pressure or the heart experienced volume overload. This caused the heart to adapt by developing a larger than normal ventricular cavity, allowing a larger stroke volume or more blood per heart beat to be pumped. During the performance of resistance training exercises, blood pressure rises substantially (MacDougall, Tuxen, Sale, Moroz, & Sutton, 1985; Fleck & Dean, 1985). Because the hearts of resistance-trained athletes must pump blood at intermittently higher pressures (i.e., pressure overload), they adapt to this stress by developing thicker than normal ventricular walls.

Body size can have an affect on heart size: A large individual may have a large heart (Alpert, Terry, & Kelly, 1985). Previously cited data (Morganroth et al., 1975) demonstrated that, in absolute terms, endurance- and resistance-trained athletes have significantly larger ventricular cavities and thicker heart walls, respectively. If body surface area and body weight are taken into account, the values for athletes' ventricular cavity size and heart wall thickness are not significantly different from the values for normal individuals.

More recent cross-sectional studies of body builders and power and Olympic lifters have not necessarily agreed either with the above results or with each other (Brown, Byrd, Jayasinghe, & Jones, 1983; Longhurst,

Kelley, Gonyea, & Mitchell, 1980; Menapace et al., 1982). Some of these studies report significant and others nonsignificant differences between resistance-trained athletes and normal individuals for ventricular size and heart wall thickness, both in absolute terms and relative to body surface area. A study accounting for body size found resistance-trained males to have a significantly greater wall thickness but a nonsignificant difference in volume of the left ventricle compared to sedentary males (Fleck, Bennett, Kraemer, & Baechle, 1987). This study individually matched a group of Olympic lifters, power lifters, and body builders to sedentary males for age, height, and weight. (This eliminated the effect that age, height, and body weight may have had on the results.) This study, along with the majority of previous studies, suggests that resistance training may increase wall thickness of the left ventricle but has little or no effect on left ventricular volume.

Short-term longitudinal studies (8 to 10 weeks) involving resistance training and adaptive changes of the heart have provided inconclusive results concerning cardiac adaptations. One of these studies reports nonsignificant changes in ventricular cavity size and heart wall thickness due to strength training (Ricci et al., 1982). A second study reports no change in ventricular cavity size but a significant increase in wall thickness due to strength training (Knakis & Hickson, 1980). Unfortunately, both of these studies reported only absolute values, not accounting for body size.

The Morganroth et al. hypothesis may be too simplistic. The resistance training programs of power and Olympic lifters (i.e., low number of repetitions with heavy weights) place a high pressure overload and small volume overload on the heart; the result is an increased wall thickness with no change in ventricular cavity size. On the other hand, training for body builders (i.e., higher number of repetitions with low or moderate weights) places a larger volume overload as well as a pressure overload on the heart; the result may be increased ventricular volumes and increased wall thickness. Whether body builders or power and Olympic lifters are the subjects in cross-sectional studies may, therefore, affect the results. This same line of reasoning reveals that the number of repetitions and the chosen resistance in longitudinal training studies may also affect the results. It is possible that this accounts, in part, for the contradictory results obtained in studies concerning ventricular size and heart wall thickness.

A decrease in resting heart rate due to physical training is a familiar cardiovascular change. Studies of short-term resistance training (8 to 20 weeks) have shown small but statistically nonsignificant decreases in resting heart rate (Allen, Byrd, & Smith, 1976; Ricci et al., 1982; Stone et al., 1983) and statistically significant decreases in heart rate (seven beats per minute) (Knakis & Hickson, 1980).

Individuals experience high blood pressures during the performance of resistance type exercise (Fleck & Dean, 1985; MacDougall et al., 1983). Competitive weight lifters, however, demonstrate resting blood pressures within normal ranges (Longhurst et al., 1980). Short-term resistance training programs reveal no significant changes in resting blood pressure (Allen et al., 1976) or they reveal a small but statistically significant drop in resting systolic pressure but no change in diastolic blood pressure (Fahey et al., 1975). In addition, male body builders have lower blood pressures than either recreational resistance trainers or sedentary males during resistance exercises performed at the same relative load (Fleck & Dean, 1985).

Recent attention has been focused on the levels of cholesterol and triglycerides (fats) in the blood. High concentrations in the blood of either of these substances are associated with atherosclerosis. In addition, cholesterol is divided into two major types: high-density lipoproteins (HDL) and low-density lipoproteins (LDL). A high concentration of HDL is associated with a decreased risk of cardiovascular disease (e.g., heart attack and stroke), whereas a high level of LDL is associated with an increased risk. The total cholesterol, triglyceride, and HDL levels of male recreational resistance trainers is not different from that of normal individuals (Farrell et al., 1982); the risk of cardiovascular disease is equal for both groups. A comparison of body builders and power lifters revealed that the former have a more favorable lipid profile than the latter for the reduction of the potential for cardiovascular disease (Hurley et al., 1984). This is probably due to the body builders' shorter rest periods between sets and greater number of sets and repetitions as compared to the power lifters' regimen. This same study also demonstrated that steroid use affects the lipid profile of blood in such a way as to actually increase risk of coronary heart disease. A study of sedentary males and females revealed that, after a 16-week program of 3 sessions per week, their lipid profiles changed in the direction that would reduce the risk of coronary heart disease (Goldberg, Elliot, Schutz, & Kloster, 1984). It appears that certain kinds of resistance training (short rest periods and large volume) can favorably alter the lipid profile.

In summary, resistance training increases ventricular cavity size and heart wall thickness depending upon the volume and intensity of the training. Resting blood pressure as well as total cholesterol, HDL, and LDL blood concentrations may be slightly affected by resistance training. Maximal oxygen consumption is elevated by resistance training but the increase is less than that caused by a running program. In general, resistance training produces small changes in cardiovascular fitness and in variables indicating a decrease in the probability of a cardiovascular problem. Consequently, resistance training should not be the exercise of choice if the major goal of the conditioning program is cardiovascular fitness.

Muscle Contraction Time

One common misconception about resistance training is that it slows a person down. Research concerning speed-related properties of muscle, such as contraction time, demonstrates that there is no change in these characteristics with resistance training. Contraction time in humans remained unchanged after four months of dynamic resistance training, three times per week (DeLorme, Ferris, & Gallagher, 1952). Contraction time of a nonhuman primate's muscle also remained unchanged after resistance training (Edgerton, 1976). In female rats the contraction time of fast muscle and slow muscle has been reported to decrease and increase 20%, respectively, following isometric training (Exner et al., 1973). These changes are, however, inconsistent with previous studies. What this research does reveal is that resistance training does not affect a muscle's contraction time and, therefore, will not slow one down.

Connective Tissue

Connective tissue is abundantly distributed throughout the body. Physiological adaptations in ligaments and tendons due to physical training do occur and may aid in injury prevention. Physical activity causes increased metabolism, thickness, weight, and strength of ligaments (Staff, 1982; Tipton, Matthes, Maynard, & Carey, 1975). Damaged ligaments regain their strength at a faster rate if physical activity is performed after the damage has occurred (Staff, 1982; Tipton et al., 1975; see Figure 7.2). Both the attachment site of a ligament or tendon to a bone and the muscle-tendinous junction are frequent sites of injury. Research involving laboratory animals demonstrates that with endurance-type training the amount of force necessary to cause separation at these areas increases (Tipton et al., 1975). There is reason to believe that resistance training would produce similar results.

The connective tissue sheathes that surround the entire muscle (epimysium), groups of muscle fibers (perimysium), and individual

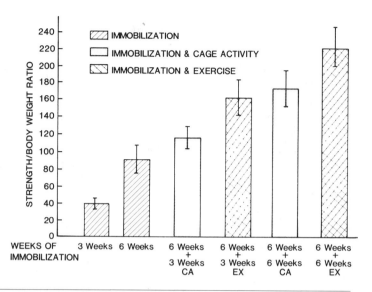

Figure 7.2 The effect of various periods of immobilization and normal cage activity (CA) and immobilization followed by exercise (EX) on ligament strength after surgical transection.

Note. From "Influence of Exercise on the Strength of the Medial Collateral Knee Ligament of Dogs" by C.M. Tipton, S.L. James, W. Mergner, and T.K. Tcheng, 1970, *American Journal of Physiology*, **218**, p. 898. Copyright 1970 by the American Physiological Society. Adapted by permission.

muscle fibers (endomysium) may also adapt to resistance training. These sheaths are of major importance in the tensil strength and elastic properties of muscle; they form the framework that supports an overload of the muscle. Compensatory hypertrophy induced in the muscle of laboratory animals also caused an increase in the collagen content of these connective tissue sheaths (Laurent, Sparrow, Bates, & Millward, 1978; Turto, Lindy, & Halme). It has been reported, however, that body builders do not differ from age-mated control subjects in the relative amount of connective tissue in the biceps brachii (Mac-Dougall et al., 1985).

Resistance training has been found to increase the thickness of hyaline cartilage on the articular surfaces of bone (Holmdahl & Ingelmark, 1948; Ingelmark & Elsholm, 1948). One major function of hyaline cartilage is to act as a shock absorber between the bony surfaces of a joint. Increasing the thickness of this cartilage could facilitate the performance of this shock absorber function.

Bone Density

A fractured bone is an all too common occurrence in daily life and in sports. Immobilization produces local or generalized bone loss (Falch, 1982; Krolner, Tondevold, Toft, Berthelsen, & Pors Nielsen, 1982). Cross-sectional studies which have examined bone mineral content in athletes demonstrate that weight-trained athletes have greater bone mineral content than both other athletes and sedentary individuals (Nilsson & Westlin, 1977), and that the dominant or more active arm has greater bone mineral content than its nondominant counterpart (Montoye, Smith, Fardon, & Howley, 1980). Longitudinal training studies involving humans (Williams, Wagner, Wasnich, & Heilbrun, 1984) and dogs (Martin, Albright, Clarke, & Niffenegger, 1981) conclusively demonstrate that physical activity can cause increased bone mineral content. The study involving dogs consisted of walking on a treadmill carrying weighted jackets of up to 130% of the dog's weight. This closely simulated resistance training and provided strong evidence that resistance training can increase bone mineral content.

Prevention of Injuries

Athletic training and coaching literature contain numerous reports concerning resistance training and injury prevention. Most of these reports suggest exercise to prevent various injuries which have not been scientifically tested. The role of resistance training in injury prevention for tennis and swimming has, however, received some attention.

Resistance training of the wrist extensors and flexors has been shown to aid in preventing tennis elbow (Gruchow & Pelleiter, 1979; Kuland, McCue, Rockwell, & Gieck, 1979). Athletes who do not include some form of resistance training in their physical conditioning have a higher incidence of tennis elbow complaints (Gruchow & Pelleiter, 1979). In addition, 31% of the athletes who undergo a preventative resistance training program after developing tennis elbow have a recurrence of tennis elbow symptoms, whereas 41% of the athletes who do not perform preventative resistance training have a recurrence of tennis elbow symptoms (Gruchow & Pelleiter, 1979). Resistance training has also been proven effective in pain prevention from tennis shoulder (Priest & Nagle, 1976).

Resistance training is effective in reducing shoulder pain in age group swimmers (Dominguez, 1978) and collegiate swimmers (Falkel, Murphy, Murray, & Cox, 1985). Isokinetic resistance training of the shoulder has also been demonstrated to reduce the incidence of shoulder pain in other groups of athletes who utilize the shoulder extensively (Hawkins & Kennedy, 1980). These studies demonstrate the value of resistance training in reducing the incidence of injuries due to athletic competition and training.

The information in this chapter describes the many physiological adaptations that occur in response to resistance training. Equally important in the design of sound resistance training programs is an understanding of the physiological processes that occur during periods of detraining or less activity. Detraining is the subject of chapter 8.

Chapter 8

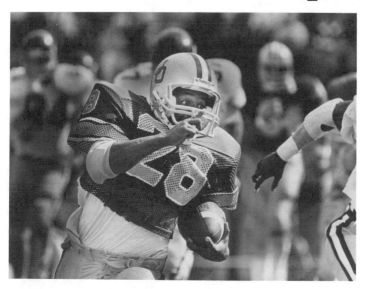

Detraining

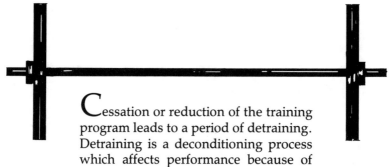

Cessation or reduction of the training program leads to a period of detraining. Detraining is a deconditioning process which affects performance because of diminished physiological capacity. During this period, there is a loss of physiological adaptations associated with the training stimulus. A basic understanding of detraining will facilitate the design of exercise programs for improving or maintaining the various fitness components.

Strength Loss

Previous studies have indicated that gains in strength are typically maintained with minimal maintenance programs. In one study, Berger (1962a) demonstrated that strength could be improved over a six-week detraining period using only one set of one RM and training only one day a week. Even when training ceases completely or is drastically reduced, strength gains decline at a much slower rate than the rate at which they increased (McMorris & Elkins, 1954; Morehouse, 1967; Rasch, 1971; Rasch & Morehouse, 1957; Waldman & Stull, 1969). Research has not yet indicated the exact loading, frequency of training, and type of program needed to maintain the training gains achieved by an individual. Maintenance programs are probably as specific as the strength development prescription. These studies indicate that it is possible to maintain gains with a drastically reduced volume of training. These observations may be related to the cycling phenomenon discussed in chapter 3. To maintain strength gains the intensity should be maintained, but the volume and frequency of training can be reduced.

Unpublished data by Kraemer (see Figure 8.1) lends support to this idea. Sixty-eight college football players performed a one RM on three

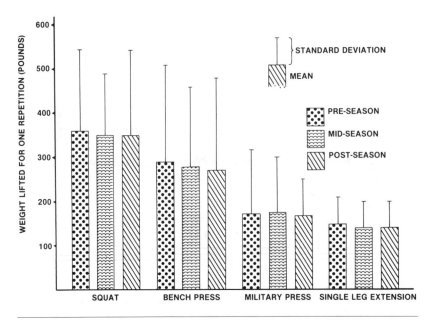

Figure 8.1 Results of in-season resistance program on 1 RM lifts.

separate occasions: preseason, midseason, and postseason. All athletes trained two times per week during the 14-week season. The in-season program consisted of the following exercises; two-minute rests were allowed between sets and exercises:

Bench Press	8, 5, 5, 8
Squats	8, 5, 5, 5
Single Leg Extensions	10, 10
Single Leg Curls	10, 10
Military Press	8, 8, 8
Power Cleans	8, 8, 8

Each player completed winter and summer resistance training programs consisting of four to five days per week with a much larger training volume and more exercises than the in-season program. The entire group exhibited no significant decreases in one RM for any of the exercises between the time periods evaluated. A separate evaluation of backs and linemen produced similar results.

In-season programs are considered a form of detraining due to the reduction in volume and frequency of training. In a study by Campbell (1967) isometric elbow flexion strength increased over spring football practice, but isometric leg extension strength significantly decreased.

The study did not use an in-season resistance training program. The amount of both weight-bearing activity and leg stress involved in the sport might have contributed to the impaired isometric leg strength performances. In comparing in-season standing long jump performances to preseason and postseason measures, Hammer (1965) found in-season distances to be significantly shorter. All of these data suggest that a competitive sport season taxes sport-specific musculature and produces strength performance decrements. The use of an in-season resistance training program may eliminate these decrements. Data from Thorstensson (1977) suggest that performance in complex skills involving strength components (e.g., vertical jump) may be lost if not included in the training program. Thus, off-season sport training programs should include practice of vital skills.

Muscle Fiber Responses

Training adaptations are extensively discussed in chapter 7. Few studies have examined the effects of detraining on cellular level variables. In the absence of a resistance training exercise stimulus, muscle fibers tend toward their pretrained sizes (Thorstensson, 1977; Staron, Hagerman, & Hikida, 1981).

Table 8.1 depicts the effects of 7 months of detraining and dieting on an elite power lifter. The individual performed no resistance training during this period.

The data from this study (Staron et al., 1981) suggest that detraining results in a physiological shift from a strength profile to an improved aerobic profile. Three observations reflected this shift: the improvement of maximum oxygen consumption ($\dot{V}O_2$max), the improvement of mitochondrial density, and the improved oxidative enzyme profile of the muscle fibers. These changes occurred without any aerobic training stimulus during the seven-month detraining period. The large weight loss (27.5 kg) and reduction in body fat during this period may have accounted for some of these changes. The decrease in muscle fiber area contributed to the decrease in thigh girth. These observations are consistent with the traditional changes attributed to muscle atrophy (Fox & Mathews, 1981).

Data from Houston, Bentzen, and Larsen (1979) showed that muscle fiber areas in three of six well-trained runners tended to be larger after 15 days of detraining. In spite of the methodological errors related to the biopsy technique, it appears that complete detraining of endurance athletes may result in a shift to normal values of muscle fiber metabolism and size. In cases where training is necessary to maintain

Table 8.1   Physiological Changes After Seven Months of Detraining

Variable		Trained	Detrained
Ht (cm)		170.0	170.0
Wt (kg)		121.5	94.0
% body fat		25.2	14.8
Thigh girth (cm)		82.5	66.5
BP		146/96	137/76
$\dot{V}O_2$max ml/kg/min		32.6	49.1
HR max		200	198
Volume % mitochondria			
	slow-twitch	3.04	4.41
	fast-twitch	1.76	2.46
SO(%)		31.2	38.1
FG(%)		53.2	34.7
FOG(%)		15.6	27.2
Cross-sectional	SO	5,625	3,855
area (μm²)	FG	8,539	5,075
	FOG	9,618	5,835
(SO fibers smaller than fast-twitch fibers and smaller than FOG fibers)			

BP = blood pressure
HR = heart rate
SO = slow oxidative
FG = fast glycolytic
FOG = fast oxidative glycolytic

Note. From "The Effects of Detraining on an Elite Power Lifter" by R.S. Staron, F.C. Hagerman, and R.S. Hikida, 1981, *Journal of Neurological Sciences, 51,* 247–257. Copyright 1981 by the *Journal of Neurological Sciences.* Adapted by permission.

a competitive edge, physiological adaptations involving the muscle cell seem to be very sensitive to periods of complete detraining (i.e., no training activity). Detraining in athletes (strength or endurance) apparently shifts muscle fiber characteristics toward more control or untrained values. These data strongly support the need for year-round training to maintain adaptations of the muscle cell.

Aerobic Fitness

It has been well documented that aerobic fitness for both men and women is severely compromised following a period of complete detraining (Chi et al., 1983; Coyle, Martin, Bloomfield, Lowry, & Holloszy, 1985; Drinkwater & Horvath, 1972; Hendriksson & Reitman, 1977; Michael, Evert, & Jeffers, 1972). Reductions in aerobic fitness are related to metabolic and cardiovascular decrements resulting from a lack of training. Reduction in blood flow, oxidative enzymes, capillary density, and mitochondrial density all contribute to a reduction in aerobic capacity (Fox & Mathews, 1981).

Aerobic fitness, measured by maximum oxygen consumption, is not retained unless exercise intensity is maintained in training. In a study by Hickson, Foster, Pollock, Galassi, and Rich (1985) reductions in training intensity of one-third and two-thirds resulted in a 21% and 30% reduction in aerobic fitness, respectively. It has been shown previously that maintaining aerobic fitness gained during a five-days-per-week training program required a minimum of three days per week of training at the same intensity (80%) (Brynteson & Sinning, 1973). A maintenance program for aerobic fitness can decrease training frequency and duration but must maintain training intensity. Hickson et al. also revealed the importance of intensity in maintaining short-term endurance. Short-term endurance ($\cong$ 5 min) was maintained with a one-third reduction in intensity but not a two-thirds reduction. Thus, high-intensity, short-term endurance is very sensitive to drastic reductions in training intensity.

Few studies have documented the effects of detraining on competitive athletes. Examining competitive swimmers, Costill, Fink, Hargreaves, King, and Thomas (1985) discovered that in only one to four weeks significant changes occurred in the muscle which might reduce athletic performance. These major changes included a greater dependence on glycolysis and a reduced removal rate of lactate from the blood. A diminished oxygen transport system arising from a decline in the muscle's aerobic enzyme concentration as well as a greater concentration of lactate in the blood led to a reduction in performance. Another study observed significant decreases in exercise forearm blood flow in competitive swimmers in the third week of detraining, further supporting the hypothesis of a reduced oxygen transport system (Rochter, Rochelle, & Hyman, 1963). Two additional projects observed a reduction in muscle capillary density within three weeks of endurance detraining; the results point to the potential of underlying mechanisms to compromise the endurance ability of an athlete (Klausen, Andersen, & Pelle, 1981; Saltin & Rowell, 1980).

Physiological Detraining Summary

The effects of detraining are dramatic, especially for the competitive athlete who can lose in a short time period physiological adaptations associated with long-term training. In comparison with endurance adaptations, strength adaptations appear to be maintained for longer periods of time with a reduced training program. Exercise intensity is a key variable to stress in the design of maintenance programs for strength and especially for aerobic endurance. Periodization techniques enable the development of year-round training programs; this eliminates the periods of inactivity which lead to detraining effects. Figure 8.2 depicts the general effects of detraining.

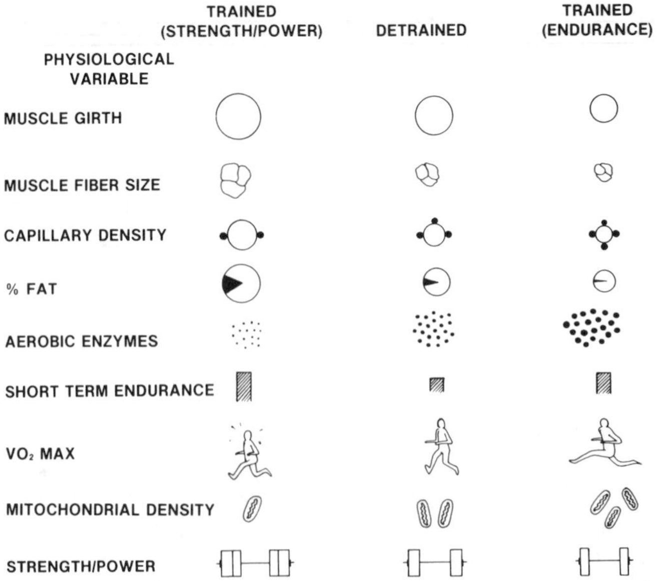

Figure 8.2 General detraining effects are presented.

Detraining the Bulked-Up Athlete

Little attention has been given to the detraining of the bulked-up athlete. Through resistance training many athletes gain substantial amounts of body weight. These weight gains are probably related to increased muscle mass necessary for successful participation in sports such as football.

Following an athletic career, chronic detraining leads to the potential of health and fitness problems. Obesity and a sedentary life-style often contribute to an increased risk of cardiovascular disease (Kraemer, 1983a). Many athletes who exercise for increased muscle mass and strength do not know how to exercise for health and recreation using other types of training (e.g., aerobic training). Consequently, the ex-athlete needs to start training again with new objectives, and to examine dietary habits in order to avoid large weight gains.

Studies have shown that, compared to nonathletes, former athletes have an advantage in cardiovascular fitness (Fardy, Maresh, & Abbott, 1976). This advantage did not exist in a comparison of former athletes with nonathletes who engaged in strenuous leisure-time activities. Little data exists with regard to specific athletic subgroups and lifelong health. One might speculate that athletes who require substantial body weight gains during their sport careers are at the greatest risk for cardiovascular diseases (CD). To reduce this risk, ex-athletes require the proper prescription of exercise, along with diet and weight control.

The modification of objectives and goals of resistance training programs, while recognizing that one can still enjoy resistance training, should reflect new training needs. This includes lighter loads (10–12 RM) and shorter rest periods to induce a higher caloric expenditure during the workout. Detraining of the resistance-trained athlete necessitates aerobic exercise programs for improving cardiovascular function and reducing body weight. As one grows older, a primary goal should be to reduce CD risk. The primary risk factors are as follows:

- Smoking
- High cholesterol levels
- High blood pressure

Other secondary risk factors include the following:

- Family history
- Diabetes
- Age
- Gender
- Overweight
- Stress

When individuals have all three primary risk factors the danger of heart attack is five times greater than when none are present (Fox & Mathews, 1981).

Management of these risk factors helps to reduce the risk of CD. It is easy to perform a risk factor analysis; this procedure has been described extensively in Kraemer (1983a) and Fox and Mathews (1981). Despite the fact that a strong genetic link is thought to be responsible for CD, former athletes should continue an active life-style with new goals and objectives for their training. The role of teachers and coaches is to educate students and athletes about lifelong health and fitness, exposing them to other forms of resistance training and cardiovascular endurance training. Frequently, it is possible to implement different programs either during certain periods in the training cycle or as a supplement to the regular exercise prescription. This adds variation to the program and also contributes to a healthy transition for athletes whose careers end after high school, college, or professional participation in sports.

Chapter 9

Women and Resistance Training

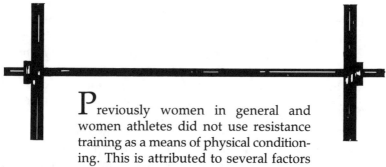

Previously women in general and women athletes did not use resistance training as a means of physical conditioning. This is attributed to several factors including the view that resistance training is not feminine, the lack of resistance training facilities available to women, and certain misconceptions about resistance training, such as the fear that it makes women look too muscular. Recently, however, the number of women and women athletes performing resistance training has increased tremendously, evidenced by the increase in the number of private resistance training facilities available to women, the number of women athletes using high school and university weight rooms, and the increased popularity of female body building and weight lifting contests. This chapter examines areas of interest concerning women and resistance training.

Sex Differences in Strength

Women's mean total body strength is 63.5% of men's total body strength (Laubach, 1976). There is a great deal of variation, however, from one body part to the next and in different movements of the same body part. Laubach found that upper extremity dynamic strength of women varies from 35% to 79% of men's, averaging 55.8%. Examples of the movements included within this range are lifting and/or lowering a resistance from shoulder height to full arm reach and pushing and pulling movements involving the arms. Women's lower extremity strength measurements vary from 57% to 86%, averaging 71.9% of men's. Lower body movements included knee and hip extension and flexion. All of these relationships are for the average male and female and are in absolute terms (i.e., not accounting for body size). Possible reasons for the difference in strength are variations in muscle mass distribution and quality of the muscle tissue; in addition, the difference may be attributed in part to the fact that in our society the majority of heavy physical labor is performed by males.

Several studies have examined the role of body size in the strength differences between men and women. One of these studies reports that, when body size is accounted for, women are weaker than men in upper body strength; but when body size is accounted for in leg strength, women are actually slightly stronger than men (Wilmore, 1974). Men proved 63% stronger in the bench press than women; accounting for body weight and LBM, men were still 54% and 45% stronger, respectively. In leg strength (squat and/or leg press) the men were 27% stronger; accounting for body weight, men exhibited approximately 8% more strength than women. Accounting for LBM, however, women demonstrated 6% greater leg strength than men.

A project using isokinetic testing of strength (Hoffman, Stauffer, & Jackson, 1979) supports the results of the Wilmore study (1974). The bench press of men was found to be 50% and 24% greater than women of average fitness in absolute terms and when adjusted for height and LBM, respectively. The leg press of men was 26% greater in absolute terms than women, but women had a 4% greater leg press than men when adjusted for height and LBM. The parity of leg strength in men and women, when expressed relative to LBM, may be attributed to a similar use of legs in daily life; that is, both sexes walk and run. The greater arm strength in men indicates a dissimilar use of the arms; that is, on the average men lift heavy objects with their arms more frequently.

A recent study (Falkel, Sawka, Levine, & Pandolf, 1985) involving isokinetic testing demonstrated that women's arm and leg strength is as great as men's when expressed relative to LBM. The study tested for elbow and knee extension and flexion. This study matched the men and women for absolute aerobic fitness: Relative to their own gender, however, the women were very fit and the men were only slightly above average fitness. This may explain the parity in arm and leg strength exhibited in this study when accounting for LBM.

Studies also report that men of average fitness are significantly stronger than women in both arm and leg strength, accounting for LBM; this proved true as well in a comparison with women on college basketball and volleyball teams (Morrow & Hosler, 1981). This study reported that women basketball and volleyball players exhibited strengths of 71% and 50%, in absolute terms, of the average college-aged male in isokinetic leg and bench press, respectively. Relative to LBM, the women athletes demonstrated 75% and 56% as much strength as the males in the leg and bench press, respectively (see Figure 9.1).

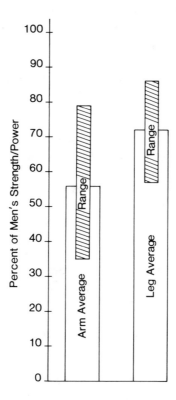

Figure 9.1 Range and average of various dynamic strength measurements of the average woman compared to the average man.
Note. From "Comparative Muscular Strength of Men and Women: A Review of the Literature" by L.L. Lauback, 1976, *Aviation, Space, and Environmental Medicine,* **47,** pp. 534-542. Copyright 1976 by *Aviation, Space, and Environmental Medicine.* Adapted by permission.

In summary the majority of research indicates that the average woman's absolute arm and leg strength is less than the average man's. If expressed relative to LBM, however, leg strength is equal for men and women. Arm strength expressed relative to LBM is normally less in women.

Training Effects

Does resistance training produce the same training effects in women as it does in men? Many people believe that women benefit less from resistance training than men (Wells, 1978). The research to date, however, demonstrates that resistance training is at least as beneficial, if not more so, to women as it is to men.

Women's $\dot{V}O_2$max (an indicator of cardiovascular endurance capabilities) increases 8% on the average with circuit weight training programs compared to the men's average of 5% (Gettman & Pollock, 1981). Endurance capabilities of the average women, therefore, increase more than that of the average man with circuit weight training. This difference in gains in $\dot{V}O_2$max may, in part, be due to higher cardiovascular fitness levels in the male trainees than the female trainees prior to the onset of the circuit weight training. Increases in LBM and decreases in percentage of body fat due to short-term resistance training programs (8 to 20 weeks) are of the same magnitude for women as for men (see Table 7.1).

Women can become very strong due to resistance training; at the 1985 Women's National Powerlifting Championships, a contestant squatted 534 lb, deadlifted 551 lb, and bench pressed 270 lb at a body weight of 165 lb. Due to resistance training, women gain strength at the same or greater rate than men (Wilmore, 1974; Wilmore et al., 1978). Over the course of a 10-week training period, women increased their leg and bench press 29.5% and 28.6%, respectively, and men increased 26% and 16.5%, respectively (Wilmore, 1974). The greater relative increase in strength of women compared to men, especially in the arms, is normally attributed to the fact that the average woman starts training at a lower level of fitness. Consequently, she is not as close to her genetic potential for strength and therefore makes greater initial gains in strength (see Figure 9.2).

Misconceptions about Women and Resistance Training

Many women don't perform resistance training because they are afraid that their muscles will excessively hypertrophy and subsequently look less feminine. This is not true for the average woman. The greatest increase in various body circumferences in women due to 10 weeks of resistance training was 0.6 cm (Wilmore, 1974). Such gains are virtually unnoticeable. In addition, hip, thigh, and abdomen circumferences actually decreased from 0.2 cm to 0.7 cm during the same time period. The trend of strength increases in women accompanied by very small increases in limb circumference is also apparent in other studies (Capen, Bright, & Line, 1961; Wells, Jokl, & Bohanen, 1973). The lack of large increases in limb circumference is good news to women who

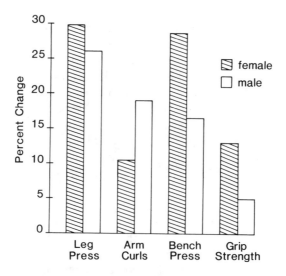

Figure 9.2 Male and female strength changes due to a 10-week resistance training program. *Note.* Data from "Alterations in Strength, Body Composition, and Anthropometric Measurements Consequent to a 10-Week Weight Training Program" by J.H. Wilmore, 1974, *Medicine and Science in Sports,* **6,** pp. 133-138.

want increased strength without increased size. Limb circumference does not increase in part because of the combination of small increases in muscle mass and a decrease in adipose tissue in the limb (Mayhew & Gross, 1974). Because muscle tissue is denser than adipose tissue, these two changes together yield no overall change (except perhaps a slight decrease) in limb circumference. The toned quality of firm, trained muscle tissue is also much more attractive than excess adipose tissue.

The inability of the average women to develop large bulky muscles is normally attributed to her low testosterone (male hormone) to estrogen (female hormone) levels. Males at rest normally have ten times the testosterone blood levels of females (Wright, 1980). Normally the relatively large increases in strength experienced by females in resistance training is accompanied by only small increases in muscle mass and either decreases in or constant total body weight. Any increase in muscle mass is typically balanced by a loss of adipose tissue, yielding no change or a slight decrease in total body weight (see Table 7.1).

Hetrick and Wilmore (1979) found that resting testosterone levels of women remain unchanged in an 8-week resistance training program. No relationship has been observed between blood testosterone levels and strength in college women (Fahey, Rolph, Moungmee, Nagel, & Mortara, 1976). This further suggests that resistance training will not cause excessive hypertrophy in the average female. In addition, some other mechanism must exist if muscle hypertrophy is not the major mechanism of the strength increases. Enhancement of motor unit recruitment as well as learning to perform the exercise are the likely mechanisms producing the strength increases (see chapter 6, neural adaptations).

Some women, however, do show increases in limb circumferences due to resistance training. A group of women athletes, after a 6-month resistance training program, exhibited an increase of 37% in upper body strength and 3.5 cm and 1.1 cm (5% and 4%) increases in shoulder girth and upper arm girth, respectively (Brown & Wilmore, 1974). Thigh girth in this same study increased 0.9 cm (2%). These larger increases in the limb circumferences of women athletes are probably due to several factors including: (a) higher than normal testosterone levels, (b) lower than normal estrogen to testosterone levels, (c) a genetic disposition to develop a greater muscle mass, and (d) more intense resistance training than the average woman may be willing to tolerate.

Another misconception is that women's resistance training should differ from men's. Comparisons of males and females who used identical resistance training programs demonstrate that women make the same, if not greater, gains in strength as men. This indicates that resistance training programs for women do not have to be different from those for men.

Female muscle has the same physiological characteristics as male muscle and, therefore, responds to training in the same fashion. Arm flexor strength of males and females is directly related to the arm flexor muscle's cross-sectional area (Ikai & Fukunaga, 1968). Muscles from both sexes are capable of producing approximately 6 kg/cm² of muscle (Ikai & Fukunaga, 1968); the quality of the muscle is equal for both sexes. An untrained woman's muscle, however, has only 68% and 71% of the fast- and slow-twitch fiber areas, respectively, as an untrained male's muscle (Drinkwater, 1984). In strength sports which rely predominantly on the anaerobic energy sources women athletes have 66% and 71% of the fast- and slow-twitch fiber areas, respectively, as their male counterparts. An untrained female's muscle (medial tibialis anteria) also has 20% fewer muscle fibers than has an untrained male's. There are some conflicting data concerning the concentrations of aerobic and anaerobic enzymes in male and female muscles. The majority of evidence, however, suggests that there is no difference between the genders with respect to enzyme concentrations (Drinkwater, 1984). It appears that the difference in strength between men and women is due not to a difference in the quality of the muscle but to the greater cross-sectional area and number of fast- and slow-twitch muscle fibers in males (see Figure 9.3).

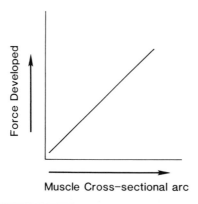

Muscle Cross-sectional arc

Figure 9.3 Male and female muscle have the same direct relationship concerning force developed and cross-sectional arc.

The preceding studies also reveal that there is no major physiological difference between female and male muscle tissue. Females may, however, have a tendency to store fat between the muscle fasicles (bundles) to a greater extent than males (Prince, Hikida, & Hagerman, 1977). This has no effect upon the trainability of the muscle tissue. From a physiological point of view, resistance training programs for women do not have to differ from those for men.

Many women as well as men don't perform resistance training because they are afraid they will become muscle bound: a reference to the lack of flexibility sometimes associated with improper resistance training programs. Resistance training can cause increases in flexibility. Women and men increased 6% and 8% in the sit-and-reach test (a common flexibility measure), respectively, during 10 weeks of resistance training (Wilmore et al., 1978). Weight lifters show no difference from various other groups of athletes in flexibility at the shoulder, elbow, knee, wrist, ankle, and hip (Leighton, 1957a, 1957b). When performed properly resistance training does not have a deleterious effect upon flexibility.

The beliefs that women will become excessively hypertrophied, that their resistance training programs must be different from those of men, and that resistance training will leave them muscle bound are unfounded. The scientific research leads to the conclusions that women will not become excessively hypertrophied, do not need programs different from men, and will in fact gain in flexibility during a properly performed resistance training program.

Menstrual Cycle Irregularities

Some women engaged in physical training experience variations in their menstrual cycles. Irregularities in the menstrual cycle which have been associated with physical training include: (1) oligomenorrhea, or an irregular menstrual pattern in women who previously had a normal menstrual pattern; (b) secondary amenorrhea, or the absence of menstruation in women who previously periodically menstruated; and (c) dysmenorrhea, or pain during menstruation. Research concerning any or all of the previously mentioned menstrual problems is not equivocal; the possible mechanisms responsible for these problems have not been fully determined. It should be noted that, in general, differences between individual females are considerable; it is therefore difficult to determine what is a regular, as opposed to an irregular, menstrual cycle.

Oligomenorrhea and Secondary Amenorrhea

Oligomenorrhea and secondary amenorrhea have been reported to be more common in women engaged in vigorous physical activity than in sedentary women (Gray and Dale, 1984; Loucks & Horvath). Of women participating in a body building contest, 33% not taking oral contraceptives reported having oligomenorrhea or amenorrhea (Elliot & Goldberg, 1983). Several factors have been implicated as possibly contributing to these menstrual irregularities. A low percentage of body fat, low body weight for height, and a rapid loss of body weight have been associated with menstrual irregularities (Gray & Dale, 1984; Loucks & Horvath, 1985). Changes in body composition may affect the menstrual cycle because adipose tissue is the site for conversion of androgens (male hormones) to estrogens (female hormones) and for conversion of certain kinds of estrogen to others. An alteration in body composition may change the estrogen levels in the body and therefore affect the menstrual cycle. It should be noted, however, that some athletes with a low percentage of body fat are not amenorrheic, some high-fat and heavy weight athletes are amenorrheic, and some athletes regain normal menstrual cycles with no change in body weight (Loucks & Horvath, 1985). Because of this variation, the exact role of body composition and oligomenorrhea and secondary amenorrhea is unclear.

In runners, greater training distance, speed, frequency, and duration of training season have all been implicated in causing menstrual irregularities (Gray & Dale, 1984; Loucks & Horvath, 1985). This indicates that athletes who train for long periods of time (daily and yearly) at high intensities have a greater risk of experiencing oligomenorrhea or secondary amenorrhea. Again, not all runners who train intensely for long time periods experience menstrual irregularities.

Aspects of reproductive history and maturity have also been associated with menstrual irregularities. The incidence of amenorrhea is higher in younger than in older women. One study reported that 85% of the runners experiencing amenorrhea were under 30 years of age (Speroff & Redwine, 1980). It has also been proposed that physical training at an early age delays menarche and that late menarche is associated with a greater chance of experiencing amenorrhea (Gray & Dale, 1984; Louck & Horvath, 1985). In one study, young ballet dancers reported an average age of menarche of 15.4 years, whereas normal females reported an average age of menarche of 12.5 years; this was a statistically significant difference (Warren, 1980). A previous pregnancy has also been associated with a decreased risk of amenorrhea (Loucks & Horvath, 1985). The mechanisms for any of these possible causes of menstrual cycle irregularities have not, however, been fully elucidated.

Psychological stress has also been associated with amenorrhea (Loucks & Horvath, 1985). Though psychological stress may cause changes in various neurotransmitters that regulate the reproductive system, exact mechanisms have not been fully determined.

Information to date indicates that women who have the highest risk of oligomenorrhea and secondary amenorrhea are young, engaged in intense daily physical training, and have both low body weight and low percentage of body fat. Some available evidence, however, contradicts the role of all of these factors in menstrual cycle irregularities. Therefore, the role physical training plays in precipitating oligomenorrhea and secondary amenorrhea is unclear.

Many physicians and athletes have assumed that menstrual irregularities are not serious and can be reversed by gaining body weight and decreasing training intensity and duration. There are reports of amenorrheic athlete's becoming cyclic after making these types of life-style changes (Loucks & Horvath, 1985). It is wise to consult a physician any time an athlete develops menstrual cycle irregularities to rule out other possible causes; such causes include anatomic defects and tumors on the glands controlling the reproductive system.

Dysmenorrhea

Dysmenorrhea, or abdominal pain due to menstruation, is reported by 60% to 70% of adult women, and it increases with chronologic and gynecologic age (Brooks-Gunn & Ruble, 1983; Widholm, 1979). Athletes report symptoms of dysmenorrhea less frequently and of less severity than the normal population (Dale, Gerlach, & Wilhite, 1979; Timonen & Procope, 1971).

An increased production of a hormone (prostaglandin) is associated with uterine cramping and is thought to be the cause of dysmenorrhea (Dawood, 1983). The lower frequency and severity of symptoms of dysmenorrhea in athletes could be due to several factors: lower levels of prostaglandin, or a higher pain threshold in athletes. In either case it appears that physical training decreases the incidence of dysmenorrhea.

Performance and Menstrual Problems

Dysmenorrhea could have a detrimental effect upon athletic performance due to the associated pain. Oligomenorrhea or secondary amenorrhea should, however, have no effect upon performance. Research indicates that the best physical performance probably occurs between the immediate postmenstrual period and the 15th day of the cycle (Allsen, Parsons, & Bryce, 1977; Doolittle & Engebretsen, 1972). Olympic medal performances have occurred during all portions of the menstrual cycle. Participation in physical training and athletic events should not be discouraged during menstruation and should have no detrimental effects upon physical performance.

Needs Analysis

The needs analysis for a woman in a particular sport or for general strength is conducted according to the outline in chapter 3. What it takes to be successful in a particular sport is dictated by the sport and not the sex of the participant. A training program for a particular sport is based upon what is required for successful participation in that sport; the athlete's individual weaknesses are essentially the same for either sex. Due to the absolute strength differences between the sexes, the major difference for men versus women is the amount of resistance used in the program.

The needs analysis for a woman must take into account her weak upper body musculature, in absolute and relative terms, as compared to a man's. The training program should stress upper body exercises in an attempt to correct this weakness in total upper body strength. This is accomplished by adding one or two upper body exercises and/or one or two extra sets than deemed necessary by the needs analysis.

The weak upper body musculature of most females also causes problems in the performance of structural exercises such as power cleans and squats. In these types of exercises females may find it very difficult or impossible for their upper bodies to handle the loads their lower bodies can tolerate. Good form for these exercises should never be ignored to allow the individual to lift greater loads. The sacrificing of form can cause injury to the lifter. Instead, the program should stress assistive exercises to strengthen the weak upper body musculature. It is important to be aware of the characteristics of women; this allows training programs to be better designed to the needs of this specific population. The next chapter discusses the needs and areas of concern for resistance training for prepubescent individuals.

Chapter 10

Children and Resistance Training

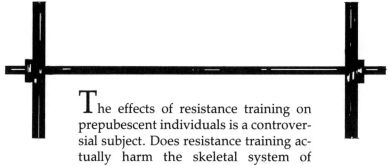

$\mathbf{T}$he effects of resistance training on prepubescent individuals is a controversial subject. Does resistance training actually harm the skeletal system of children? Will resistance training cause increased strength in children? These questions represent the core of this controversy and are addressed in this chapter.

The information in this chapter, especially that concerning skeletal injuries, stresses the difference between resistance training and weight lifting. Resistance training involves the performance of exercises in an attempt to make the individual stronger and more powerful. Resistance training *does not* have to involve the use of maximal or near-maximal resistances. In weight lifting (e.g., Olympic and power lifting) the object is to lift as much as possible of a particular exercise for one repetition. Training for weight lifting, consequently, does require lifting maximal resistances.

Skeletal System Damage

In addition to the possibility of injury normally associated with adults, the prepubescent individual is subject to injury of the growth cartilage. Growth cartilage is located at three sites: (a) the epiphyseal plate or growth plate, (b) the epiphysis or joint surface, and (c) the tendon insertion or apophyseal insertions (see Figure 10.1). The long bones of the body grow in length from the epiphyseal plates located at each of their ends. Normally, due to hormonal changes, these epiphyseal plates ossify after puberty. Once they ossify, growth of the long bones is no longer possible; an increase in the height of an individual is also no longer possible. Joint surface cartilage acts as a shock absorber between the bones that form a joint. Damage to this articular cartilage

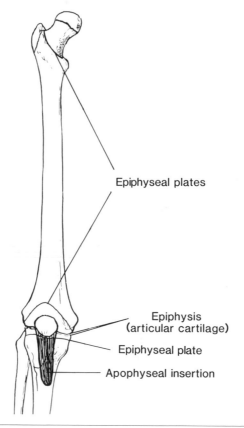

Epiphyseal plates

Epiphysis
(articular cartilage)

Epiphyseal plate

Apophyseal insertion

Figure 10.1   Locations of growth cartilage at the knee joint.

may lead to a rough articular surface and subsequent pain during movement of the joint. The growth cartilage at apophyseal insertions of major muscle-tendon-bone units insures a solid connection between the tendon and bone. Damage to the growth cartilage here may cause pain and also increase the chance of separation between the tendon and bone.

Acute Injuries

Acute injury refers to a single trauma causing an injury. The most commonly referred to acute injury risk for prepubescent weight trainers is a fracture at an epiphyseal plate. Cases of epiphyseal plate fractures in prepubescent weight trainers have been reported (Grumbs, Segal, Halligan, & Lower, 1982; Rowe, 1979; Ryan & Salcicioli, 1976). This area is prone to fracture in children because the epiphyseal plate has not yet ossified and does not have the structural strength of mature adult bone. All of these case reports involved overhead lifts (i.e., overhead press, clean and jerk) with near maximal resistances. These case reports reveal two precautions for prepubescent programs. First, maximal or near-maximal lifts (1 RMs) should be avoided in prepubescent weight trainers. Second, because improper form is a contributing factor to any injury, proper form of all exercises (particularly overhead lifts) should especially be emphasized with young resistance trainees.

Chronic Injuries

Chronic injury refers to repeated microtraumas causing injury; another common reference for this is overuse injury. Shin splints and stress fractures are common overuse injuries.

It is possible to damage all three growth cartilage sites due to physical stress. Kato and Ishiko (1976) have proposed that early heavy work by children may result in epiphyseal plate damage resulting in bone deformation. Repeated microtrauma to the shoulder due to baseball pitching results in damage to the epiphyseal plate of the humerus. This damage causes pain with shoulder movement and is often called little league shoulder (Barnett, 1985; Torg, Pollack, & Sweterlitsch, 1972).

The growth cartilage on the articular surface of prepubescent joints is more prone to injury than that of adults. This is especially true for the articular cartilage at the ankle, knee, and elbow. Repeated microtrauma appears to be responsible for many cases of osteochondritis dissecans at the elbow of young baseball pitchers (Adams, 1965; Lipscomb, 1975) and the ankle joint of young runners (Conale & Belding, 1980). The growth cartilage at the site of a tendon insertion onto a bone may be connected to the pain associated with Osgood-Schlatter disease. Although the cause of Osgood-Schlatter disease is not completely known, there is increasing evidence that it may in part be due to tiny avulusion fractures (i.e., pulling the tendon from the bone) (Micheli, 1983).

Back Problems

Repeated microtrauma can cause a compression fracture of the vetebral bodies (Hensinger, 1982) resulting in pain. During the growth spurt of many children there is a tendency to develop lordosis of the lumbar spine. Lordosis is an anterior bending of the spine, usually accompanied by flexion of the pelvis. Several factors contribute to the lordosis including enhanced growth in the anterior portion of the vetebral bodies and tight hamstrings causing the hips to assume a flexed position (Micheli, 1983). Acute trauma can also cause lower back problems, in adults as well as in children. In resistance training the acute trauma is equivalent to the frequent lifting of maximal or near-maximal resistances. In many cases, back pain is associated with improper form in the squat or dead lift exercises. In the performance of these exercises it is essential to keep the back in an upright position using the legs as much as possible. This keeps the torque on the lower back small and the resistance over the individual's feet, protecting the lower back from excessive stress. Back pain arising from overstress is caused by muscle spasm, damage to ligaments, or compression of vetebral discs.

Back problems due to resistance training are avoided by performing exercises that strengthen the abdominal muscles (e.g, sit-ups) and back musculature (e.g., good morning exercise, back hyperextensions). When performing exercises to strengthen the lower back, the resistance should be of light-to-moderate intensity thus allowing the performance of at least ten repetitions.

Strength Gains

Whether resistance training causes increases in strength in prepubescent individuals is controversial. Opponents of prepubescent resistance training claim that little if any gains in strength or muscle hypertrophy (beyond that due to normal growth) will take place in prepubescents due to their immature hormonal systems (Legwold, 1982). Serum testosterone levels do not rise after exercise in prepubescent males as they do in adults (see Figure 10.2). Testosterone is believed to be necessary for increases in muscle mass.

Significant strength gains in prepubescent males and females have, however, been reported (Micheli, 1983; Sewall & Micheli, 1984; Servedio et al., 1985). In all three of these studies prepubescents performed resistance training three times per week for 8 to 24 weeks; training involved both free-weight and machine-type exercises. The children's ages averaged 11–12 years. All three studies reported significant gains in strength in the resistance-trained groups over a similar group of children who did not perform resistance training. One study reported that after 24 weeks of resistance training the trained and untrained groups showed mean improvements in static strength of 52% and 2% percent, respectively (Micheli, 1983). After 18 weeks of training, a second study demonstrated a mean increase in strength

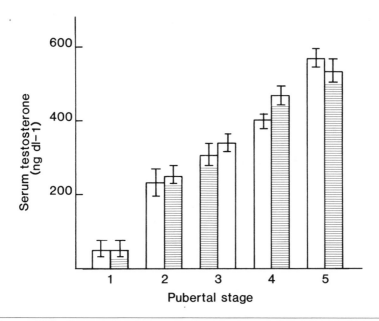

Figure 10.2 Serum testosterone levels prior to and following an exercise bout in prepubescent children. Pubertal Stages 1 through 5 refer to the maturity of the individual with 1 being very immature and 5 just reaching full maturity. *Note.* From "Pubertal Stage Differences in Hormonal and Hematological Responses to Maximal Exercise in Males" by T.D. Fahey, A. DelValle-Zuris, G. Oehlsen, M. Trieb, and J. Seymour, 1979, *Journal of Applied Physiology,* **46**, p. 825. Copyright 1979 by the American Physiological Society. Adapted by permission.

in the trained and untrained groups of 42.9% and 9.5%, respectively (Sewall & Micheli, 1984). All three studies noted no injuries to the children who performed resistance training. These studies clearly indicate that prepubescent males and females can both increase their strength due to resistance training and safely perform resistance training including free-weight exercises. An increased participation of young athletes in sports requires injury prevention programs. Resistance training facilitates the prevention of injuries in adults (see chapter 7, Prevention of Injuries); there is also evidence that resistance training helps to prevent injuries in adolescent athletes (Hejna, Rosenberg, Buturusis, & Krieger, 1982).

The research clearly demonstrates that resistance training of prepubescent males and females can cause significant increases in strength. These increases in strength can be achieved without injury to the children in a well-organized and supervised program. The possibility of acute and chronic injuries to children's growth cartilage is a valid concern. Therefore a resistance training program for children should not focus on lifting maximal or near-maximal amounts of resistance. The number of repetitions per set of an exercise should be at minimum approximately 10, with a resistance of no greater than a ten RM.

Programs for Children

The development of a prepubescent resistance training program should follow the same steps as that of a program for adults. These considerations are addressed in detail in chapters 1 and 3. In addition, the concern for possible injury to the child's growth cartilage must be considered in program development.

Needs Analysis

Children need to develop cardiovascular fitness, flexibility, and motor skills as well as strength. A resistance training program should not be so time-consuming as to ignore these other aspects of fitness in a child's development and to interfere with a child's play time. A well-organized and well-supervised program for children need not be any longer than 30 to 60 min per training session, three times per week. The resistance training program should be conducted in an atmosphere conducive both to the child's safety and to the child's enjoyment.

Prior to any exercise program including resistance training, all children should have a medical examination by a physician knowledgeable in sports medicine. This serves to prevent injury to a child whose physical condition is unsuitable for participation in a resistance training program.

Precautions Taken with Children

The concern for injury to growth cartilage and subsequently the need to use moderate resistances (10 RM) and high repetitions (10 minimum) per set are precautions that have already been discussed. Certain other precautions should be taken with children who perform a resistance training program.

All children participating in a resistance training program must be emotionally mature enough to follow directions. It must be impressed upon them that horseplay and failure to follow directions may lead to injury to themselves and/or their friends.

Proper form of all exercises must be explained and reiterated in a manner the children understand. Improper form of individual children should be corrected as soon as it is identified. This helps the children learn proper form and aids in injury prevention. This is especially true for exercises involving the lower back (squats, dead lifts, clean and jerk) and an overhead press movement (military press, clean and jerk). Contests of technique in various lifts rather than lifting of maximal resistances should be encouraged. This motivates the children to learn and use proper technique, and provides an outlet for the competitive urge found in many children.

The facility should have enough floor space to allow for the safe performance of the exercises. Spotting techniques should be continually stressed. The supervisor should monitor resistances to ensure that the appropriate resistances are being used by individual children. Because of the competitive nature of some children, they will want to attempt to lift as much weight as possible for one repetition. The supervisor must stress to these children that if they can lift 10 lb more for 10 repetitions they are obviously stronger and more powerful.

The age at which maximal lifts may be safely attempted by children is controversial. Though it depends on the physical and mental maturity of the individual child, a general rule is that maximal lifts are not to be attempted until the child is 16 years old.

Sample Programs

This section outlines two sample programs: one involves the use of either the child's body weight or another child's body weight as resistance; the other requires some resistance training equipment.

Programs Using Own Body Weight. Table 10.1 outlines the program involving the child's own body weight as resistance. This program can be performed in a circuit manner, moving from one exercise to the next, or in a set-repetition manner, performing all three sets of an exercise with a rest between sets before moving on to the next exercise. The proper execution of the exercises is shown in Figure 10.3.

The push-ups should be varied to include those performed with hands at shoulder width and those with hands wider than shoulder width. The latter place a greater stress on the chest muscles whereas the former stress the shoulder and upper arm to a greater extent. A modified push-up (i.e., knees as opposed to feet touching the ground) should be used by those children who cannot perform a normal push-up.

Table 10-1   Resistance Training Program for Children Involving the Use of Body Weight for Resistance

Exercise	Sets and repetitions
Push-ups	3 × 10–20
Bent leg sit-ups	3 × 15–30
Parallel squats	3 × 10–20
Self-resistance arm curls	10 contractions of 6 s duration
Toe raises	3 × 20–30
Partner-resisted lateral arm raises	10 contractions of 6 s duration
Lying back hyperextensions	3 × 10–15

Figure 10.3   Illustrations of exercises presented in Table 10.1.

The bent leg sit-ups require a partner to hold the individual's feet down. Parallel squats involve squatting until the thigh is parallel to the ground. During this exercise the feet should be kept flat on the ground or as near to this position as possible. Resistance can be added to this exercise by placing an object in the children's hands or, for older children, placing a partner on their back.

The self-resistance arm curls are performed in this manner: Place the elbow of the exercising arm in a fully extended position, with the hand palm up in front of the body; then grasp that hand with the opposite hand. During performance of the exercise, contract the elbow flexors, resisting with the opposite arm but allowing the exercising arm to reach the fully flexed position in six seconds. Then assume the fully extended position and repeat. This is performed 10 times with each arm.

Toe raises are performed by raising as high as possible on the toes. Resistance can be added by placing either an object in the hands or a partner on the child's back.

Lying back hyperextensions are performed by lying on the stomach and clasping the hands behind the head. A partner holds the child's legs down by placing his or her hands on the back of the exerciser's legs just above the knees. The individual then attempts to raise the chest and shoulders as high as possible. This should be performed in a slow, controlled manner. Finally, the chest is lowered to the ground and the exercise is repeated.

Partner-resisted lateral arm raises are performed by children's placing their arms at their sides. Partners grasp the arms slightly above the wrists, and each child then attempts to raise the arms laterally from the body while the partner resists. Each partner allows the exercising child's arms to reach the horizontal position in six seconds.

Program Using Free Weights. Table 10.2 outlines the program involving the use of free weights or resistance training machines. Initially, the resistance used for each exercise should be such that the minimum number of repetitions can be performed. Once it is possible to perform the maximum number of repetitions the resistance is increased so that again the minimum number of repetitions can be performed. Form and spotting techniques of all exercises should be continually stressed. The exercises should be performed in a controlled manner. This helps prevent injury to the trainees due to lost control of the weights. It also prevents damage to the weight stack of a machine or the free weights.

As with the push-ups in the first program hand spacing in the bench press is varied from narrow to wide. This varies the involvement of the shoulder, back of arm, and chest in the exercise.

Table 10.2   Resistance Training Program for Children Using Equipment

Exercise	Sets and repetitions
Leg press (or Squat)	3 × 10–15
Bench press	3 × 10–15
Leg curls	3 × 10–15
Arm curls	3 × 10–15
Leg extensions	3 × 10–15
Military press	3 × 10–15
Bent leg sit-ups	3 × 15–20
Back hyperextensions (or good mornings)	3 × 10–15

Bent leg sit-ups are performed with a sit-up board or on the floor. Resistance can be increased by raising the inclination of the sit-up board or by holding a weight against the chest during the exercise.

Back hyperextensions are performed either with one of the pieces of equipment for back hyperextensions or on the floor as described in the previous program. In either case, resistance is added by holding a weight behind the neck. Good mornings involve standing and bending over from the waist as far as possible, heavily involving the lower back. Resistance is added by holding a weight behind the head.

Resistance training is safe for prepubescent individuals and does cause gains in strength. Several precautions are, however, recommended: maximal or near-maximal lifts should not be performed, overhead lifts should be avoided, and the training needs to be supervised.

Suggested Reading

Position Paper on Prepubescent Strength Training of the National Strength and Conditioning Association. (1985). *National Strength and Conditioning Journal*, **7**, 27–31.

Chapter 11

Resistance Training Sports

We gratefully acknowledge the assistance of Tom Baechle, Creighton University, Omaha, NE; Keith Kephart, University of South Carolina, Columbia, SC; Dinni McCurry, Boston, MA; and Leo Toten, Littletown, PA in the preparation of this chapter.

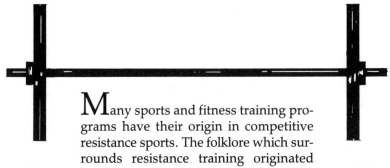

Many sports and fitness training programs have their origin in competitive resistance sports. The folklore which surrounds resistance training originated from the resistance sports of body building, power lifting, and Olympic lifting. A great deal of empirical evidence about training has been generated by athletes in these sports. Consequently, when resistance training became popular, coaches, athletes, and fitness enthusiasts looked to these individuals for help in designing exercise programs. Each resistance sport has very specific needs and objectives; it is important for a coach to have a broad understanding of resistance training in order to individually prescribe exercise based on the specific needs of the individual.

Patterning a program after body building, power lifting, or Olympic lifting is appropriate if the individual is interested in one of these sports; if the individual is an athlete in another sport or is simply interested in basic muscular fitness, however, improvements using one style of training may not be specific to that person's individual needs. In order to reach desired goals, combinations of training styles may be required. Using one style of training for both athletics and fitness is a common mistake in the prescription of resistance exercise. One who prescribes exercise to a wide variety of people (e.g., a strength and conditioning coach) must draw upon more than just his or her own competitive training experience. Some successful individuals in resistance training link their competitive experience to a solid educational background, an open mind, and an appreciation for the other resistance training sports. If the conditioning coach has neither a good resistance training background nor a basic understanding of research findings, that person's exercise prescription for other sports are frequently not specific enough to fully address the needs of the individual.

When examining published examples of competitive styles of training, it is important to realize that these training techniques are being used by experienced weight trainers with years of background experience. Some routines are too advanced for beginning and novice weight trainers. It is important for one to have a systematic approach to training goals (chapter 3) and then to work to achieve these goals. The purpose of this chapter is to give the individual a basic review of the three resistance training sports and the general concepts used in the different training programs they employ.

Body Building

The sport of body building gained great popularity in the 1970s. Today there are many amateur and professional body building competitions for men, women, and couples. Body builders have specific programs designed to address the following need for balanced muscular (a) size, (b) symmetry, and (c) definition (cuts). Body builders also spend a great deal of time developing their posing ability and specific routines for competition. A body building competition consists of judging each contestant on the three characteristics of balanced muscularity in different compulsory poses (flexed and unflexed) and a free posing routine. Body builders must also pay attention to cosmetic appearance (e.g., body tan, hair cut, etc.), which helps to enhance their competitiveness. Dietary habits which reduce body fat to a minimum also play a large role in final preparations for the contest.

As with any sport, body building has a wide range of training styles. There are, however, several basic components to all body building programs. In general, body building workouts are characterized for acute program variables according to (a) choice of exercise, (b) order of exercise, (c) load, (d) number of sets, and (e) rest periods.

Choice of Exercise

Body building workouts in general contain more exercises than the other resistance training sports. This stems from the belief that working a particular muscle at different angles and with several exercises will lead to optimal gains in muscle size. The use of many different exercise angles is also thought to contribute to the symmetrical appearance of the hypertrophied muscle. The body builder selects exercises which will develop and balance the body's appearance. In body building the aim is balance; certain parts of the body should not overshadow others. Beginners frequently concentrate on upper body musculature, letting their lower body lag behind. This nonsymmetrical development scores poorly in competitions. Because the sport involves posing, the competitor chooses exercises which develop the muscles used in mandatory or free posing routines.

Order of Exercise

Generally a body builder progresses from large muscle group to small muscle group exercises. Order is believed to be more important concerning the exercises that pertain to a certain body part than it is concerning the choice of which body part precedes the others. Many workouts are performed in a split-routine fashion: only certain body parts (e.g., back and chest) are exercised during a particular workout. This allows for a maximum amount of time to be spent on each body part. Body builders use many systems of resistance training but the most common is super setting (see chapter 4). The order of exercise becomes more important if super sets are performed in a workout.

Load

The majority of loads used by body builders typically range from 8 to 12 RM. Because the sport does not require the athlete to exhibit superior maximal strength there is no real need to train with exceptionally heavy loads. Many exercises prohibit the use of heavy weights because of the angles used, a poor mechanical advantage, and a small relative size of many of the muscle groups exercised. The load factor (8–12 RM) appears to be important in the performance of the large volumes (load × repetitions × sets) of exercise in body building workouts. This high-intensity volume stress may be a primary stimulus to the tissue hypertrophy observed in these athletes.

Number of Sets

It is most common for body builders to use multiple sets of an exercise. Sometimes as many as 10 to 15 sets are performed for a particular exercise, but usually 3 to 6 sets are used and a particular muscle is stressed from a number of angles. This requires several exercises for each muscle group.

Rest Periods

Probably the most distinctive feature of a body building workout, in addition to the high volume of exercise, is the short length of the rest periods. Rest between sets and exercises are rarely above 90 seconds and sometimes are less than 30 seconds. This variable appears to be important in promoting the muscular definition and vascularity observed in these athletes. It may also be a vital factor in helping individuals to maintain a high metabolic intensity which, along with diet, may contribute to the low body fat observed in these athletes.

Figure 11.1 shows a series of pictures which demonstrate various poses and the high level of body development exhibited by these athletes in competition. The following is a basic description of a typical body building workout. Notice the basic features that are common to all types of body building programs.

Figure 11.1 Sample body building poses.

Sample Body Building Workout
(Heavy = 80% of maximal lift or greater)

Monday
6:00 A.M. (BACK - HEAVY)

Warm-Up
2 × 12—Wide Grip Lat Pulls to Chest

Lat Pulls (Wide Grip)
2 × 10 to Chest
2 × 10 Behind the Neck
Low Cable Pulls
3 × 10-8-6 (Heavy)

Close-Grip Pull Downs
3 × 10-8-6 (Heavy)

Straight Leg Deadlifts
2 × 12-10 (Medium to Heavy)

Hyperextensions
2 × 25

10:00 A.M. (CHEST - HEAVY)

Warm-Up
2 × 12 Dumbbell Laterals   1 × 10 Flat Bench (135 lb)
1 × 10 Incline Bench   1 × 10 Flat Bench (Medium Wt)

Bench Press
3 × 10-8-8 (Heavy)

Semi-Incline
3 × 8

Incline Press (Bar or Dumbbell)
3 × 8

Dumbbell Fly
2 × 8

Tuesday
6:00 A.M. (SHOULDERS)

Warm-Up
2 × 12 Dumbbell or Machine Lateral Raises
1 × 10 Shoulder Press (Fronts)

Dumbbell Laterals
3 × 10-8-8 (Heavy)

Seated Press (Behind or in Front of Neck)
3 × 10-8-6 (Heavy)

Dumbbell Posterior Pulls
3 × 10-8-8

Upright Row
2 × 10

Shrugs
2 × 12-10

Neck Machine
2 × 12

Note the overlap and flow of the exercises. Also remember that on the previous day you did chest which involves a lot of anterior deltoid work. Be prepared to make necessary adjustments.

10:00 A.M. (ARMS)

Warm-Up
2 × 10 Curls   2 × 10 Tricep Extensions   1 × 8 Dips } SUPER SET

Preacher Curls (Low Cable)
3 × 10-8-6 (Heavy)

Tricep Extensions
3 × 12-10-8 (Heavy)

Straight Bar Curl (E-Z Curls)
3 × 8 (Heavy) } SUPER SET

Close-Grip Press
3 × 10-8-6 (Heavy)

Concentration Curls
2 × 8 } SUPER SET

Flat Back Tricep Extensions
2 × 10

Wednesday
10:00 A.M. (LEGS)

Warm-Up
2 × 12 Leg Extensions

Leg Extensions
3 × 12-10-10 (Heavy)

Front Squats
3 × 10-8-8 (Heavy)

Leg Press
3 × 10-8-8 (Heavy)

Double Leg Curl
3 × 10-8-8 (Heavy)

Single Leg Curl
3 × 10-8-8 (Medium)

Note. The front end of the week is *heavy* (80% or greater), concentrated exercise.

The second time through, the exercise is medium to moderate heavy, with higher reps.

Thursday
6:00 A.M. (BACK)

Warm-Up
Same as Monday

Low Cables (Standard or Reverse Grip)
2 × 12-10 (Slide second set—i.e., do 10, drop the pin 4 or 5 plates and do
        2 × 12-10-8 to 10 more)

Lat Pulls (Wide Grip)
2 × 12-10 Pull to Front—Slide Second Set
2 × 12-10 Pull to Back of Neck—Slide Second Set

Close-Grip High Pull Downs
2 × 12-10 (Slide Second Set)

Prone Leg Raises
2 × 20 (Use 10 lb Dumbbell)

Hyperextensions
2 × 20

} SUPER SET

10:00 A.M. (CHEST)

Warm-Up
Same as Monday

Incline Press Press (Bar or Dumbbell)
3 × 12-10-8

Semi-Incline (Dumbbell)
3 × 12-10-10

Flat Bench
2 × 10 (Slide second set, i.e., 1 × 10 at 255—Slide 50 lb
               1 × 8 to 10 at 205—NO REST)

Dumbbell Flys
2 × 10

Friday
 6:00 A.M. (SHOULDERS)

Warm-Up
Same as Tuesday

Dumbbell or Machine Lateral Raises
2 × 12-10 (Slide Second Set, i.e., Dumbbell = 35 lb × 8; 20 lb × 8)

Front Press
2 × 10

Cable Posterior Pulls
2 × 12-10 (Slide Second Set 10-8-8)

Upright Row (Low Cable)
1 × 12-10-10 (Drop the lb once, i.e., 8 Plates for 10
                                4 Plates for 10)

Shrugs
1 × 12-10-10 (Drop the resistance twice)

Neck
1 × 12-10-10 (Front & Back) (Slide Same as Above)

10:00 A.M. (ARMS)

Warm-Up
Same as Tuesday

Dumbbell Concentration Curl
3 × 10   } SUPER SET

Tricep Extension
3 × 12-10-10

Spider Curls (Arms raised laterally to shoulder height
               and curled in from that position)
3 × 10-8-8   } SUPER SET

Dips (With Weight)
3 × 10

Preacher Curls
2 × 10-8   } SUPER SET

Reverse Grip Push Downs
2 × 12-10

Saturday
10:00 A.M. (LEGS)

Warm-Up
Same as Wednesday

Leg Extensions
3 × 12-10

Hack Squats
3 × 12-10-10

Leg Press
2 × 12

Single Leg Curl
2 × 12-10

Double Leg Curl
3 × 12-10-8 (Forced Reps on Last Set to Failure)

Monday - Friday (Afternoon)
        Calves
1. Leg Press   Pick two movements-train one heavier
2. Calf Raisers   and try more isolation on the other
                                exercise
3. Seated Calf Raisers   Do 3 × 12 for each exercise (3 & 4)
4. Donkeys (Calf Raisers)

Tuesday - Thursday (Afternoon)
        Abdominals
1. Incline Hip Flexor   Start out with one general exercise (i.e,
2. Incline Sit-Ups   incline sit-ups) and as you fatigue, isolate
3. Incline Leg Raises   exercise to the part of the abdomen on
4. Rope Crunches   which you want to concentrate. As you
5. Weight Semi-Crunch become more fit add other exercises to
6. Crunches   your abdominal routine.
7. V-Ups

                    1. Incline Sit-Ups
                    2. V-Ups 3 × 20 for each exercise
                    3. Rope Crunches

This is primarily an off-season program. As you approach competition, adjustment must be made in sets, repetitions, length of rest periods, and number of days you exercise certain muscle groups such as the
abdominals. Diet and posing must be considered in the total training

program, so adjustments will be essential. (Above program developed by Keith Kephart, University of South Carolina.)

The above program is an example of one possible set of workouts. By manipulating the acute variables there are many other workout possibilities. The workouts have to be geared to the competition schedule. The primary systems of training (chapter 4) used by body builders are the following:

1. Super setting (exercising the muscle group at multiple angles with several exercises)
   Example: Back

Lat pull	10	10	10
Seated row	10	10	10
Bent over row	10	10	10
Wide-grip pull up	10↓	10↓	10↓
	Rest	Rest	Rest
	1 min	1 min	1 min

2. Burn sets (chapter 4)
3. Descending sets

10	10	10	10
Reduce	Reduce	Reduce	to
Load	Load	Load	Failure

   (one takes resistance off as each set progresses)

4. Multiple sets of an exercise
5. Agonist/antagonist orders
   Example:

Arm curls	10	10	10
Tricep extension	10	10	10
Rest period	1 min	1 min	1 min

Power Lifting

Power lifting is a relatively new sport, gaining Amateur Athletic Union (AAU) acceptance only in the early 1960s. Today men and women participate in local, state, national, and world championship competitions. The sport of power lifting consists of three lifts: (a) bench press, (b) squat, and (c) dead lift (see Figure 11.2). The winner in each weight class is the athlete who totals the most weight for all three lifts. Each competitor gets three attempts at each lift; competition entails giving

Figure 11.2 Executing the (a) bench press (b) squat and (c) deadlift.

a maximal effort every time a lift is attempted. Consequently, training is geared to performance of one RM lifts. A wide variety of training routines are used according to individual preferences. The deciding factor in evaluating a training program for power lifting is 1-RM strength in the three competition lifts. This is the primary objective of all training programs; the needs analysis for power lifting is well defined.

Choice of Exercise

In power lifting the training revolves around the three competition lifts. The bench press, squat, and dead lift are the core lifts in the program. Assistance exercises are then chosen which develop those muscles which assist or stabilize the primary movements of the core lifts.

Order of Exercise

The workout is typically centered around one or two of the competition exercises (bench press, squat or dead lift). The progression is from the larger (major lifts) to the smaller muscle groups (assistance exercises). This is done to allow for a maximal intensity during performance of the competition lifts.

Load

Since the criterion of this sport is one RM strength almost all loading is heavy. Typically, the load ranges from one to eight RM. Ten and 12 RM loads are used for warm-ups or when training is in a high-volume/low-intensity period. Most power lifters do not frequently perform singles or one RM lifts in training.

Number of Sets

Multiple sets are used in training. The number of sets can range from 3 to 10 for a primary exercise, followed by 3 or 4 sets of assistance exercises. The use of different loads for each set (i.e., pyramid programming) is a popular style of training.

Rest Periods

In this sport rest periods are long and are related to the particular load they follow. The heavier the load, the longer the rest period will be to prepare for the next set. Rest periods may range from two to five minutes, depending on the load.

Training Styles

Basic training style commonly includes the following:

1. Pyramid programming: (Full = 10 8 6 4 2 1 1 2 4 6 8 10)
   (Ascending Half 10 8 6 4 2 1)
   Singles (1 RM) are not usually performed on a regular basis. Performance of singles is reserved for the physical and mental preparation prior to a competition.
2. Multiple sets
   5 Sets of 5 or 6 RM
3. Forced repetitions
   The training partners help in completion of the lift when failure is reached. The bench press and other assistance exercises using smaller musculature are the most common exercises performed in this fashion.
4. Eccentric training
   This is commonly used when a variation in training is needed. One must be aware of the high amount of delayed muscular soreness associated with this type of training.
5. Functional isometrics
   This is typically used at sticking points within the range of motion of a competitive lift.

Cycling (Periodization)

Today most athletes utilize some form of cycling in their training. This concept was discussed in chapter 3. Another form of cycling includes the following program:

3 weeks	10 RM	3-4 d/w
3 weeks	6 RM	4 d/w
3 weeks	3 RM	5 d/w
3 weeks	1 or 2 RM	6 d/w

The number of weeks (two to six weeks) in each cycle and the RM load used for each exercise are highly variable and subject to individual preference. Some athletes will vary the number of training weeks for each training load. For example:

2 weeks	10 RM
6 weeks	6 RM

3 weeks	3 RM
2 weeks	1-2 RM

By manipulating the load and frequency of exercise the volume of exercise is controlled. Training cycles progress from high-volume/low-intensity to low-volume/high-intensity. This is done both to allow for a maximal exercise stimulus and to give the body time to recover and adapt to training. Specifically it allows the body to adapt to the heavy loads which are encountered in competition. Periodization plays an important role in developing maximal strength capabilities.

Sample Power Lifting Program:

All repetitions listed in this program are RM loads unless otherwise noted.

Monday
Warm-up – stretching

Bench Press: 10, 8, 6, 4, 2, 2, 4, 6, 8, 10; or multiple sets using RM load cycles

Assistance Exercises
  Incline Presses: 8, 8, 8
  Press Behind the Neck: 8, 8, 8
  Tricep Extensions: 8, 8, 8
  Bicep Curls: 10, 10, 10

Sit-Ups (Bent Leg) with load: 2 × 20
Crunches: 10, 10, 10

Calf Raisers: 10, 10, 10

Tuesday
Squats: 10, 8, 6, 4, 2, 2, 2, 6, 8, 10; or multiple sets using RM load cycles

Assistance Exercises
  Lat Pull Downs: 8, 8, 8
  Seated Rows: 8, 8, 8
  T-Bar Rows: 8, 8, 8
  Upright Rows: 10, 10, 10
  Leg Extensions: 10, 10, 10
  Leg Curls: 10, 10, 10

Thursday
Bench Press (Close-Grip): 6 × 8 (light day)

Assistance Exercises
  Incline Bench: 8, 8, 8

Press Behind Neck: 8, 8, 8
Tricep Extensions: 8, 8, 8
Bicep Curls: 10, 10, 10

Sit-Ups: 20, 20, 20
Hanging Knee-Ups: 10, 10, 10

Calf Raisers: 10, 10, 10

Friday
Dead Lift: 10, 8, 6, 4, 2, 2, 4, 6, 8, 10; or multiple sets using RM load cycles

Squats: 6 × 8 (light day)

Assistance Exercises
  Lat Pull Downs: 8, 8, 8
  Seated Rows: 8, 8, 8
  T-Bar Rows: 8, 8, 8
  Leg Extensions (doubles): 6, 6, 6, 6
  Leg Curls: 10, 10, 10

Wednesday, Saturday, and Sunday are days of active rest or complete rest. (Active rest consists of doing other recreational sport activities.)

Olympic Lifting

The sport of Olympic lifting has become popular throughout the world and is an Olympic event with over 60 nations competing. The two competitive lifts are the snatch and the clean and jerk (see Figure 11.3(a) and (b)). In this sport, as in power lifting, the goal is to total the most weight for the two combined lifts. Each competitor receives three attempts for both competitive lifts. The training goal is maximal strength development.

Choice of Exercise

Almost all of the exercises used in training for Olympic lifting are related to the two competitive lifts. The major component of both lifts is the pull movement; this involves pulling the weight as high as possible off the floor before the second phase of each lift. The legs, shoulders and back are the primary muscle groups which require strength for this sport. In addition, a great deal of work is focused on technique for the two lifts. Of all the resistance training sports, Olympic lifting

(a)   (b)

Figure 11.3 Executing the (a) snatch and (b) the clean and jerk.

involves the highest skill component; attention must be given to technique during each set.

Order of Exercise

Olympic lifting workouts progress from large to small muscle group exercises. In Olympic lifting very few exercises concentrate on small or single muscle groups. Some lifters, however, regularly perform leg curls to maintain a balance between the hamstrings and the quadriceps. Abdominal exercises are also regularly performed to balance the extreme hypertrophy of the spinal erectors and to prevent back problems.

Load

Olympic lifting loads are usually heavy (1 RM to 6 RM) and primarily directed toward strength development. When lighter loads (8 RM to 10 RM) are used, the primary concerns are cycling and technique work. The loads are frequently calculated based on the lifters best snatch, and clean and jerk. This is especially true for the primary exercises (i.e., snatch pull, clean pull, power snatch, power clean). Load varies considerably according to individual preference and to the particular cycling phase in which the lifter is training.

Number of Sets

The Olympic lifter uses multiple sets (three to six) of each exercise. With the importance of technique, the load and the number of sets are related not only to the training effect but also to skill development.

Rest Periods

As with power lifting, the rest periods for this sport are related to the loads used in training. Because of the high loads and the large skill component in the lifting movements, rest periods are relatively long; this allows sufficient recovery time so that the next lift can be executed in good form. Usual rest periods range from two to three minutes between both sets and exercises. As lifts become very heavy (1 RM to 3 RM), rest periods may range from three to five minutes. In an attempt to sustain high intensities, many lifters perform two training sessions per day with little or no increase in the number of exercises. The

Olympic lifter, in this manner, experiences almost complete recovery after completion of approximately half of the day's training.

Sample Olympic Lifting Program

Stretching should be performed for fifteen to twenty minutes prior to each workout session. Special attention to technique during all lifting movements is necessary. In addition, in all pulling-type movements it is important to move the load as quickly as possible. This develops skill at the speed necessary to successfully complete a snatch or clean and jerk.

(Loads for all exercises are calculated based on the lifter's maximal snatch and clean and jerk.)

Monday
AM

Front Squats	4 × 5 at 75%
Shoulder Shrugs (snatch grip)	4 × 5 at 80%
Jerk from Rack	4 × 4 at 70%

PM

Power Snatch	4 × 4 at 70%
Military Press	4 × 4 at 80%
Good mornings	3 × 6 at 40% (best clean and jerk)
Sit-ups	3 × 30 (20 lb)

Tuesday
AM

Back Squats	4 × 5 at 75% (maximal back squat)
Shoulder Shrugs (clean grip)	4 × 5 at 80%

PM

Power Clean	4 × 4 at 75%
Hyperextensions	3 × 6 (40 lb)
Sit-ups	3 × 30 (20 lb)

Thursday
AM

Snatch High Pull (from floor)	5 × 4 at 85%
Pull to Knees (from floor)	4 × 4 at 85%
Snatch Pulls from Hang	4 × 4 at 75%

PM

Shoulder Shrugs (snatch grip)	4 × 4 at 85%
Jerks from Rack	4 × 4 at 75%
Leg Curls	3 × 6 at 6 RM

Friday

	AM
Clean High Pulls	5 × 5 at 80%
Clean Pull to Knees (from floor)	4 × 4 at 90%
Power Clean from Hang	4 × 5 at 75%

	PM
Back Squats	5 × 5 at 80% (maximal back squat)
Shoulder Shrugs (clean grip)	4 × 4 at 85%
Leg Curls	3 × 6 at 6 RM
Sit-ups	3 × 30 (20 lb behind neck)

The AM and PM sessions may be combined if necessary due to time constraints. This, however, requires a decrease in the load as the training session progresses.

Wednesday and Saturday are active rest days with the performance of stretching and jumping drills. This sample training week is specifically for the start of the power phase of cycling. During other phases the load and the number of sets and repetitions are varied accordingly. Other exercises may be periodically substituted for the core exercises. Such substitutions include behind the neck press for military press or combination exercises (e.g., two power cleans followed by a jerk) for another primary exercise.

During the hypertrophy phase (early preparatory) the primary exercises are performed for 8 to 15 repetitions per set with resistances varying 60% to 70% of maximal load for an exercise. Heavier loads (95% to 100%) and fewer repetitions (one to three) are utilized during the peaking phase. In addition full snatches, full cleans, and full clean and jerks are substituted for the primary exercises during a peaking phase.

Closing Word to All Lifters

When designing a resistance program it is important to develop the goals of the program. Common goals are muscular hypertrophy, increasing the 1 RM of various lifts, and increased performance in a particular sport. Do not make the mistake of blindly adapting a program because it is used by a successful weight-trained athlete. Use the principles presented in this text, add your own creativity, and design a program individualized to meet your needs and situation.

References

Adams, J.E. (1965). Injuries to the throwing arm: A study of traumatic changes in the elbow joints of boy baseball players. *California Medicine*, **102**, 127–132.

Allen, T.E., Byrd, R.J., & Smith, D.P. (1976). Hemodynamic consequences of circuit weight training. *Research Quarterly*, **47**, 299–307.

Allsen, P.E., Parsons, P., & Bryce, G.R. (1977). Effect of menstrual cycle on maximum oxygen uptake. *The Physician and Sportsmedicine*, **5**, 53–55.

Alpert, M.A., Terry, B.E., & Kelly, D.L. (1985). Effect of weight loss on cardiac chamber size, wall thickness and left ventricular function in morbid obesity. *American Journal of Cardiology*, **55**, 783–786.

American College of Sports Medicine. (1978). The recommended quantity and quality of exercise for developing and maintaining fitness in healthy adults. *Medicine and Science in Sports*, **10**, vii–x.

American College of Sports Medicine. (1980). *Guidelines for graded exercise testing and exercise prescription*. Philadelphia: Lea & Febiger.

Anderson, B., Beaulieu, J.E., Cornelius, W.L., Dominguez, R.H., Prentice, W.E., & Wallace, L. (1984). Flexibility. *National Strength and Conditioning Association Journal*, **6**, 10–22.

Anderson, T., & Kearney, J.T. (1982). Muscular strength and absolute and relative endurance. *Research Quarterly for Exercise and Sport*, **53**, 1–7.

Ariel, G. (1977). Barbell vs dynamic variable resistance. *U.S. Sports Association News*, **1**, 7.

Atha, J. (1981). Strengthening muscle. *Exercise and Sport Science Reviews*, **9**, 1–73.

Barnett, L.S. (1985). Little league shoulder syndrome: Proximal humeral epiphyseolysis in adolescent baseball pitchers. *The Journal of Bone and Joint Surgery*, **67-A**, 495–496.

Barnham, J.N. (1960). *A comparison of the effectiveness of isometric and isotonic exercise when performed at different frequencies per week*. Unpublished doctoral dissertation, Louisiana State University.

Bass, A., Mackova, E., & Vitek, V. (1973). Activity of some enzymes of energy-supplying metabolism in rat soleus after tenotomy of synergistic muscles and in contralateral control muscle. *Physiologia Bohemoslovaca*, **22**, 613–621.

Belanger, A., & McComas, A.J. (1981). Extent of motor unit activation during effort. *Journal of Applied Physiology,* **51**, 1131-1135.

Berger, R.A. (1962a). Effect of varied weight training programs on strength. *Research Quarterly,* **33**, 168-181.

Berger, R.A. (1962b). Optimum repetitions for the development of strength. *Research Quarterly,* **33**, 334-338.

Berger, R.A. (1963a). Comparative effects of three weight training programs. *Research Quarterly,* **34**, 396-398.

Berger, R.A. (1963b). Comparison between static training and various dynamic training programs. *Research Quarterly,* **34**, 131-135.

Berger, R.A. (1965). Application of research findings in progressive resistance exercise to physical therapy. *Journal of the Association of Physical and Mental Rehabilitation,* **19**, 200-203.

Berger, R.A., & Hardage, B. (1967). Effect of maximum loads for each of ten repetitions on strength improvement. *Research Quarterly,* **38**, 715-718.

Blatther, S.E., & Noble, L. (1979). Relative effects of isokinetic and polymetric training on vertical jumping performance. *Research Quarterly,* **50**, 583-588.

Bonde-Peterson, F. (1960). Muscle training by static, concentric and eccentric contractions. *Acta Physiologica Scandinavica,* **48**, 406-416.

Bonde-Peterson, F., & Knuttgen, H.G. (1971). Effect of training with eccentric muscle contractions on human skeletal muscle metabolites. *Acta Physiologica Scandinavica,* **80**, 16A-17A.

Brooks, G.A., & Fahey, T.D. (1984). *Exercise physiology: Human bioenergetics and its applications.* New York: Wiley & Sons.

Brooks-Gunn, J., & Rubb, D.N. (1983). The experience of menarche from a developmental perspective. In J. Brooks-Gunn & A.C. Peterson (Eds.), *Girls at puberty: Biological and psychosocial perspectives* (pp. 155-177). New York: Plenum Press.

Brose, D.E., & Hanson, D.L. (1967). Effects of overload training on velocity and accuracy of throwing. *Research Quarterly,* **38**, 528-533.

Brown, S., Byrd, R., Jayasinghe, M.O., & Jones, D. (1983). Echocardiographic characteristics of competitive and recreational weight lifters. *Journal of Cardiovascular Ultrasonograph,* **2**, 163-165.

Brown, C.H., & Wilmore, J.H. (1974). The effects of maximal resistance training on the strength and body composition of women athletes. *Medicine and Science in Sports,* **6**, 174-177.

Brynteson, P., & Sinning, W.E. (1974). The effects of training frequencies on the retention of cardiovascular fitness. *Medicine and Science in Sports*, **5**, 29–30.

Caiozzo, V.J., Laird, T., Chow, K., Prietto, C.A., & McMaster, W.C. (1983). The use of precontractions to enhance the in-vivo force velocity relationship. *Medicine and Science in Sports and Exercise*, **14**, 162.

Caiozzo, V.J., Perrine, J.J., & Edgerton, V.R. (1981). Training-induced alterations of the in vivo force-velocity relationship of human muscle. *Journal of Applied Physiology: Respiratory, Environmental and Exercise Physiology*, **51**, 750–754.

Campbell, D.E. (1967). Maintenance of strength during a season of sports participation. *American Corrective Therapy Journal*, **21**, 193–195.

Campbell, R.C. (1962). Effects of supplemental weight training on the physical fitness of athletic squads. *Research Quarterly*, **33**, 343–348.

Capen, E.K. (1950). The effect of systematic weight training on power, strength and endurance. *Research Quarterly*, **21**, 83–93.

Capen, E.K. (1956). Study of four programs of heavy resistance exercises for the development of muscular strength. *Research Quarterly*, **27**, 132–142.

Capen, E.K., Bright, J.A., & Line, P.Q. (1961). The effects of weight training on strength, power, muscular endurance and anthropometric measurements on a select group of college women. *Journal of the Association for Physical and Mental Rehabilitation*, **15**, 169–173.

Chi, M.M.Y., Hintz, C.S., Coyle, E.F., Martin, W.H., Ivy, J.L., Nemeth, P.M., Holloszy, J.O., & Lowery, O.H. (1983). Effects of detraining on enzymes of energy metabolism in individual human muscle fibers. *American Journal of Physiology*, **244**, 276–287.

Chu, E. (1950). The effect of systematic weight training on athletic power. *Research Quarterly*, **21**, 188–194.

Ciriello, V.M., Holden, W.C., & Evans, W.J. (1983). The effects of two isokinetic training regimens on muscle strength and fiber composition. In H.G. Knuttgen, J.A. Vogel, & S. Poortmans (Eds.), *Biochemistry of Exercise* (pp. 787–793). Champaign, IL: Human Kinetics.

Clark, D.H. (1973). Adaptations in strength and muscular endurance resulting from exercise. *Exercise and Sport Science Reviews*, **1**, 73–102.

Clow, A.E.S. (1962). Treatment of dysmenorrhea by exercise. *British Medical Journal*, **1**, 4–5.

Cohen, C. (1975). The protein switch of muscle contraction. *Scientific American*, **233**, 36–45.

Coleman, A.E. (1977). Nautilus vs universal gym strength training in adult males. *American Corrective Therapy Journal*, **31**, 103–107.

Conale, S.T., & Belding, R.H. (1980). Osteochondral lesions of the talus. *The Journal of Bone and Joint Surgery*, **62A**, 97–102.

Cornelius, W.L. (1985). Flexibility: The effective way. *National Strength and Conditioning Association Journal*, **7**, 62–64.

Costill, D.L., Coyle, E.F., Fink, W.F., Lesmes, G.R., & Witzmann, F.A. (1979). Adaptations in skeletal muscle following strength training. *Journal of Applied Physiology: Respiratory, Environmental and Exercise Physiology*, **46**, 96–99.

Costill, D.L., Fink, W.J., Hargreaves, M., King, D.S., & Thomas, R. (1985). Metabolic characteristics of skeletal muscle during detraining from competitive swimming. *Medicine and Science in Sports and Exercise*, **17**, 339–343.

Coyle, E.F., Feiring, D.C., Rotkis, T.C., Cote, R.W., Roby, F.B., Lee, W., & Wilmore, J.H. (1981). Specificity of power improvements through slow and fast isokinetic training. *Journal of Applied Physiology*, **51**, 1437–1442.

Coyle, E.F., Martin, W.H., Bloomfield, S.A., Lowry, O.H., & Holloszy, J.O. (1985). Effects of detraining on responses to submaximal exercise. *Journal of Applied Physiology: Respiratory, Environmental and Exercise Physiology*, **59**, 853–859.

Cureton, T.K., & Phillips, E.E. (1964). Physical fitness changes in middle-aged men attributable to equal eight-week periods of training, non-training, and re-training. *Journal of Sports Medicine and Physical Fitness*, **4**, 87–93.

Dale, E., Gerlach, D., & Wilhite, A. (1979). Menstrual dysfunction in distance runners. *Obstetrics and Gynecology*, **54**, 47–53.

Darden, E. (1973). Weight training systems in the U.S.A. *Journal of Physical Education*, **44**, 72–80.

Davies, A.H. (1977). Chronic effects of isokinetic and allokinetic training on muscle force, endurance, and muscular hypertrophy. *Dissertation Abstracts International*, **38**, 153A.

Davies, C.T.M., & Young, K. (1983). Effects of training at 30 and 100% maximal isometric force on the contractile properties of the triceps surae of man. *Journal of Physiology*, **336**, 22–23.

Davies, R. (1966). A molecular theory of muscle contraction: Calcium dependent contractions with hydrogen bond formation plus ATP-dependent extensions of part of the myosin-actin cross-bridges. *Nature*, **199**, 1068–1074.

Dawood, M.Y. (1983). Dysmenorrhea. *Clinical Obstetrics and Gynecology,* **26**, 719–727.

DeKoning, F.L., Binkhorst, R.A., Vissers, A.C.A., & Vos, J.A. (1982). Influence of static strength training on the force-velocity relationship of the arm flexors. *International Journal of Sports Medicine,* **3**, 25–28.

DeLorme, T.L., Ferris, B.G., & Gallagher, J.R. (1952). Effect of progressive exercise on muscular contraction time. *Archives of Physical Medicine,* **33**, 86–97.

DeLorme, T.L., & Watkins, A.L. (1948). Techniques of progressive resistance exercise. *Archives of Physical Medicine,* **29**, 263–273.

DeLuca, C.J., LeFever, R.S., McCue, M.P., & Xenakis, A.P. (1982). Behavior of human motor units in different muscles during linearly varying contractions. *Journal of Physiology,* **329**, 113–128.

Desmedt, J.E., & Godaux, E. (1977). Ballistic contractions in man: Characteristic recruitment pattern of single motor units of the tibialis muscle. *Journal of Physiology,* **264**, 673–694.

DeVries, H.A. (1980). *Physiology of exercise for physical education and athletics.* Dubuque: Brown.

DiPrampero, P.E., & Margaria, R. (1978). Relationship between O_2 consumption, high energy phosphates and the kinetics of the O_2 debt in exercise. *Pflugers Archives,* **304**, 11–19.

Dohm, G.L., Williams, R.T., Kasperek, G.J., & Van, R.J. (1982). Increased excretion of urea and N - methylhistidine of exercise. *Journal of Applied Physiology,* **52**, 458–466.

Dominguez, R.H. (1978). Shoulder pain in age group swimmers. In B. Ericksson & B. Furong (Eds.), *Swimming Medicine IV* (pp. 105–109). Baltimore: University Park Press.

Dons, B., Bollerup, K., Bonde-Peterson, F., & Hancke, S. (1979). The effect of weight lifting exercise related to muscle fiber composition and muscle cross-sectional area in humans. *European Journal of Applied Physiology,* **40**, 95–106.

Doolittle, R.L., & Engebretsen, J. (1972). Performance variations during the menstrual cycle. *Journal of Sports Medicine and Physical Fitness,* **12**, 54–58.

Drinkwater, B.L. (1984). Women and exercise: Physiological aspects. In R.L. Terjung (Ed.), *Exercise and Sport Science Reviews* (pp. 21–52). Lexington, MA: Callamore Press.

Drinkwater, B.L., & Horvath, S.M. (1972). Detraining effects on young women. *Medicine and Science in Sports,* **4**, 91–95.

Dudley, G.A. & Djamil, R. (1985). Incompatibility of endurance and strength training modes of exercise. *Journal of Applied Physiology: Respiratory, Environmental and Exercise Physiology*, **59**, 1336-1451.

Edgerton, V.R. (1976). Neuromuscular adaptation to power and endurance work. *Canadian Journal of Applied Sport Science*, **1**, 49-58.

Edgerton, V.R. (1978). Mammalian muscle fiber types and their adaptability. *American Zoologist*, **18**, 113-125.

Elliot, D.L., & Goldberg, L. (1983). Weight lifting and amenorrhea. *Journal of the American Medical Association*, **249**, 354.

Essen, B., Jansson, E., Henriksson, J., Taylor, A.W., & Saltin, B. (1975). Metabolic characteristics of fiber types in human skeletal muscle. *Acta Physiologica Scandinavica*, **95**, 153-165.

Exner, G.U., Staudte, H.W., & Pette, D. (1973). Isometric training of rats—effects upon fast and slow muscle and modification by an anabolic hormone in female rats. *Pflugers Archives*, **345**, 1-14.

Fahey, T.D., Akka, L., & Rolph, R. (1975). Body composition and VO₂max of exceptional weight trained athletes. *Journal of Applied Physiology*, **39**, 559-561.

Fahey, T.D., & Brown, C.H. (1973). The effects of anabolic steroid on the strength, body composition and endurance of college males when accompanied by a weight training program. *Medicine and Science in Sports*, **5**, 272-276.

Fahey, T.D., DelValle-Zuris, A., Oehlsen, G., Trieb, M., & Seymour, J. (1979). Pubertal stage differences in hormonal and hematological responses to maximal exercise in males. *Journal of Applied Physiology*, **46**, 823-827.

Fahey, T.D., Rolph, R., Moungmee, P., Nagel, J., & Mortara, S. (1976). Serum testosterone, body composition and strength of young adults. *Medicine and Science in Sports*, **8**, 31-34.

Falch, J.A. (1982). The effect of physical activity on the skeleton. *Scandinavian Journal of Social Medicine*, **29** (Suppl.), 55-58.

Falkel, J.E., Murphy, J.A., Murray, T.F., & Cox, J.B. *Effect of resistive exercise on shoulder external rotation strength and endurance in swimmers*. Manuscript submitted for publication.

Falkel, J.E., Sawka, M.N., Levine, L., & Pandolf, K.B. (1985). Upper to lower body muscular strength and endurance ratios for women and men. *Ergonomics*, **28** (12), 1661-1670.

Fardy, P.S. (1969). Effects of soccer training and detraining upon selected cardiac and metabolic measures. *Research Quarterly*, **40**, 503-509.

Fardy, P.S. (1977). Training for aerobic power. In E.J. Burke (Ed.), *Toward an understanding of human performance* (pp. 10-14). Ithaca: Movement.

Fardey, P.S., Maresh, C.M., Abbott, R., & Kristiansen, T. (1976). An assessment of the influence of habitual physical activity, prior sport participation, smoking habits and aging upon indices of cardio-vascular fitness: Preliminary report of a cross-section and retrospective study. *Journal of Sports Medicine and Physical Fitness*, **16**, 77-90.

Farrell, P.A., Maksud, M.G., Pollock, M.L., Foster, C., Anholm, J., Hare, J., & Leon, A.S. (1982). A comparison of plasma cholesterol, triglycerides and high density lipoprotein-cholesterol in speed skaters, weightlifters and non-athletes. *European Journal of Applied Physiology*, **48**, 77-82.

Fleck, S.J. (1979). Varying frequency and intensity of isokinetic strength training. *Dissertation Abstracts International*, **39**, 2126A.

Fleck, S.J. (1983). Body composition of elite American athletes. *American Journal of Sports Medicine*, **11**, 298-403.

Fleck, S.J., Bennett, J.B., Kraemer, W.J., & Baechle, T. (in press). Echocardiography in highly strength trained males. *Proceedings: 2nd International Congress on Sports Cardiology.*

Fleck, S.J., Case, S., Puhl, J., & Van Handle, P. (1985). Physical and physiological characteristics of elite women volleyball players. *Canadian Journal of Applied Sport Sciences*, **10**, 122-126.

Fleck, S.J., & Dean, L.S. (in press). Influence of weight training experience on blood pressure response to exercise. *Journal of Applied Physiology.*

Fleck, S.J., & Falkel, J.E. (1986). Value of resistance training for the reduction of sports injuries. *Sports Medicine*, **3**, 61-68.

Fleck, S.J., & Schutt, R.C. (1985). Types of strength training. *Clinics in Sports Medicine*, **4**, 159-168.

Fox, E.L. (1979). *Sports physiology.* Philadelphia: Saunders.

Fox, E.L., & Mathews, D.K. (1974). *Interval training.* Philadelphia: Saunders.

Fox, E.L., & Mathews, D.K. (1981). *The physiological basis of physical education and athletics.* Philadelphia: Saunders.

Freedson, P.S., Michevic, P.M., Loucks, A.B., & Birandola, R.N. (1983). Physique, body composition, and psychological characteristics of competitive female body builders. *The Physician and Sportsmedicine*, **11**, 85-93.

Frisch, R.E., & McArthur, J.W. (1974). Menstrual cycles: Fatness as a determinant of minimum weight and height necessary for their maintenance or onset. *Science, 185*, 949–951.

Froelicher, V.F. (1983). *Exercise testing and training.* New York: LeJacq.

Gajda, B. (1965). The new revolutionary phase or sequence system of training. *Iron Man, 26*, 14–17.

Galbo, H. (1983). *Hormonal and metabolic adaptation to exercise.* New York: Thieme-Stratton.

Gardner, G. (1963). Specificity of strength changes of the exercised and nonexercised limb following isometric training. *Research Quarterly, 34*, 98–101.

Garhammer, J. (1981). Equipment for the development of athletic strength and power. *National Strength and Conditioning Association Journal, 3*, 24–26.

Gasser, G.A., & Brooks, G.A. (1979). Metabolism and lactate after prolonged exercise to exhaustion. *Medicine and Science in Sports, 11*, 76.

Gettman, L.R., Ayres, J.J., Pollock, M.L., Durstine, J.C., & Grantham, W. (1979). Physiological effects on adult men of circuit strength training and jogging. *Archives of Physical Medicine and Rehabilitation, 60*, 115–120.

Gettman, L.R., Ayres, J.J., Pollock, M.L., & Jackson, A. (1978). The effect of circuit weight training on strength, cardiorespiratory function and body composition of adult men. *Medicine and Science in Sports, 10*, 171–176.

Gettman, L.R., Culter, L.A., & Strathman, T. (1980). Physiological changes after 20 weeks of isotonic vs isokinetic circuit training. *Journal of Sports Medicine and Physical Fitness, 20*, 265–274.

Gettman, L.R., & Pollock, M.L. (1981). Circuit weight training: A critical review of its physiological benefits. *The Physician and Sportsmedicine, 9*, 44–60.

Gilliam, G.M. (1981). Effects of frequency of weight training on muscle strength enhancement. *Journal of Sports Medicine, 21*, 432–436.

Gladden, L.B., & Colacino, D. (1978). Characteristics of volleyball players and success in a national tournament. *Journal of Sports Medicine and Physical Fitness, 18*, 57–64.

Goldberg, A.L. (1971). Biochemical events during hypertrophy of skeletal muscle. In N. Alpert (Ed.), *Cardiac hypertrophy* (pp. 301-314). New York: Academic Press.

Goldberg, A.L., Elliot, D.L., Schutz, R.W., & Kloster, F.E. (1984). Changes in lipid and lipoprotein levels after weight training. *Journal of the American Medical Association, 252,* 504-506.

Goldberg, A.L., Eltinger, J.D., Goldspink, L.F., & Jablecki, D. (1975). Mechanism of work-induced hypertrophy of skeletal muscle. *Medicine in Science and Sports, 7,* 248-261.

Goldberg, A.L., & Goodman, H. (1969). Relationship between growth hormone and muscular work in determining muscle size. *Journal of Physiology, 200,* 655-666.

Goldspink, G., Larson, R.E., & Davies, R.E. (1970). The immediate energy supply and the cost of maintenance of isometric tension for different muscles in the hamster. *Aeitschrift Fuer Vergleichende Physioloigie, 66,* 389-397.

Gollnick, P.D., Parsons, D., Reidy, M., & Moore, R.L. (1983). Fiber number and size in overloaded chicken anterior latissimus dorsi muscle. *Journal of Applied Physiology: Respiratory, Environmental and Exercise Physiology, 54,* 1291-1297.

Gollnick, P.D., Timson, B.F., Moore, R.L., & Riedy, M. (1981). Muscular enlargement and number of fibers in skeletal muscles of rats. *Journal of Applied Physiology: Respiratory, Environmental and Exercise Physiology, 50,* 936-943.

Gonyea, W.J. (1980). Role of exercise in inducing increases in skeletal muscle fiber number. *Journal of Applied Physiology: Respiratory, Environmental and Exercise Physiology, 48,* 421-426.

Gonyea, W.J., & Sale, D. (1982). Physiology of weight-lifting exercise. *Archives of Physical Medicine and Rehabilitation, 63,* 235-237.

Gordon, E. (1967). Anatomical and biochemical adaptations of muscle to different exercises. *Journal of the American Medical Association, 201,* 755-758.

Gray, D.P., & Dale, E. (1984). Variables associated with secondary amenorrhea in women runners. *Journal of Sports Sciences, 1,* 55-67.

Grimby, G., Bjorntrop, P., Fahlen, M., Hoskins, T.A., Hook, O., Oxhof, H., & Saltin, B. (1973). Metabolic effects of isometric training. *Scandinavian Journal of Clinical Laboratory Investigation, 31,* 301-305.

Grimby, L., & Hannerz, J. (1977). Firing rate and recruitment order of toe extensor motor units in different modes of voluntary contraction. *Journal of Physiology* (London), *264,* 865-879.

Grimby, L., Hannerz, J., & Hedman, B. (1981). The fatigue and voluntary discharge properties of single motor units in man. *Journal of Physiology, 36,* 545-554.

Gruchow, W., & Pelleiter, P. (1979). An epidemiologic study of tennis elbow. *American Journal of Sports Medicine, 7,* 234-238.

Grumbs, V.L., Segal, D., Halligan, J.B., & Lower, G. (1982). Bilateral distal radius and ulnar fractures in adolescent weight lifters. *American Journal of Sports Medicine, 10,* 375-379.

Haar, Romeny, B.M., Denier Van Der Gon, J.J., & Gielen, C.C. (1982). Changes in recruitment order of motor units in the human biceps muscle. *Experimental Neurology, 78,* 360-368.

Haggmark, T., Jansson, E., & Eriksson, E. (1982). Fiber type area and metabolic potential of the thigh muscle in man after knee surgery and immobilization. *International Journal of Sports Medicine, 2,* 12-17.

Haggmark, T., Jansson, E., & Svane, B. (1978). Cross-sectional area of the thigh muscle in man measured by computed tomography. *Scandinavian Journal of Clinical Laboratory Investigation, 38,* 355-360.

Hakkinen, K. (1985). Factors influencing trainability of muscular strength during short term and prolonged training. *National Strength and Conditioning Association Journal, 7,* 32-37.

Hakkinen, K., Alen, M., & Komi, P.V. (1984). Neuromuscular, anaerobic, and aerobic performance of elite power athletes. *European Journal of Applied Physiology, 53,* 97-105.

Hakkinen, K., & Komi, P.V. (1981). Effect of different combined concentric and eccentric muscle work regimens on maximal strength development. *Journal of Human Movement Studies, 7,* 33-44.

Hakkinen, K., & Komi, P.V. (1983). Changes in neuromuscular performance in voluntary and reflex contraction during strength training in man. *International Journal of Sports Medicine, 4,* 282-288.

Hammer, W.M. (1965). Physiological and performance changes during periods of football training and detraining. *Journal of Sports Medicine and Physical Fitness, 5,* 72-75.

Harman, E. (1983). Resistive torque analysis of 5 nautilus exercise machines. *Medicine and Science in Sports and Exercise, 15,* 113.

Hatfield, F.C., & Krotee, M.L. (1978). *Personalized weight training for fitness and athletics from theory to practice.* Dubuque: Kendall/Hunt.

Hawkins, R.J., & Kennedy, J.C. (1980). Impingement syndrome in athletes. *American Journal of Sports Medicine, 8,* 151-158.

Hejna, W.F., Rosenberg, A., Buturusis, D.J., & Krieger, A. (1982). The prevention of sports injuries in high school students through strength training. *National Strength and Conditioning Association Journal, 4,* 28-31.

Henderson, J.M. (1970). The effects of weight loadings and repetitions, frequency of exercise and knowledge of theoretical principles of weight training on changes in muscular strength. *Dissertation Abstracts International,* **31A**, 3320.

Henriksson, J., & Reitman, J.S. (1977). Time course of changes in human skeletal muscle succinate dehydrogenase and cytochrome-oxidases activities and maximal oxygen uptake with physical activity and inactivity. *Acta Physiologica Scandinavica,* **99**, 91–97.

Henriksson-Larsen, K. (1985). Distribution, number, and size of different types of fibers in whole cross-sections of female in tibialis anterior: An enzyme histochemical study. *Acta Physiologica Scandinavica,* **123**, 229–235.

Hensinger, R.N. (1982). Back pain and vertebral changes simulating Scheuermann's disease. *Orthopaedic Transactions,* **6**, 1.

Hermansen, L., Machlum, S., Pruett, E.R., Vaage, O., Waldrum, H., & Wessel-Aas, T. (1976). Lactate removal at rest and during exercise. In H. Howard & J.R. Pootsmans (Eds.), *Metabolic adaptation to prolonged physical exercise* (pp. 101–105). Basel, Switzerland: Birhauser Verlag.

Hetrick, G.A., & Wilmore, J.H. (1979). Androgen levels and muscle hypertrophy during an eight week weight training program for men/women. *Medicine and Science in Sports,* **11**, 102.

Hettinger, R. (1961). *Physiology of strength.* Springfield, IL: Charles C. Thomas.

Hettinger, R., & Muller, E. (1953). Muskelleistung und muskeltraining. *Arbeits Physiology,* **15**, 111–126.

Hickson, R.C. (1980). Interference of strength development by simultaneously training strength and endurance. *European Journal of Applied Physiology,* **45**, 255–263.

Hickson, R.C., Foster, C., Pollock, M.L., Galassi, T.M., & Rich, S. (1985). Reduced training intensities and loss of aerobic power, endurance and cardiac growth. *Journal of Applied Physiology,* **58**, 492–499.

Ho, K.W., Roy, R.R., Tweedle, C.D., Heusner, W.W., Van Huss, W.D., & Carrow, R. (1980). Skeletal muscle fiber splitting with weight-lifting exercise in rats. *American Journal of Anatomy,* **157**, 433–440.

Hoffman, T., Stauffer, R.W., & Jackson, A.S. (1979). Sex difference in strength. *American Journal of Sports Medicine,* **7**, 265–267.

Holmdahl, D.C., & Ingelmark, R.E. (1948). Der bau des gelenknorpels unterverschiedenen funktionellen verhaltnissen. *Acta Anatomy,* **6,** 113–116.

Horvath, B. (1959). What's new in muscles? *Muscle Sculpture,* **2,** 39–44.

Houston, M.E., Bentzen, H., & Larsen, H. (1979). Interrelationship between skeletal muscle adaptations and performance as studied by detraining and retraining. *Acta Physiologica Scandinavica,* **105,** 163–170.

Howald, H. (1982). Training-induced morphological and functional changes in skeletal muscle. *International Journal of Sports Medicine,* **3,** 1–12.

Hultman, E., Bergtrom, J., & McLennan, N.A. (1967). Breakdown and resynthesis of phosphorylcreatine and adenosine triphosphate in connection with muscular work in man. *Scandinavian Journal of Clinical Laboratory Investigation,* **19,** 56–66.

Hunter, G.R. (1985). Changes in body composition, body build and performance associated with different weight training frequencies in males and females. *National Strength and Conditioning Association Journal,* **7,** 26–28.

Hurley, B.F., Seals, D.R., Ehsani, A.A., Cartier, L.J., Dalsky, G.P., Hagberg, J.M., & Holloszy, J.O. (1984a). Effects of high-intensity strength training on cardiovascular function. *Medicine and Science in Sports and Exercise,* **16,** 483–488.

Hurley, B.F., Seals, D.R., Hagberg, J.M., Goldberg, A.C., Ostrove, S.M., Holloszy, J.O., Wiest, W.G., & Goldberg, A.P. (1984b). High density lipoprotein cholesterol in body builders vs power lifters. *Journal of the American Medical Association,* **252,** 507–513.

Huxley, H. (1969). The mechanism of muscular contraction. *Science,* **164,** 1356–1366.

Ikai, M., & Fukunaga, T. (1968). Calculation of muscle strength per unit cross-sectional area of human muscle by means of ultrasonic measurements. *International Zeitschrift Fur Angewandte Physiologie,* **26,** 26–32.

Ikai, M., & Fukunaga, T. (1970). A study on training effect on strength per unit cross-sectional area of muscle by means of ultrasonic measurement. *European Journal of Applied Physiology,* **28,** 173–180.

Ikai, M., & Steinhaus, A.H. (1961). Some factors modifying the expression of human strength. *Journal of Applied Physiology,* **16,** 157–163.

Ingelmark, B.E., & Elsholm, R. (1948). A study on variations in the thickness of the articular cartilage in association with rest and periodical load. *Uppsala Lakaretorenings Foxhandlingar, 53,* 61–64.

Ingjer, F. (1979). Effects of endurance training on muscle fiber ATP-ase activity, capillary supply and mitochondrial content in man. *Journal of Physiology, 294,* 419–432.

Jackson, A., Jackson, T., Hnatek, J., & West, J. (1985). Strength development: Using functional isometrics in an isotonic strength training program. *Research Quarterly for Exercise and Sport, 56,* 234-237.

Jensen, C., & Fisher, G. (1979). *Scientific basis of athletic conditioning.* Philadelphia: Lea and Febiger.

Johnson, B.L., Adamczy, K.J.W., Tennoe, K.O., & Stromme, S.B. (1976). A comparison of concentric and eccentric muscle training. *Medicine and Science in Sports, 8,* 35–38.

Jones, A. (1973). The best kind of exercise. *Ironman, 32,* 36–38.

Kamen, G., Kroll, W., & Zigon, S.T. (1984). Exercise effects upon reflex time components in weight lifters and distance runners. *Medicine and Science in Sports and Exercise, 13,* 198–204.

Kanehisa, H., & Miyashita, M. (1983a). Effect of isometric and isokinetic muscle training on static strength and dynamic power. *European Journal of Applied Physiology, 50,* 365–371.

Kanehisa, H., & Miyashita, M. (1983b). Specificity of velocity in strength training. *European Journal of Applied Physiology, 52,* 104–106.

Karlsson, J., Bonde-Petersen, F., Henriksson, J., & Knuttgen, H.G. (1975). Effects of previous exercise with arms or legs on metabolism and performance in exhaustive exercise. *Journal of Applied Physiology, 38,* 208–211.

Katch, F.I., Pechar, G.S., Pardew, D., & Smith, L.E. (1975). Neuromotor specificity of isokinetic bench training in women. *Medicine and Science in Sports, 7,* 77.

Katch, V.L., Katch, F.I., Moffatt, R., & Gittleson, M. (1980). Muscular development and lean body weight in body builders and weight lifters. *Medicine and Science in Sports and Exercise, 12,* 340–344.

Kato, S., & Ishiko, T. (1976). Obstructed growth of children's bones due to excessive labor in remote corners. In K. Kato (Ed.), *Proceedings of the International Congress of Sports Sciences.* Tokyo: Japanese Union of Sport Sciences.

Keul, J., Haralambei, G., Bruder, M., & Gottstein, H.J. (1978). The effect of weight lifting exercise on heart rate and metabolism in experienced lifters. *Medicine and Science in Sports*, **10**, 13-15.

Klausen, K., Andersen, L.B., & Pelle, I. (1981). Adaptive changes in work capacity, skeletal muscle capillarization and enzyme levels during training and detraining. *Acta Physiologica Scandinavica*, **113**, 9-16.

Knakis, C., & Hickson, R.C. (1980). Left ventricular responses to a program of lower limb strength training. *Chest*, **78**, 618-621.

Knapik, J.J., Mawdsley, R.H., & Ramos, M.U. (1983). Angular specificity and test mode specificity of isometric and isokinetic strength training. *Journal of Orthopedic Sports Physical Therapy*, **5**, 58-65.

Knuttgen, H.G., & Kraemer, W.J. (1987). Terminology and measurement in exercise performance. *The Journal of Applied Sport Science Research*, **1**, 1-10.

Komi, P.V. (1979). Neuromuscular performance: Factors influencing force and speed production. *Scandinavian Journal of Sports Sciences*, **1**, 2-15.

Komi, P.V., & Buskirk, E.R. (1972). Effect of eccentric and concentric muscle conditioning on tension and electrical activity of human muscle. *Ergonomics*, **15**, 417-434.

Kraemer, W.J. (1983a). Detraining the "bulked up" athlete: Prospects for lifetime health and fitness. *National Strength and Conditioning Association Journal*, **5**, 10-12.

Kraemer, W.J. (1983b). Exercise prescription in weight training: A needs analysis. *National Strength and Conditioning Association Journal*, **5**, 64-65.

Kraemer, W.J. (1983c). Exercise prescription in weight training: Manipulating program variables. *National Strength and Conditioning Association Journal*, **5**, 58-59.

Krolner, B., Tondevold, E., Toft, B., Berthelsen, B., & Pors Nielsen, S. (1982). Bone mass of the axial and the appendicular skeleton in women with colles' fracture: Its relation to physical activity. *Clinical Physiology*, **2**, 147-157.

Kuland, D.N., McCue, F.C., Rockwell, D.A., & Gieck, J.A. (1979). Tennis injuries: Prevention and treatment. *American Journal of Sports Medicine*, **7**, 249-253.

Kusintz, I., & Kenney, C. (1958). Effects of progressive weight training on health and physical fitness of adolescent boys. *Research Quarterly*, **29**, 295-301.

Lamb, D.R. (1978). *Physiology of exercise: Responses and adaptations.* New York: Macmillan.

Lander, J.E., Bates, B.T., Sawhill, J.A., & Hamill, J.A. (1985). Comparison between free-weight and isokinetic bench pressing. *Medicine and Science in Sports and Exercise,* **17,** 344–353.

Laubach, L.L. (1976). Comparative muscular strength of men and women: A review of the literature. *Aviation, Space and Environmental Medicine,* **47,** 534–542.

Laurent, G.J., Sparrow, M.P., Bates, P.C., & Millward, D.J. (1978). Collagen content and turnover in cardiac and skeletal muscles of the adult fowl and the changes during stretch-induced growth. *Biochemistry Journal,* **176,** 419–427.

Laycoe, R.R., & Marteniuk, R.G. (1971). Leaning and tension as factors in strength gains produced by static and eccentric training. *Research Quarterly,* **42,** 299–305.

Legwold, G. (1982). Does lifting weights harm a prepubescent athlete? *The Physician and Sportsmedicine,* **10,** 141–144.

Leighton, J. (1955). Instrument and technique for measurement of range of joint motion. *Archives of Physical and Mental Rehabilitation,* **36,** 571–578.

Leighton, J. (1957a). Flexibility characteristics of four specialized skill groups of college athletes. *Archives of Physical Medicine and Rehabilitation,* **38,** 24–28.

Leighton, J. (1957b). Flexibility characteristics of three specialized skill groups of champion athletes. *Archives of Physical Medicine and Rehabilitation,* **38,** 580–583.

Leighton, J.R., Holmes, D., Benson, J., Wooten, B., & Schmerer, R. (1967). A study of the effectiveness of ten different methods of progressive resistance exercise on the development of strength, flexibility, girth and body weight. *Journal of the Association of Physical and Mental Rehabilitation,* **21,** 78–81.

Lemon, P.W., & Mullin, J.P. (1980). Effect of initial muscle glycogen levels on protein catabolism during exercise. *Journal of Applied Physiology: Respiratory, Environmental and Exercise Physiology,* **48,** 624–629.

Lesmes, G.R., Costill, D.L., Coyle, E.F., & Fink, W.J. (1978). Muscle strength and power changes during maximal isokinetic training. *Medicine and Science in Sports,* **4,** 266–269.

Liederman, E. (1925). *Secrets of strength.* New York: Earle Liederman.

Lind, A.R., & Petrofsky, J.S. (1978). Isometric tension from rotary stimulation of fast and slow cat muscles. *Muscle and Nerve,* **1,** 213–218.

Lipscomb, A.B., (1975). Baseball pitching in growing athletes. *Journal of Sports Medicine*, **3**, 25–34.

Longhurst, J.C., Kelly, A.R., Gonyea, W.J., & Mitchell, J.H. (1980). Echocardiographic left ventricular masses in distance runners and weight lifters. *Journal of Applied Physiology: Respiratory, Environmental and Exercise Physiology*, **48**, 154–162.

Loucks, A.B., & Horvath, S.M. (1985). Athletic amenorrhea: A review. *Medicine and Science in Sports and Exercise*, **17**, 56–72.

MacDougall, J.D., Elder, G.C.B., Sale, D.G., Moroz, J.R., & Sutton, J.R. (1980). Effects of strength training and immobilization of human muscle fibers. *European Journal of Applied Physiology*, **43**, 25–34.

MacDougall, J.D., Sale, D.G., Alway, S.E., & Sutton, J.R. (1984). Muscle fiber number in biceps brachii in body builders and control subjects. *Journal of Applied Physiology: Respiratory, Environmental and Exercise Physiology*, **57**, 1399–1403.

MacDougall, J.D., Sale, D.G., Elder, G.C.B., & Sutton, J.R. (1982). Muscle ultrastructural characteristics of elite power lifters and body builders. *European Journal of Applied Physiology*, **48**, 117–126.

MacDougall, J.D., Sale, D.G., Moroz, J.R., Elder, G.C.B., Sutton, J.R., & Howard, H. (1979). Mitochondrial volume density in human skeletal muscle following heavy resistance training. *Medicine and Science in Sports*, **11**, 164–166.

MacDougall, J.D., Tuxen, D., Sale, D.G., Moroz, R., & Sutton, J.R. (1985). Arterial blood pressure response to heavy resistance exercise. *Journal of Applied Physiology*, **58**, 785–790.

MacDougall, J.D., Ward, G.R., Sale, D.G., & Sutton, J.R. (1977). Biochemical adaptation of human skeletal muscle to heavy resistance training and immobilization. *Journal of Applied Physiology*, **43**, 700–703.

Madsen, N., & McLaughlin, T. (1984). Kinematic factors influencing performance and injury risk in the bench press exercise. *Medicine and Science in Sports and Exercise*, **16**, 429–437.

Marshall, J.L., Johanson, N., Wickiewicz, T.L., Tishler, H.M., Koslin, B.L., Zeno, S., & Myers, A. (1980). Joint looseness: A function of the person and the joint. *Medicine and Science in Sports and Exercise*, **12**, 189–194.

Martin, R.K., Albright, J.P., Clarke, W.R., & Niffenegger, J.A. (1981). Load-carrying effects on the adult beagle tibia. *Medicine and Science in Sports and Exercise*, **13**, 343–349.

Massey, B.H., & Chaudet, N.L. (1956). Effects of heavy resistance exercise on range of joint movement in young male adults. *Research Quarterly*, **27**, 41–51.

Matvey, L. (1981). *Fundamentals of sports training*. Moscow: Progress.

Mayhew, J.L., & Gross, P.M. (1974). Body composition changes in young women with high intensity weight training. *Research Quarterly*, **45**, 433–440.

McDonagh, M.J.N., & Davies, C.T.M. (1984). Adaptive responses of mammalian skeletal muscle to exercise with high loads. *European Journal of Applied Physiology*, **52**, 139–155.

McDonagh, M.J.N., Hayward, C.M., & Davies, C.T.M. (1983). Isometric training in human elbow flexor muscles. *Journal of Bone and Joint Surgery*, **65**, 355–358.

McLaughlin, T.M., Dillman, C.J., & Lardner, T.J. (1977). A kinematic model of performance of the parallel squat. *Medicine and Science in Sports*, **9**, 128–133.

McMorris, R.O., & Elkins, E.C. (1954). A study of production and evaluation of muscular hypertrophy. *Archives of Physical Medicine and Rehabilitation*, **35**, 420–426.

Menapace, F.J., Hammer, W.J., Ritzer, T.F., Kessler, K.M., Warner, H.F., Spann, J.F., & Bove, A.A. (1982). Left ventricular size in competitive weight lifters: An echocardiographic study. *Medicine and Science in Sports and Exercise*, **14**, 72–75.

Meyer, R.A., & Terjung, R.L. (1979). Differences in ammonia and adenylate metabolism in contracting fast and slow muscle. *American Journal of Physiology*, **237**, C11–C18.

Meyers, C.R. (1967). Effect of two isometric routines on strength, size and endurance in exercised and non-exercised arms. *Research Quarterly*, **38**, 430–440.

Michael, E.M., Evert, J., & Jeffers, K. (1972). Physiological changes of teenage girls during five months of detraining. *Medicine and Science in Sports*, **4**, 214–218.

Micheli, L.J. (1983). Overuse injuries in children's sports: The growth factor. *The Orthopedic Clinics of North America*, **14**, 337–360.

Milner-Brown, H.S., Stein, R.B., & Yemin, R. (1973). The orderly recruitment of human motor units during voluntary contractions. *Journal of Physiology*, **230**, 359–370.

Misner, S.E., Broileau, R.A., Massey, B.H., & Mayhew, J. (1974). Alterations in the body composition of adult men during selected physical training. *Journal of the American Geriatrics Society*, **22**, 33–38.

Moffroid, M.T., & Whipple, R.H. (1970). Specificity of speed of exercise. *Physical Therapy*, **50**, 1693-1699.

Moffroid, M., Whipple, R., Hofkosh, J., Lowman, E., & Thistle, H. (1969). A study of isokinetic exercise. *Physical Therapy*, **49**, 735-747.

Montoye, H.J., Smith, E.L., Fardon, D.F., & Howley, E.T. (1980). Bone mineral in senior tennis players. *Scandinavian Journal of Sports Science*, **2**, 26-32.

Moore, M.A., & Hutton, R.S. (1980). Electromyographic investigation of muscle stretching techniques. *Medicine and Science in Sports and Exercise*, **12**, 322-329.

Morehouse, C. (1967). Development and maintenance of isometric strength of subjects with diverse initial strengths. *Research Quarterly*, **38**, 449-456.

Morganroth, J., Maron, B.J., Henry, W.L., & Epstein, J.E. (1975). Comparative left ventricular dimensions in trained athletes. *Annals of Internal Medicine*, **82**, 521-524.

Moritani, T., & DeVries, H.A. (1979). Neural factors versus hypertrophy in the time course of muscle strength gain. *American Journal of Physical Medicine*, **82**, 521-524.

Moritani, T., & DeVries, H.A. (1980). Potential for gross hypertrophy in older men. *Journal of Gerontology*, **35**, 672-682.

Morrow, J.R., Jackson, A.S., Hosler, W.W., & Kachurick, J.K. (1979). The importance of strength, speed and body size for team success in women's intercollegiate volleyball. *Research Quarterly*, **50**, 429-437.

Morrow, J.R., & Hosler, W.W. (1981). Strength comparisons in untrained men and trained women athletes. *Medicine and Science in Sports and Exercise*, **13**, 194-198.

Nakamura, Y., & Schwartz, S. (1972). The influence of hydrogen ion concentration calcium binding and release by skeletal muscle sarcoplasmic reticulum. *Journal of General Physiology*, **59**, 22-32.

Nelson, A.G., Conlee, R.K., Arnall, D.A., Loy, S.F., & Silvester, L.J. (1984). Adaptations to simultaneous training for strength and endurance. *Medicine and Science in Sports and Exercise*, **16**, 184.

Nemoto, E.M., Hoff, J.T., & Sereringhaus, J.W. (1974). Lactate uptake and metabolism by brain during hyperlactacidemia and hypoglycemia. *Stroke*, **5**, 48-53.

Nilsson, B.E., & Westlin, N.E. (1971). Bone density in athletes. *Clinical Orthopedics and Related Research*, **7**, 179-182.

Noble, B.J., Kraemer, W.J., Clark, M.J., & Culver, B.W. (1984). Stress response to high intensity circuit weight training in experienced weight trainers. *Medicine and Science in Sports and Exercise, 16*, 164.

Norris, D.O. (1980). *Vertebrate endocrinology.* Philadelphia: Lea and Febiger.

Ohtsuki, T. (1981). Decrease in grip strength induced by simultaneous bilateral exertion with reference to finger strength. *Ergonomics, 24,* 37–48.

Olson, V.L., Schmidt, G.L., & Johnson, R.C. (1972). The maximum torque generated by eccentric, isometric, and concentric contractions of the hip abduction muscles. *Physical Therapy, 52,* 148–149.

O'Shea, P. (1966). Effects of selected weight training programs on the development of strength and muscle hypertrophy. *Research Quarterly, 37,* 95–102.

Oteghen, S.L. (1975). Two speeds of isokinetic exercise as related to the vertical jump performance of women. *Research Quarterly, 46,* 78–84.

Page, B. (1966). Latest muscle building technique. *Muscle Builder, 14,* 20–21.

Perrine, J.A., & Edgerton, V.R. (1975). Isokinetic anaerobic ergometry. *Medicine and Science in Sports, 7,* 78.

Peterson, J.A. (1975). Total conditioning: A case study. *Athletic Journal, 56,* 40–55.

Phillips, L.S., & Vassilopoulou-Sellin, R. (1980). Somatomedins. *The New England Journal of Medicine, 302,* 438–446.

Pipes, T.V. (1978). Variable resistance versus constant resistance strength training in adult males. *European Journal of Applied Physiology, 39,* 27–35.

Pipes, T.V. (1979). Physiological characteristics of elite body builders. *The Physician and Sportsmedicine, 7,* 116–126.

Pollock, M.L., Wilmore, J.H., & Fox, S.M. (1978). *Health and fitness through physical activity.* New York: Wiley and Sons.

Poole, H. (1964). Multi-poundage sets. *Muscle Builder, 14,* 20–21.

Priest, J.P., & Nagle, P.A. (1976). Tennis shoulder. *American Journal of Sports Medicine, 4,* 28–42.

Prince, F.P., Hikida, R.S., & Hagerman, F.C. (1976). Human muscle fiber types in power lifters, distance runners and untrained subjects. *Pflugers Archives, 371,* 161–165.

Prince, F.P., Hikida, R.S., & Hagerman, F.C. (1977). Muscle fiber types in women athletes and non-athletes. *Pflugers Archives, 371*, 161–165.

Rack, D.M.H., & Westbury, D.R. (1969). The effects of length and stimulus rate on isometric tension in the cat soleus muscle. *Journal of Physiology, 204*, 443–460.

Rarick, G.L., & Larson, G.L. (1958). Observations on frequency and intensity of isometric muscular effort in developing static muscular strength in post-pubescent males. *Research Quarterly, 29*, 333–341.

Rasch, P. (1971). Isometric exercise and gains of muscular strength. In R. Shepard (Ed.), *Frontiers of fitness* (pp. 98–111). Springfield: Thomas.

Rasch, P., & Morehouse, L. (1957). Effect of static and dynamic exercises on muscular strength and hypertrophy. *Journal of Applied Physiology, 11*, 29–34.

Ricci, G., LaJoie, D., Petitclere, R., Peronnet, F., Ferguson, R.J., Fournier, M., & Taylor, A.W. (1982). Left ventricular size following endurance, sprint, and strength training. *Medicine and Science in Sports and Exercise, 14*, 344–347.

Richford, C. (1966). *Principles of successful body building.* Alliance, NE: Iron Man Industries.

Rieger, J. (1985). Upgrading your conditioning facility: Equipment evaluation and selection. *Cardinal Conditioning, University of Louisville Athletics and Sports Medicine, 4*, 1–4.

Rochter, F.D., Rochelle, R.H., & Hyman, C. (1963). Exercise blood flow changes in the human forearm during physical training. *Journal of Applied Physiology, 18*, 789–793.

Rowe, T.A. (1979). Cartilage fracture due to weight lifting. *British Journal of Sports Medicine, 13*, 130–131.

Rowell, L.B., Kranning, K.K., Evans, T.O., Kennedy, J.W., Blackman, J.R., & Kusumi, F. (1966). Splanchnic removal of lactate and pyruvate during prolonged exercise in man. *Journal of Applied Physiology, 21*, 1773–1783.

Ryan, A.J. (1975). Gynecological considerations. *Journal of Physical Education and Recreation, 4*, 205–209.

Ryan, J.R., & Salciccioli, G.G. (1976). Fractures of the distal radial epiphysis in adolescent weight lifters. *Sports Medicine, 4*, 26–27.

Sale, D.G., MacDougall, J.D., Upton, A.R.M., & McComas, A.J. (1983). Effects of strength training upon motoneuron excitability in man. *Medicine and Science in Sports and Exercise, 15*, 57–62.

Saltin, B., & Astrand, P.O. (1967). Maximal oxygen uptake in athletes. *Journal of Applied Physiology, 23*, 353–358.

Saltin, B., & Rowell, L.B. (1980). Functional adaptations to physical activity and inactivity. *Federation Proceedings, 39*, 1506–1513.

Schantz, P. (1982). Capillary supply in hypertrophied human skeletal muscle. *Acta Physiologica Scandinavica, 114*, 635–637.

Schultz, R.W. (1967). Effect of direct practice and repetitive sprinting and weight training on selected motor performance tasks. *Research Quarterly, 38*, 108–118.

Secher, N.H. (1975). Isometric rowing strength of experienced and inexperienced oarsmen. *Medicine and Science in Sports, 7*, 280–283.

Secher, N.H., Rorsgaard, S., & Secher, O. (1978). Contralateral influence on recruitment of curanized muscle fibers during maximal voluntary extension of the legs. *Acta Physiologica Scandinavica, 130*, 455–462.

Servedio, F.J., Bartels, R.L., Hamlin, R.L., Teske, D., Shaffer, T., & Servedio, A. (1985). The effects of weight training using olympic style lifts on various physiological variables in pre-pubescent boys. *Medicine and Science in Sports and Exercise, 17*, 158.

Sewall, L., & Micheli, L.J. (1984). Strength development in children. *Medicine and Science in Sports and Exercise, 16*, 158.

Sheehan, G. (1985, June). Health vs fitness. *The Runner,* pp. 14–15.

Shellock, F.G., & Prentice, W.E. (1985). Warming-up and stretching for improved physical performance and prevention of sports related injuries. *Sports Medicine, 2*, 267–278.

Silvester, L.J., Stiggins, C., McGown, C., & Bryce, G. (1984). The effect of variable resistance and free-weight training programs on strength and vertical jump. *National Strength and Conditioning Association Journal, 5*, 30–33.

Sinning, W.E. (1974). Body composition assessment of college wrestlers. *Medicine and Science in Sports, 6*, 139–145.

Smith, M.J., & Melton, P. (1981). Isokinetic versus isotonic variable resistance training. *American Journal of Sports Medicine, 9*, 275–279.

Spence, D.W., Disch, J.G., Fred, H.C., & Coleman, A.E. (1980). Descriptive profiles of highly skilled women volleyball players. *Medicine and Science in Sports and Exercise, 12*, 299–302.

Speroff, L., & Redwine, D.B. (1980). Exercise and menstrual function. *The Physician and Sportsmedicine, 8*, 42–48.

Spitzer, J.J. (1974). Effect of lactate infusion on canine myocardial free fatty acid metabolism in vivo. *American Journal of Physiology, 22,* 213–217.

Sprynarova, S., & Parizkova, J. (1971). Functional capacity and body composition in top weight lifters, swimmers, runners and skiers. *International Zeitschrift Fur Angewandte Physiologie, 29,* 184–194.

Staff, P.H. (1982). The effect of physical activity on joints, cartilage, tendons and ligaments. *Scandinavian Journal of Social Medicine,* 29(Suppl.), 59–63.

Staron, R.S., Hagerman, F.C., & Hikida, R.S. (1981). The effects of detraining on an elite power lifter. *Journal of Neurological Sciences, 51,* 247–257.

Staron, R.S., Hikida, R.S., & Hagerman, F.C. (1983). Reevaluation of human muscle fast-twitch subtypes evidence for a continuum. *Histochemistry, 78,* 33–39.

Steinhaus, A.H. (1954, September). *Some selected facts from physiology and the physiology of exercise applicable to physical rehabilitation.* Paper presented to the study group on body mechanics, Washington, DC.

Stone, M.H., Byrd, R., & Johnson, C. (1984). Observation on serum androgen response to short term resistive training in middle age sedentary males. *National Strength and Conditioning Association Journal, 6,* 30–31.

Stone, M.H., Johnson, R.C., & Carter, D.R. (1979). A short term comparison of two different methods of resistance training on leg strength and power. *Athletic Training, 14,* 158–160.

Stone, M.H., O'Bryant, H., & Garhammer, J.G. (1981). A hypothetical model for strength training. *Journal of Sports Medicine and Physical Fitness, 21,* 342–351.

Stone, M.H., O'Bryant, H., Garhammer, J.G., McMillian, J., & Rozenek, R. (1982). A theoretical model for strength training. *National Strength and Conditioning Association Journal, 4,* 36–39.

Stone, M.H., Wilson, G.D., Blessing, D., & Rozenek, R. (1983). Cardiovascular responses to short-term olympic style weight training in young men. *Canadian Journal of Applied Sport Science, 8,* 134–139.

Stowers, T., McMillian, J., Scala, D., Davis, V., Wilson, D., & Stone, M. (1983). The short-term effects of three different strength-power training methods. *National Strength and Conditioning Association Journal, 5,* 24–27.

Straub, W.F. (1968). Effect of overload training procedures upon velocity and accuracy of the overarm throw. *Research Quarterly,* **39,** 370–379.

Sutton, J.R., Coleman, M.J., Casey, J., & Lazarus, L. (1973). Androgen responses during physical exercise. *British Medical Journal,* **1,** 520–522.

Swegan, D.B. (1957). The comparison of static contraction with standard weight training and effect on certain movement speeds and endurance. Unpublished doctoral dissertation, Penn State University.

Talag, T.S. (1973). Residual muscular soreness as influenced by concentric, eccentric and static contractions. *Research Quarterly,* **44,** 458–461.

Tanner, J.M. (1964). *The physique of the Olympic athlete.* London: Allen and Unwin.

Tcheng, T.K., & Tipton, C.M. (1973). Iowa wrestling study: Anthropometric measurements and prediction of a minimal body weight of high school wrestlers. *Medicine and Science in Sports,* **5,** 1–10.

Tepperman, J. (1980). *Metabolic and endocrine physiology.* Chicago: Year Book Medical.

Tesch, P.A., & Larsson, L. (1982). Muscle hypertrophy in bodybuilders. *European Journal of Applied Physiology,* **49,** 301–306.

Tesch, P.A., Thorsson, A., & Kaiser, P. (1984). Muscle capillary supply and fiber type characteristics in weight and power lifters. *Journal of Applied Physiology: Respiratory, Environmental and Exercise Physiology,* **56,** 35–38.

Thistle, H.G., Hislop, H.J., Moffroid, M., & Lowman, E.W. (1967). Isokinetic contraction: A new concept in resistive exercise. *Archives of Physical Medicine and Rehabilitation,* **48,** 279–282.

Thorstensson, A. (1977). Observations on strength training and detraining. *Acta Physiologica Scandinavica,* **100,** 491–493.

Thorstensson, A., Karlsson, J., Viitasalso, J.H.T., Luhtanen, P., & Komi, P.V. (1976). Effect of strength training on EMG of human skeletal muscle. *Acta Physiologica Scandinavica,* **98,** 232–236.

Timonen, S., & Procope, B.J. (1971). Premenstrual syndrome and physical exercise. *Acta Obstetrica et Gynaecologica Scandinavica,* **50,** 331–337.

Timson, B.F., Bowlin, B.K., Dudenhoeffer, G.A., & George, J.B. (1985). Fiber number, area, and composition of mouse soleus muscle following enlargement. *Journal of Applied Physiology: Respiratory, Environmental and Exercise Physiology, 58*, 619–624.

Tipton, C.M., James, S.L., Mergner, W., & Tchern, T.K. (1970). Influence of exercise on the strength of the medial collateral knee ligament of dogs. *American Journal of Physiology, 218*, 894–902.

Tipton, C.M., Matthes, R.D., Maynard, J.A., & Carey, R.A. (1975). The influence of physical activity on ligaments and tendons. *Medicine and Science and Sports, 7*, 34–41.

Todd, T. (1985). Historical perspective: The myth of the muscle-bound lifter. *National Strength and Conditioning Association Journal, 7*, 37–41.

Torg, J.S., Pollack, H., & Sweterlitsch, P. (1972). The effect of competitive pitching on the shoulders and elbows of preadolescent baseball players. *Pediatrics, 49*, 267–272.

Trivedi, B., & Danforth, W.H. (1966). Effect of pH on the kinetics of frog muscle phosphofructokinase. *Journal of Biological Chemistry, 241*, 4110–4112.

Turto, H., Lindy, S., & Halme, J. (1974). Protocollagen proline hydroxylase activity in work-induced hypertrophy of rat muscle. *American Journal of Physiology, 226*, 63–65.

Vandervoot, A.A., Sale, D.G., & Moroz, J. (1984). Comparison of motor unit activation during unilateral and bilateral leg extension. *Journal of Applied Physiology: Respiratory, Environmental and Exercise Physiology, 56*, 46–51.

Vanhelder, W.P., Radomski, M.W., & Goode, R.C. (1984). Growth hormone responses during intermittent weight lifting exercise in men. *European Journal of Applied Physiology, 53*, 31–34.

Vorobyev, A.N. (1978). *A textbook on weightlifting* (J. Bryant, Trans.). Budapest, Hungary: International Weightlifting Federation.

Waldman, R., & Stull, G. (1969). Effects of various periods of inactivity on retention of newly acquired levels of muscular endurance. *Research Quarterly, 40*, 393–401.

Ward, J., & Fisk, G.H. (1964). The difference in response of the quadriceps and biceps brachii muscles to isometric and isotonic exercise. *Archives of Physical Medicine and Rehabilitation, 45*, 612–620.

Warren, M.P. (1980). The effects of exercise on pubertal progression and reproductive function in girls. *Journal of Clinical Endocrinology and Metabolism, 51*, 1150–1156.

Weider, J. (1954). Cheating exercises build the biggest muscles. *Muscle Builder, 3,* 60–61.

Weiss, L.W., Cureton, K.J., & Thompson, F.N. (1983). Comparison of serum testosterone and androstenedione responses to weight lifting in men and women. *European Journal of Applied Physiology, 50,* 413–419.

Wells, C.L. (1978). The female athlete: Myths and superstitions put to rest. In E.J. Burke (Ed.) *Toward an understanding of human performance* (pp. 37–40). Ithaca, NY: Movement Press.

Wells, J.B., Jokl, E., & Bohanen, J. (1973). The effect of intense physical training upon body composition of adolescent girls. *Journal of the Association for Physical and Mental Rehabilitation, 17,* 63–72.

Wickiewicz, T.L., Roy, R.R., Powell, P.L., Perrine, J.J., & Edgerton, V.R. (1984). Muscle architecture and force-velocity relationships in humans. *Journal of Applied Physiology: Respiratory, Environmental and Exercise Physiology, 57,* 435–443.

Widholm, O. (1979). Dysmenorrhea during adolescence. *Acta Obstetrica et Gynaecologica Scandinavica, 87,* 61–66.

Williams, J.A., Wagner, J., Wasnich, R., & Heilbrun, L. (1984). The effect of long-distance running upon appendicular bone mineral content. *Medicine and Science in Sports and Exercise, 16,* 223–227.

Williams, M., & Stutzman, L. (1959). Strength variation throughout the range of joint motion. *Physical Therapy Review, 39,* 145–152.

Wilmore, J.H. (1974). Alterations in strength, body composition, and anthropometric measurements consequent to a 10-week weight training program. *Medicine and Science in Sports, 6,* 133–138.

Wilmore, J.H., Parr, R.B., Girandola, R.N., Ward, P., Vodak, P.A., Barstow, T.J., Pipes, T.V., Romero, G.T., & Leslie, P. (1978). Physiological alterations consequent to circuit weight training. *Medicine and Science in Sports, 10,* 79–84.

Wilt, F. (1968). Training for competitive running. In H.B. Falls (Ed.), *Exercise physiology* (pp. 395–414). New York: Academic Press.

Withers, R.T. (1970). Effect of varied weight-training loads on the strength of university freshmen. *Research Quarterly, 41,* 110–114.

Wright, J.E. (1980). Anabolic steroids and athletics. In R.S. Hutton & D.I. Miller (Eds.), *Exercise and Sport Science Review* (pp. 149–202). The Franklin Institute.

Yates, J.W., & Kamon, E. (1983). A comparison of peak and constant angle torque-velocity curves in fast and slow twitch populations. *European Journal of Applied Physiology, 51,* 67–74.

Yudkin, J., & Cohen, R.D. (1974). The contribution of the kidney to the removal of a lactic acid load under normal and acidotic conditions in the conscious rat. *Clinical Sciences and Molecular Medicine, 46,* 8.

Zinovieff, A.N. (1951). Heavy resistance exercise: The Oxford technique. *British Journal of Physical Medicine, 14,* 129–132.

Zrubak, A. (1972). Body composition and muscle strength of body builders. *Acta Facultatis Rerum Naturalium Universitatis Comenianae Anthropologia, XI,* 135–144.

Index